REFLECTIONS ON
AMERICAN PHILOSOPHY
FROM
WITHIN

REFLECTIONS ON AMERICAN PHILOSOPHY FROM WITHIN

ROY WOOD SELLARS

UNIVERSITY OF NOTRE DAME PRESS

NOTRE DAME — LONDON

Other works by the same author include: *Critical Realism, Evolutionary Naturalism, The Philosophy of Physical Realism, The Next Step in Religion.*

FOREWORD

Philosophy should seek a clear-cut framework. It is this that I have sought. The principle is that sensations guide perceiving in action and, at the human, cognitive level, give rise to well-founded *facts about* the objects perceived. What is involved? As I explored perceiving, as a referential act, I connected it with directed response. I called this the from-and-to circuit. When I *see* a tree, I find that I am looking at it and using my visual sensations to disclose it. The visual field is not terminal, as it was regarded by traditional empiricism, but informative. It is the external object which we are concerned with in perceiving. The function of the sense-organs was not understood by philosophers, I fear. Nature was too ingenious for them. A tradition got started, ending, in our day, in positivism and phenomenalism.

The path I took was towards a new type of direct realism. I call it a referentially direct realism. Sensations function in perceiving as informational. There is a good deal of selective activity here, as the psychologist knows. And human cognizing is an achievement emerging from this setting. Its foundational postulate is that the mechanism of sense-perception furthers the transmission of information in the way of appearing or manifesting. And this is used as evidence. On its basis we sensuously think the object we are reacting to and develop our thought conceptually and linguistically into facts about. Common sense takes this natural road and then science takes over at a new level.

I have come to speak here of the "fallacy" of the unthought-of possibility. Perry, Dewey, Montague, Blanshard and Schneider seem to have thought of me as a sort of maverick. They never saw what I was driving at. What I was doing was to undercut both presentationalism and representationalism. I was working towards a new kind of direct realism.

If I am a little hard on various movements of the time, it is because I believe that much of their ingenuity is misplaced. Young philosophers work hard but start from traditional premises. As I see it, phenomenologists and existentialists have no clear epistemology. Neither like empiricism, evolution and naturalism. I have protested, more than once, at what

v

I called the neo-colonialism of recent American philosophy. Peirce, alone, seems to have survived. A recent book jumps over critical realism altogether and devotes itself to logical positivism. Now I take logical positivism to have been more of the nature of a crusade of Viennese scientists who did not like German speculative extravagances. They seem to have known little about epistemological explorations in the United States. But, then, as I have indicated, many young American philosophers spoke of a stalemate here.

Some people have condemned me for being a materialist, even though an emergent or non-reductive one. And so I will end with something shocking. As I point out, Lenin wanted to start from things but found sensations intervening. Passmore rather taunts him with it. So do other empiricists. But I have shown, I think, that perceiving does start with things and that sensations function within it. I think human knowing is a wonderful achievement but that it emerged out of a biological situation. This book is, in part, an intellectual autobiography; in part, an oriented critique of various positions of great vogue.

Oct. 12, 1967, Ann Arbor

Roy Wood Sellars

TABLE OF CONTENTS

CONTENTS

1

THE NATURE
OF THE PROJECT

What I shall be concerned with in this book is a comparison of what may be called philosophical profiles in the Western World during the last fifty or so years. And I shall select United States, Great Britain and the European Continent as particularly interesting cases. I am quite ready to admit that such selection involves omission of other centers of thought; but I am best acquainted with these centers and I shall leave it to others to supplement my work of exploration.

It so happened that I was introduced to philosophy in the year nineteen hundred, that is, at the very turn of the century, by a Scotsman, Robert Mark Wenley, who had been a pupil of the Cairds, John and Edward, of Glasgow. John was Principal of Glasgow and, I was given to understand, an eloquent preacher on set occasions. Edward became Master of Balliol. They worked largely within the Kantian-Hegelian framework.

A few words about Professor Wenley are in order. He stressed the history of philosophy rather than the analysis of problems. That is, he concerned himself with the presentation of varying outlooks from Ancient to Modern times. He was also rather a polymath, proud of the fact that he had been a pupil of Kelvin in physics and Jebb in Greek. While he retained the general outlook of his teachers, he was, I think, a little puzzled by the situation which was developing. This comes out in his contribution, toward the end of his life, to the enterprise, called *Contemporary American Philosophy* (1930). He called it *An Unborn Idealism*. It is interesting because it is so largely autobiographical and reflects the currents playing on him. As I recall it, he felt himself nearest in thought to Bernard Bosanquet. He was a striking personality, witty, and with a fund of stories of a Caledonian flavor. Perhaps his puzzlement prevented him from trying to indoctrinate me. And I was left with a rather open mind to find my way about.

Since, in the following chapters, I shall be engaged in making running commentaries on persons and movements of my time, it may be as well to say something about my development and the niche I occupied.

1

I had not specialized but had taken a large range of subjects. As yet, graduate work in philosophy had not developed except as a minor topic, as it was then called. So I did not think of it as a professional outlet. My father was a village doctor—in those days, a very hard life, indeed. My brother took that line and so I cast around for another. Comparative religions seemed an opening for I had pursued courses under the guidance of a very able man, Professor Craig, one of the early workers in Assyriology and the teacher of a man who later became a professor of that subject at Oxford. And so I secured a fellowship at Hartford Theological Seminary to study under Paton and Duncan Black MacDonald. But the next year an opening occurred in the way of a teaching fellowship in philosophy at the University of Wisconsin. F. C. Sharp was the chairman of the department and Boyd Bode was an instructor. Professor Sharp specialized in ethics and worked along the lines of a kind of experimental and statistical development of utilitarianism. I think the book he later published was too much neglected. He had studied in Berlin, as so many Americans of that day had. He was empirical-minded and used Stout's *Analytic Psychology* as a text in his seminar. Bode was just in process of making a transition from objective idealism to pragmatism. I had long talks with both but especially with Bode, a very friendly and unassuming person.

The next year I was called back to Michigan and actually spent my life at Ann Arbor. In the summer of 1906, I attended a summer session at the University of Chicago in order to hear James Mark Baldwin. I found him very stimulating and he encouraged me to write a paper, for the *Psychological Review* of which he was the editor, taking up critically a point in his treatment of the mind-body problem. I have sometimes wondered why he has been so neglected in histories of American philosophy. His approach was genetic. So my first two papers were published in a psychological journal at that time ready to accept papers with a philosophical background. That policy altered sharply when Watson succeeded Baldwin. I remember Watson very well for he used to come in to chat with Baldwin before class. It so happened that Michigan became a center of study in animal psychology under John F. Shepard and Norman Maier. So I had to reflect on behaviorism long before it reached England. It hardly fitted in with idealism. In these surroundings I was led to develop a course called *The Main Concepts of Science* which has been regarded as the first course in the philosophy of science.

It was not long after this that the realistic movement in the United States began. I participated in it from the beginning but took the line I called critical realism. It was not easy to work out an adequate theory of perceiving which would allow the mediating role of sensations and yet make perceiving cognitively direct. Clarification of what this involved has been a life-work. I have always been skeptical of men like Wittgenstein and Carnap who brushed this problem aside and tried to work out a framework largely based on logic and semantics. Of course, logic and semantics should have their place.

And so it turned out that I was the only one in the middle west who helped to initiate philosophical thinking along the lines of critical realism, evolutionary naturalism and humanism. It is this framework which I shall use in my critiques of the profiles of philosophy in the cultural areas of United States, Great Britain and the Continent. One can see that I developed a kind of momentum which I found contrasting with winds of fashion as time went on. That is, I got deep roots. There are many dimensions to philosophy as I saw it, the epistemological, the ontological, the moral and valuational. And these should, if possible, be tied together. It could hardly be a work of improvisation.

Science and Philosophy

I undertook the task of being a philosopher and of facing what seemed to be fundamental problems at the time when the sciences were showing their fruitfulness. I would not quite put it the way Parrington did but, in essentials, he was correct. The old systems of philosophy were turning out to be irrelevant, particularly the idealist ones which I shall shortly examine. I quote from his book *Main Currents in American Thought*. "A new spirit of realism was abroad, probing and questioning the material world, pushing the realm of exact knowledge into the earlier regions of faith. The conquest of nature was the great business of the day, and as that conquest went forward triumphantly the solid fruits of the new mastery were gathered by industrialism."*

Now this did not mean that, when confronted by the general problems philosophy and religion had together raised, the scientist would offhand have an answer for them. I had read my Huxley and my Tyndall and saw where they diverged. My sympathies were more with Tyndall but I saw that Huxley was aware of the problems connected with perceiving and with the mind-body issue. These were inherited epistemological

---

*p. 4.

questions connected with Locke, Berkeley and Hume and with Cartesian dualism and had to be met. As time went on, I focussed my attention on perceiving as the starting-point of knowing, on the mind-body problem, and on the import of evolution. These, I felt, were tied in together.

What, then, had science and philosophy in common? It was clear that scientific method had gradually been worked out and was being applied in the various special sciences in accordance with the demands of particular problems. It was, likewise, clear that philosophy was not equipped to do this kind of work. What, then, was its point of contact and relevance?

Looking back, I saw philosophy as logical scrutiny of systems of ideas or, as we say, categories, characteristic of an epoch, such as mechanism, teleology, cognition, mind, the transcendent, etc. I saw the increasing importance of tools and experimentation but recognized the matrix of ideas and queries. These accompanied one another and undoubtedly interacted. But it was the accepted job of philosophy to keep the categories before its attention and to raise issues. If it thought that mechanical ideas needed qualification, it felt free to do so. It might go to the other extreme and advocate vitalism or stress the importance of time, as Bergson did. All this was part of the dialogue. On the whole, I found science self-correcting but I would not exclude the qualifying effect of such dialogues.

Since I am going to take the development of American philosophy in the twentieth century—something in which I participated from the beginning—as a base-line for my estimation of the movement of philosophy in Great Britain and on the Continent, it may be well to note at this point the reaction to this question of the differing roles of science and philosophy, made by A. K. Rogers, a contemporary of mine who was keenly alive to the issue. In his contribution to *Contemporary American Philosophy* he pointed to the value of following through the logical development of ideas in systems of philosophy, like those of Aristotle, Descartes, Leibnitz and Locke. These were, undoubtedly, able men. One might not agree with their preliminary axioms—a cultural shift might well account for this disagreement—but there would be mental training in the effort. And then he goes on to say: "To the philosopher must go a very large portion of the credit for rendering precise the terms of intellectual discourse and bringing them into something like an intelligible connection; apart from that subtle and technical tracing of the links of logical relationship which so irritates the unfriendly critic, the mind of man would be ruled even more universally than it is by a mass of desultory catchwords."*

*Vol. 2, p. 225.

Now I have been a systematic thinker from the start with one eye on philosophy and another on the sciences. And it may well be that I shall show myself too critical of men like Wittgenstein and Carnap who largely ignore philosophical dialogue and go off on a tangent of their own. It has been pointed out to me that Descartes did much the same in his attempt to make a new beginning in line with developments in science, though Gilson has argued that he owed more than he realized to past philosophy. I agree that originality is very desirable and is likely to make issues sharper. But I must postpone farther comment on this point until later. I merely remark that unsolved problems are easily locatable in the context of philosophy; and it is better to face up to them than to turn one's back on them. That, at least, is what I have found. I have in mind Dewey as well as Wittgenstein and Carnap. The nature of perceiving is a case in point. It has always seemed to me very fundamental. It was so assessed by the generation of American philosophers to whom I belong. And then, strangely enough, it was ignored for a time. I kept on working at it with, I shall try to show, increasing clarification.

In concluding this section on philosophy and science, I wish to remark by way of anticipation that I have the impression that American philosophy, as it developed in the twentieth century, as the universities got under way, had more intimate contact with science than did British philosophy or German philosophy. In those countries it had more or less culturally isolated itself. I fear that Germany thought of itself as the home of modern philosophy because of the Kant-Hegel tradition, while Great Britain had its inter-necine disputes into which I shall look later. It is not surprising that the next generation after mine of American thinkers turned to Great Britain with its cultural prestige, and what seemed to me, as an onlooker, its immersion in debate between Oxford and Cambridge. I do not want to oversimplify. But since I could not agree with either Russell or Moore on fundamental points—as I shall try to show later—it seemed to me that the so-called *analytic philosophy* which got quite a vogue was ambivalent. In one sense, I liked its emphasis. In another sense, it did not seem to me very creative in either epistemology or ontology. American addiction to it and disregard of its own momentum struck me as a form of neo-colonialism.

I shall, of course, go into this quite thoroughly in later chapters. I shall have occasion to discuss German thought, particularly in connection with *existentialism*. I by no means think of this as exhaustive of German thought for one of my best friends is a phenomenologist. But it is a striking phenomenon. And it has engrossed much attention because of its emphasis on the individual and his anxiety in the face of death. In it we hear much of freedom and of the authentic life. It is rather inclined to be hortatory rather than analytic and it does not pay much attention to science. But of all that later.

One other general remark. Recently, in lecturing on philosophy at Syracuse University, I had occasion to criticize rather severely both logical positivism and existentialism and was accused of being rather anti-foreign in the stand I took. I replied that I did not feel that way about it. Rather I was trying to redress the balance. I thought that, for a while, American philosophers had neglected some rather vital contributions that had been made here. It is to me interesting that I am told that logical positivism is held to have shot its bolt and shown certain inadequacies. Even existentialism, so I am told, is thought of more as a sort of ideology than as a well-worked-out philosophy. I am encouraged to think that a dialogue concerning philosophical profiles, such as I have in mind, may be profitable.

I spoke of a tendency, after the Second World War, to a kind of neo-colonialism in the United States. It seemed that it was believed that there had been a kind of stalemate here. In any case, British philosophy had gained a new vitality and self-confidence. And the British had the advantage that they could write very well, indeed. And so they secured attention. Analysis was a word to conjure with and then came the movement called that of "ordinary language." But all this was, in effect, a clearing of the ground. Philosophy in partnership with science could not be made that easy, as Bertrand Russell pointed out. And with increased communication at work something of the nature of interplay between the United States and Great Britain is occurring. I hope much from it. I expect that a better balance in ethical theory may even take place. I, myself, never considered G. E. Moore's theory of goodness as a simple, indefinable quality as a good starting point. I was persuaded that F. C. Sharp, John Dewey, Walter Everett, Warner Fite, Ralph B. Perry, A. K. Rogers and even my own analysis should be considered. There are, however, fashions in these things. It is against a temporary swing of the pendulum that I have protested. As I have indicated, I think a broader base is developing.

And I would hope that Germany and France will be included. The Continent seems to be going its own way. Perhaps it was more affected by the two great wars, driven in on itself, and looking backward for leads. And so it turned to Kierkegaard and Nietzsche. Kant and Hegel were, of course, always there as backgrounds. I find little account taken of British empiricism and American naturalism. I do not think this is healthy. I conclude this section with an illustration of the temptation to look at things in a kind of journalistic way. I have found that literary circles absorb a kind of journalistic version of philosophical affairs. This means that fashions and what Santayana called Winds of Doctrine move to the front. But to my illustration. In reading recently Denis De Rougemont's book on *The Meaning of Europe* I came across an instance he gives of what he regards as the perennial dominance of Europe in cultural matters. He pointed to the large acceptance in the United States of the writings of Maritain, Tillich and Barth.

Now it so happens that the conspicuousness of these three names is, technically, rather a journalistic illusion. Maritain is, undoubtedly, a man of great ability but he has had little influence on philosophy in the universities. I shall later examine his rather odd combination of an Aristotelian theory of sense-perception with acceptance of positivistic phenomenalism as regards the scientific view of the physical world. I do not believe that he has paid very much attention to currents in American thought. I have the impression that able Catholic thinkers in the United States do not take his emphases too seriously. So much, with due quali- fication, for De Rougemont's first example.

Now Tillich was considered here rather as a theologian than as a philosopher. And even here he was a mediator, half liberal, half conservative. Formally, he was allied with existentialism. I shall later give my critique of his theses. It so happens that *humanism* was gaining headway in the United States and I think still is. We even hear at times of a strange "theology without God." It was presented to Tillich shortly before his death (though I doubt it surprised him). The neo-Calvinism, or neo-orthodoxy, of Reinhold Niebuhr and of Paul Tillich repre- sented a blast against liberal, religious thought and humanism in the United States. I well remember when it came, as I was teaching philosophy of religion when it arrived. From the liberal standpoint, it was a cause of conservative reaction of a somewhat ambiguous type. Eustace Hayden, Max Otto, John Dewey and myself were opposed to it. It was a sort of half-way position likely to appeal, as it did, to those not ready for a frank naturalism. And so I do not think that De Rougemont's second exam- ple supports his thesis of the supremacy of Europe in culture. While I admire Europe and am quite ready to grant the role it has played in civili- zation, I think the time has come for recognition of the broader base which now exists. Some of my contacts have indicated that Latin America, as regards its intelligentsia, should be included.

The case of Karl Barth is also interesting. I believe that he rejects the intrusion of philosophy into the realm of theology which is based on revelation. He is, undoubtedly, a vigorous exponent of his outlook. And he has influenced established tradition in England and on the Continent. But there is more pluralism in these matters in the United States and the dialogue goes on. Here, again, I take it that De Rougemont has been misled by journalism. He must learn to look a little deeper. I conclude that while much can be said for Europe and while it is desirable that it federate, its hegemony is not as exceptional in science and in philosophy as it once was. In politics it has, perhaps, learned the lesson of retreat to its own resources while the United States is still tempted. But that is another question.

The General Plan of the Book

As I have indicated, I am interested in comparisons of philosophical perspectives. I shall take the American scene as a base-line because I participated in it and watched events as they unfolded. I shall devote the next chapters to the movement from idealism to pragmatism and realism. The chapter after that I shall give to the debate between the new realists and the critical realists. Here, again, we are largely on American soil. I shall argue that there was a rather remarkable amount of vigor and variety in the debate. Looking back on the participants, many of whom I knew, I am impressed by their obvious competence. It is clear that they felt that philosophy was in the making. They were well-trained, many having studied in Europe or with the rather exceptional galaxy of thinkers which made up the Harvard Department of Philosophy. What stands out is the freshness of their thought. They were exploring. Most of them had turned away from idealism. Philosophy in the United States had come of age.

After having studied the debate between the new realists and the critical realists and the apparent stalemate which ensued, I shall allow myself the privilege, which an author is entitled to take, to develop and explain his own position. This will constitute what I have called the base-line for my analysis of other cultural traditions in philosophy whose profiles I shall examine.

First, then, after the presentation of the general position which I regard as defensible and in harmony with the sciences, I shall take up the various strands of British thought. These are more diverse than ordinarily supposed. There was the tradition of Anglo-American idealism which we have already encountered. But this existed with other strands of thought, Platonic and Aristotelian, on the one hand, and empiricist, on the other. I cannot undertake to do justice to this diversity but must recognize it. As time went on, it was overshadowed by the influence of Bertrand Russell and G. E. Moore; but I have found it operating in unexpected ways in the background. Thus there is an obvious connection between the Aristotelian tradition and what is now called the "ordinary language" approach. Aristotle was very careful in his use of words. But, of course, words are tied in with a dominant outlook and must not be given connotative finality.

I shall be concerned, then, with dominant features of British thought in the twentieth century. And I shall not quarrel with those who give it a somewhat different profile. In my own thinking, I pass in review F. H. Bradley, James Ward, Cook Wilson and Prichard, Russell, Moore, C. D. Broad, Gilbert Ryle, and Ayer, while holding in suspense that rather enigmatic figure, Ludwig Wittgenstein. Logically and linguistically he is acute; but I am not so sure of his epistemology and ontology.

After the study of the British thought, which is both akin to the American and divergent from it, I pass to the Continent. In this connection I shall give, perhaps, stress to existentialism. I recognize this is a label applied rather arbitrarily. Heidegger, for instance, does not now approve of it for he regards himself as concerned with "*being*." But the perspective and historical leads are rather shared. We hear much of Kierkegaard, *Angst,* and existence. And we also hear little of empiricism, naturalism and science. The philosophical climate is divergent from that we have so far been accustomed to. There are ingredients of anti-intellectualism and voluntarism and of subjectivism in existentialism's historical heredity which are interesting and must be taken into account. Saint Augustine, Pascal and Nietzsche come into purview. I take it to be a question of comprehensive adjustment within a framework. As a realistic empiricist I do not accept the rather sharp contrasts between the objective and the subjective, the rational and the non-rational, which I find current in existential writings. Kierkegaard's abrupt reaction to Hegelian rationalism has hardly a parallel in British and American thought in which the transition was modified by empiricism. William James's criticism of Royce is only analogous.

While, then, I shall try to do justice to Continental thought and its emphases, I shall naturally have in mind the base-line which I have set up as paradigmatic. I do not want this to be rigid. And I should expect it to be able to do justice to justifiable demands. I hold that the subjective can be integrated with the objective in a double-knowledge approach and I can see no good reason why deductive thought should be set in opposition to observation. In short, I am skeptical of the validity of some of the abrupt contrasts I find in Continental literature. As another instance, I would bring forward my notion of levels of causality and the belief I entertain that the human organism cannot solve its problems apart from deliberation. This is, to me, the locus of what is called free-will or choosing. I am opposed to complete pre-determination and would enlarge and deepen causality at the mind-brain level. But of this more in the concluding chapter.

In another chapter I shall explore Marxist materialism. This, as is well known, is called dialectical materialism. First, it is essential to examine the theory of knowledge involved. It is a form of realism called the "reflection" view of perception. As I read Lenin, he starts from things and moves to sensations as reflecting them. But the epistemological difficulty is that of how he gets to things in the first place. Certainly, the old empirical puzzle was that thinkers made sensations terminal in experience and landed in representationalism, as Locke did. You seem shut into your sensations. How, then, do you know there are things and that your sensations reflect them? This is the gambit critics of dialectical materialism take.

Now it may be recalled that critical realism seeks to overcome this dilemma by reanalyzing perceiving and finding in it a direct response guided and informed by sensations so that sensations are not so much terminal as used as informational sources. We note how a thing looks or feels, that is, how what we are responding to looks and feels. Thus, the thought of a thing grows up in this context of response, action and used sensory information. What stands out in this setting is the decipherment of facts about things. How they look, how far away they are, how they feel. We are always busy in working out such facts by using our sensations as informative; and, of course, measuring and weighing and scientific technique take over.

I am inclined to think, therefore, that the epistemology of materialism can be worked out. I note that Thomists, who have a fairly definite epistemology along Aristotelian lines, make much of this requirement. Materialism, they rightly say, rests on the establishment of realism. I agree; and shall later examine their theory of perceiving. It stresses a kind of identity between object and experienced content in terms of forms or essences. I shall argue that critical realism has a more adequate notion of the mechanisms nature worked out. But, after clarifying perceiving, the philosopher still has problems with respect to materialism. The founders of dialectical materialism recognized this fact and appealed to the term, dialectic, as used by Hegel. It was not to be what they called vulgar materialism of a reductive type which they would defend but one more historical-minded. They held that there was a movement in nature of a progressive, logical sort, at least analogous to Hegel's scheme of thesis, antithesis and synthesis. Especially in the human scene they found indications of this kind of dialectic. A position was adopted and then negations of it, showing its inadequacy, manifested themselves. The next stage was a sort of transcendence of this tense confrontation of thesis and antithesis in a synthesis. Marxist experts used this schematism to throw light on history. They discerned conflict and struggle where liberals tended to find a kind of harmonious growth.

There is another contender in the field called emergence. It stresses novelty with organization. It has its roots in Darwinian biology rather than in Hegelian logic. It will be advisable to explore the kind of ontology involved.

While, then, I favor an evolutionary kind of materialism able to recognize the emergent categories of the human scene, such as those of politics and morality, I look upon a dialogue with dialectics as desirable. There are, certainly, ambivalences to be cleared up. Some of these were inherited from Hegelianism. I shall, then, discuss the "reflection" base of Marxism as well as its tendency to determinism.

Another chapter will discuss neo-Thomism. This, as I see it, is a form of neo-Aristotelianism, I have studied it recently with a good deal of interest. There was a realism here opposed sharply to Cartesian subjectivism and dualism and thus not taking the line of British empiricism. Yet it had to wrestle with the question of the nature and reach of perceiving. The mind-body problem also had to be faced. Except with Aristotle's rather vague postulation of the "active reason," there had been a marked naturalistic note in his later thought.

I had the impression, therefore, that neo-Aristotelianism had not faced up to recent developments in science. It still retained the old, relative use of the term "matter" and its complement "form." And with these went a corresponding vocabulary of potency and actuality. I was not blind to a certain common-sense richness in Aristotelianism. And yet I was persuaded that it had to be done all over again, starting with a different view of the mechanism of perceiving and taking account of evolutionary ideas alien to Aristotle. This meant, of course, taking the modern view of matter-energy and such constituents as electrons, protons, atoms, molecules, etc., along with scientific techniques. The necessary philosophical linkage was a solution of the problem of the nature and reach of perceiving. Cartesian and empirical subjectivism had to be overcome. Perceiving had to be direct in import and yet mediated by the informative use of sensations. Do we not note how things look and how they feel? That is, sensations are cognitively functional and not terminal. Inquisitively used, they are the sources of *facts about* objects.

When I turned to Maritain, for instance, I found him emphasizing what he called *sensible things* made up of *forms* and *matter* in the Aristotelian tradition and stressing a kind of cognitional identity of thought and thing. When it came to the scientific view of the world he found logical positivism with its essential phenomenalism to hand. What, I ask myself, will he do now that logical positivism is being rejected? I have the impression that Gilson and Maritain have not paid much attention to developments in Anglo-American philosophy. I am not surprised because these were very ambivalent as yet. I could not expect them to single out my form of critical realism since this was largely ignored. But I do think that such a confrontation is needed. It is this I shall undertake.

This, then, is my plan, a study of basic movements in the light of my own paradigms. By its very nature, such a comprehensive survey can only be sketchy and touch the high points. To carry it into detail would require the cooperation of many scholars expert in the different fields touched on. I cannot do much more than to set up guidelines. Yet I think I have a fair knowledge of cultural setting and philosophical profiles. Having participated in philosophical movements from the inside, I have a fair knowledge of the psychology of philosophers, their attachments and limitations. What I have noted in the American scene, I have also noticed abroad. There are trends and fashions but seldom basic reorientations. There is, also, a tendency to cultural isolation. It may well be that this last tendency is being offset by better communication.

I shall argue that American philosophical thought had a very healthy beginning and was carried on by exceptionally able men. In certain ways, its horizon was more open and less confined by tradition than was British, French and German thought. It tended, on the whole, to a broad empiricism and naturalism. And then came what I have called a certain stalemate and a tendency to look abroad for cues and guidance. And this tendency was reinforced by a certain vigor and self-confidence abroad. I was not unaware of this change of venue and tried to do justice to it, while pressing forward along the lines I had outlined. Not unnaturally I sometimes felt frustrated and ignored. But the only thing to do was, like a spider, to retest my web and strengthen it. There are, I believe, signs that something like critical realism and evolutionary materialism and humanism are being again considered viable possibilities. This book is an attempt to initiate a dialogue along these lines.

2

STAGES IN
THE AMERICAN SCENE

The primary purpose of this book is that of a study of contemporary profiles in philosophy. But I cannot altogether neglect historical backgrounds. It is, however, far easier to trace continuities in British and German thought than in American. The Germans, as we shall see, while recognizing the influence of Greek thought, turn to Leibnitz, Kant and Hegel, along with lesser lights, as the founding thinkers. It was these who made philosophy, in their opinion, a kind of German possession. Various gambits arise with this as a background. I do not wish to oversimplify and I acknowledge the role played by seminal thinkers, such as Nietzsche, Brentano and Husserl, but the framework was established in the way I have indicated. The British had a somewhat different history. Locke and Hume helped to enforce what is called the empirical tradition. This tradition can be traced back to the late Middle Ages, at least, with Roger Bacon, William of Ockham and others making their contribution. Here, again, one must not oversimplify. Francis Bacon picked it up as modern science was getting under way and turned against Aristotle. One must add John Stuart Mill and Jeremy Bentham. Academic philosophy keeps tab of history and revives interest in this, or that, thinker. But, on the whole, British thought has had empirical associations; that is, it has stressed human experience. It is so classified by the Germans. I shall have more to say about these traditions and continuities in later chapters so far as they have affected perspectives. But I want now to turn to the American scene.

First came the colonial era. Here I would pick out New England with its religious tradition. Then came the gradual shift in interest to the secular and political. As is well known, the increasingly federated colonies absorbed Enlightenment thought. The stress was on human rights. Jefferson enlarged his horizon and kept contact with current French and British radicalism. Even materialism was considered. One thinks here of Cooper, Priestley, Rush and Tom Paine. I glanced at this period in my chapter on "Social Philosophy and the American Scene" in the book I helped to edit in 1949 called *Philosophy for the Future* or the *Quest of*

15

Modern Materialism. Semi-materialistic ideas, in fact, were in vogue in
the Enlightenment even in the United States.

And then philosophy in the United States marked time. There were
incursions of Scottish common-sense thought which lasted in some
colleges until the undergraduate days of John Dewey and J. B. Pratt.
Here the stress was on mind-matter dualism and on intuition. Cousin's
eclecticism also had its impact, as in the case of Tappan, Chancellor of the
University of Michigan. Spencer had a virgin territory in his day and
social Darwinism had many followers among successful business men.

But the revival of technical philosophy in the United States is usually
associated with the *St. Louis Movement*. Under the leadership of Brok-
meyer and Harris interest was aroused in Kant and Hegel. This linked
up later with the Concord School associated with Alcott and Emerson.
Out of this sprang what is usually called Anglo-American idealism,
associated with the names of Harris, G. S. Morris, Howison, Creighton
and Josiah Royce. I used to hear much of G. S. Morris, who taught
at both Michigan and Johns Hopkins. He was one of the teachers, at
the latter school, of John Dewey. Thus, as we shall see, Dewey linked
Scottish common sense with Anglo-American idealism and went on to
develop his own brand of pragmatism, called instrumentalism.

Edwards and Emerson

But I want to turn back for a moment to the New England religious
tradition as represented by Jonathan Edwards and Emerson. This is
important for it, in many ways, runs parallel with recent, religious
existentialism. In the case of more secular existentialism, one can find
analogies between Edwards' stress on *Being* and that of Heidegger. The
religious note comes in Edwards' emphasis on *love of Being*. I shall have
occasion to compare Edwards and Tillich on this point. It interested me
after I picked up and read books on *The Search for Being* as the
outstanding and modish note of the present. It should be recalled that
Emerson was a contemporary of Kierkegaard and got some of his ideas of
German thought through Coleridge. As an evolutionary materialist, I
shall have to make my peace with Being. But here I am more impressed
with human beings and their stance of valuation, moral and non-moral,
than with *Being as such*. But the philosopher does well to reflect on the
whole scope of Being and its ontological status.

A few words, then, on Edwards. He is rightly regarded as a man of philosophical stature. He was a scholar and knew his Locke, his Newton, and the tradition of Cambridge (England) Platonism. God was Being in a transcendent way and the Scriptures and his faith taught love of Him. Neo-Platonism in the Augustinian tradition was always strong in Protestantism as opposed to the Aristotelian perspective of Thomism. Out of this complex comes very naturally Edwards' call to love of Being. I note the same Augustinian perspective in Tillich. As I read him, he was very little affected by British and American philosophy, any more than Maritain was. This is quite understandable but must be taken account of. These assizes must be as objective and comprehensive as possible.

I add a few words on Emerson. While later Anglo-American philosophy had a different texture, it was, on the whole, dominated by a religious interest. As we shall see, this manifests itself overtly in Howison, Bowne and Royce. Thus, in this regard, there is a certain continuity with Edwards and Emerson.

Transcendentalism was a mild, poetic type of religious thought, quite different from the tragic rendition of theology in Kierkegaard. For Emerson, God was an Oversoul from whom emanated the diverse and fruitful variety of things. There was, of course, the ingredient of skepticism of the senses so characteristic of idealism. Hence science is put in second place.

There is a certain ambiguity in Emerson. He takes an aesthetic delight in Nature and yet holds that it is a manifestation of the Universal Mind. In a semi-pantheistic way he passes from the one to the other. His aphoristic language helps him here. Consistency ceases to be a bane and his transitions from the subjective to the objective take place freely and easily. He has no clear framework by which to be bound. In the last analysis, nothing is of us for all things are of God. Thus he dances from one topic to another with the verve and license of the sage. He justifies himself by the axiom that to say the human mind creates objects is much the same as to say that God creates them. "I am part and parcel of God."

One can understand that, in contrast to the rigidities of Puritan thought, all this was emancipating. It put poetic epigram in place of dogma. Yet it must have been both enthralling and exasperating. Take the case of the role and validity of morality. "The moral law lies at the center of nature and radiates to the circumference. It is the pith and marrow of every substance, every relation, and every process." It would seem that, for Emerson, Nature is moral throughout.

In his later years, the notion of evolution confronted him but it was in the form of Lamarckism which stressed will and effort and thus fitted in with his romantic voluntarism. But there is every now and then a realistic note which warns us not to ignore the complexity of things. It is not so certain that man is the prime end of all that happens.

So Emerson must be taken as a poet-philosopher, a voice of his times, aware of dialogues that were going on in Europe and moving in the direction of liberation. His essays were at once general pronouncements and exhortations. His sincerity was manifest. I read him much as a youth and felt his appeal to integrity and self-reliance, but got no indications of systematic approach to philosophical problems. That came later in the University and even there with no great clarity. I had the task of locating them and of circling around them and envisaging them ever more sharply.

I want now to comment briefly on his Danish contemporary as regards style of thought and temper. More analytic treatment must be postponed until I examine existentialism as a movement of to-day.

Kierkegaard was more thoroughly trained in philosophy than was Emerson. But he turned to Schelling and away from the panlogism of Hegel. We find mention of Schelling in Emerson also, probably through the mediation of Coleridge.

But we come quickly to the divergence in theological and ecclesiastical setting. No sect was dominant in an established way in Emerson's America, while Kierkegaard was confronted with the Established Church of Denmark, which he was to attack for its laxities. The liberal wing of Congregationalism in Emerson's New England was veering towards Unitarianism with its rejection of biblical orthodoxy. Kierkegaard drew lessons from biblical legends, such as that of the story of Abraham and Isaac. And he reflected on the paradoxes of God becoming man in Jesus. How could eternity break into time? How could history be of continuing moment? To meet these questions he plunged into the self and away from science and the objective. The heart has its reasons. We shall find something of this appearing in William James.

Now I grant that the objective approach must do justice to what stands out in self-knowledge. And I think this adjustment is gradually taking place. In my own terminology I speak of double-knowledge, of supplementation. And I would reject the abrupt opposition adopted by Kierkegaard. But I shall take up that issue in due season. What I want to note now is the different texture and orientation of Kierkegaard's writings and those of Emerson. The first is biblically based and has the tragic intensity of legend, while the latter is optimistic and semi-romantic.

It is usually said that philosophy and science arose when the question, What is a thing made of? replaced sagas and legends. As I saw it, liberalism and humanism in religious thought followed this direction. And I was surprised when neo-orthodoxy was exported from Europe after the First World War. Was this an advance? Was Europe in the lead? I did not think so. In many ways, Europe seemed to me conservative. I did not deny that the United States spoke with no certain voice. But I thought that the enlightened trend was liberal and humanistic.

My friend Swenson was a great admirer of Kierkegaard and, being of Scandinavian descent, a good translator. I was, again, interested when Lindsey of Oxford, stopping here on cultural business during the Second World War, asked me about my attitude toward Kierkegaard, indicating his interest. And now I hear of Bishop Robinson's heretical attack on the three-stage universe of the bible, qualified, however, by appeal to Tillich's view of God as *Being*. And so the debate goes on.

Bowne's Personalism

Bowne was one of the first to bring German philosophy to the United States and in a form fairly congenial to the American temper. It was not Hegel but Kant and Lotze who gave the frame to his thinking. And his personalism has remained an influence in American thought. I shall discuss Bowne's position and add comments on its development by Brightman. I shall have occasion to examine Brightman's epistemic dualism, which he opposed to epistemic monism, and try to show that there is a middle way between these extremes. This will involve some nice points in epistemology.

As I understand it, the personalist regards the person as the category of categories and the most complex model in terms of which to think of reality. As I look back on my contacts, I would say that James Ward, the critic of the absolute idealism of F. H. Bradley, represents the nearest approach to personalism in England. He, also, stressed the self.

I may remark, in passing, that I look upon personalism as more liberal and rational in temper than the neo-orthodoxy stemming from Kier-kegaard. The personalists are temporalists and do not put time over against eternity. They do not set the subjective over against the objective but seek to make the personal the model and pass from it to their concept of reality with a finite God as the great agent and mediator. I found I could debate with Brightman on both epistemology and ontology. I, of course, took an evolutionary approach to culture and personality but sought to do justice to their quality and uniqueness. I was not reductive in my views and argued for levels of causality and the import of human agency.

Bowne, I recall, had standing, though he was overshadowed by Royce. It is curious how one finds recurrent the recognition of certain priorities. Bowne was puzzled by the fact of objective knowledge-claims. These claims involved some kind of transcendence. In re-reading Lovejoy for my paper in the Pratt memorial volume, I found the same axiom.* "The mind has the capacity to transcend itself." Lovejoy was a dualist and took this ability as somehow intrinsic to the very nature of mind. I, on the other hand, sought to trace it to biological mechanisms in which sensations are used as informative guides to reactive responses. As I saw it, explicit referential knowing emerged from this foundation. I shall shortly discuss Brightman's epistemic dualism from this angle.

Bowne held—and I think rightly—that judging has conditions in the capacity of the person to correlate subject and predicate terms, that is, to denote and connote, to realize what you are talking about and what you are saying about it. This kind of activity, he thought, involved the self. But there remained the question of what the self is. I may remark that I am more a functionalist in these matters than an old-time associationalist. That is, I think in terms of developed activities.

Quite understandably, Bowne rejected a passive imprint notion of the origin of knowledge. And so he turned to thought, somewhat after the manner of Kant. He sought to move between realism and extreme idealism. But I do not think he explored sufficiently the informative control exerted by sensations in the job of perceiving. He swung over to the innatism of Kant. And the stress is put on construction by thought with the categories as norms. The result was a kind of phenomenalism. Brightman calls it in his last book, *Person and Reality*, a quasi-phenomenalism. I think this is a good expression to distinguish it from the simplicities of logical positivism.

But the role of such quasi-phenomenalism is to set nature apart from reality as a whole. As Brightman puts it, "The object of metaphysics is the total system of reality of which the phenomena of Nature are a part." I shall point to much the same tactics by Maritain, to escape the full impact of the scientific view of things. Logical positivism was a double-edged affair. As I saw it, it represented a combination of epistemological naïveté in its phenomenalism, which made sensations terminal, and logical sophistication. Even its logic seemed unable to deal with the

_____
*Self, Religion and Metaphysics, Macmillan.

demands of language as in treating dispositional terms which had grown up in the context of natural realism. I take it that they had a bogy in mind, such as Kant's famous unknowable things-in-themselves. One can't take philosophy by storm even in Vienna.

Here, again, I take Brightman's version of personal idealism for he lived in the period of epistemological dispute. Quite understandably, he rejected the epistemic monism of the new realists. It seemed to him quite clear that perceiving did not involve the actual givenness, or openness to apprehension, that the new realists had predicated as the sole alternative to Locke's representationalism. From the start, the new realism had met serious objections in terms of error and personal perspective. Perry had devoted his energies largely to undermining idealism, as he understood it. His constructive enterprise was less marked. I have long argued that there were possibilities between presentationalism and Locke's representationalism. Why not take the act of perceiving as referentially directed at the external object which is controlling sensations in the percipient and regard these sensations as functioning in this context as informative and not terminal? So taken, the objective reference would be developed on the basis of reactive response and sensory informing would express itself as discerned *facts about* the objects. Certainly, this is the way it emerges in perceptual judgments.

In contrast to epistemic monism of the new realist's type, this could be called epistemological dualism and Brightman regards me as the coiner of this terminology. But, as a matter of fact, I was concerned with the establishment of a more adequate type of *direct realism* able to do justice to the complex mechanism of perceiving indicated above. Thus I moved between presentationalism and representationalism. I shall not go into greater detail at this point since I must go into the question in depth in a later chapter. Suffice it to say that, in perceiving, sensations are not terminal as they were for Berkeley, Hume, Mill and Russell but cognitively used for the factual information they offer. We become aware of how things look and feel.

But, to return to Brightman, he embraced epistemic dualism and did not explore this alternative. I can quite understand his motivations. He was following Bowne's semi-Kantian stress on categorial construction. The result was his quasi-phenomenalism. The advantage of this was that the metaphysical (reality) cannot be deduced from epistemic dualism; "the metaphysical stage is clear for nonmental or for idealistic objects. All that the personalist holds is that his hypothesis not be excluded arbitrarily from among the contenders." The person then becomes the category of categories. Thence the advance is to theism. This is one way of proceeding. I took the evolutionary way and sought to do justice to human personality and valuations within this context.

A Few Remarks on Howison

Howison, I take it, stood out as a defender of idealistic pluralism in opposition to the tendency to idealistic absolutism, or monism, on the part of Josiah Royce and F. H. Bradley. As his pupil A. O. Lovejoy points out, Howison was convinced that mind was primary in the world. Summing up a memorable philosophical symposium in 1895, he said, "we are all agreed" in one "great tenet," which is "the entire foundation of philosophy itself: that explanation of the world which maintains that the only thing absolutely real is mind; that all material and all temporal existences take their being from Consciousness that thinks and experiences; that out of consciousness they all issue, to consciousness they are presented, and that *presence to consciousness* constitutes their entire reality." Lovejoy comments, "With almost a whole generation of acute and powerful minds this passed for a virtual axiom." He was himself to swing to temporalism and realism.

How did Howison get that way? Well, it was the climate of the times. He got his start in philosophy in St. Louis along the lines of Hegelian idealism. Then he spent two years in Germany and, under the spell of Michelet, turned to personalism as against Hegelian stress on logic. He ended up at the University of California as a gifted teacher and director. I had no direct contact with him but my colleague, DeWitt Parker, spent a year there and told me about him.

Mind is, then, primary. What follows? I use his own words. "All existence is either (1) the existence of minds, or (2) the existence of the items and order of their experiences; all existences known as 'material' consisting in certain of these experiences. Accordingly, Time and Space, and all they contain owe their entire existence to the essential correlation and coexistence of minds."

This order is also moral. "The recognition of each other as all alike self-determining renders their coexistence a moral order." The eternal world of selves is thus constituted. It may be called the city of God. God is the living bond of their union and reigns in it not by power but by light. The members of this "Eternal Republic have no origin—no source in *time* whatever. They simply are and together constitute the eternal order."

One can see the influence of both Leibnitz and Kant here. It is said that Howison regarded his own philosophy as an attempt to break down the Kantian barrier between the practical and the theoretical consciousness. It is obvious that both empiricism and materialism are dismissed. The position lent itself to almost evangelical exhortation. Freedom, immortality and progress were assured.

But the fly in the ointment turned out to be the Absolute Idealism of Josiah Royce. Over his theses debate began to rage. As yet, idealism, itself, was not challenged. Aside from Howison, as Professor Schneider points out, there were in this period four academic centers of idealism: Bowne at Boston University, with his form of personalism; speculative or objective idealism at Cornell with Creighton; dynamic idealism at the University of Michigan with Morris; and absolute idealism at Harvard with Royce. These occupied the limelight. I shall later consider objective idealism in the form of a letter addressed to me by Bosanquet as comment on my first book, *Critical Realism*. In the same context, I shall quote from a letter by F. H. Bradley. These letters are interesting as showing the presuppositions within which they thought. I shall note Morris' type of idealism in connection with Dewey's shift away from it under the influence of Darwin and William James. But now to Royce.

Royce's Absolute Idealism

I saw and heard Royce once and that was at Madison in 1904 while I was a fellow there in philosophy. To Bode's annoyance, I was not invited to the evening reception and so I never met him personally. I heard the rumor that the governing body had it in mind to invite him to occupy the vacant chair in philosophy at the university.

I think that Santayana's sketch of Royce in his book *Character and Opinion in the United States* should by all means be read. He emphasizes Royce's omnivorous range of interest. "He had an evident sly pleasure in the degustation and savour of difficulties; biblical criticism, the struggle for life, the latest German theory of sexual insanity, had no terrors for him; it was all grist for the mill, and woe to any tender thing, any beauty or any illusion, that should get between that upper and that nether millstone." My own idealistic Head was also a polymath but one with less rigor of outlook. If knowledge, alone, would solve philosophical problems, these men would have solved them. I speak of philosophical problems for there were such problems clearly visible in the culture of the time: the nature and conditions of human knowing, the mind-brain issue, the texture of evolution, the role and status of valuation, the justification of moral judgment, etc. I do not think philosophy wanted to dictate to the growing sciences. Rather it was puzzled as to what answers to give to what it felt to be unavoidable issues and how these answers would fit into the world. I have since watched impatient empiricists and positivists giving their nostrums, Russell starting with a primary knowledge of acquaintance and constructing the world therefrom, the logical positivists beginning with similar data, now baptized protocol sentences. It was, quite obviously, not easy to dig deeper into nature's technique in the operations involved in perceiving. I know it was a step-by-step affair with me, as I circled around the problem. But I will go into that in the chapter on the development of realism.

With all his ability, Royce did not question the great German tradition of philosophy from Kant, through Hegel, to Schopenhauer and Lotze. Rather he sought to press onward within its general framework. Nothing exemplifies this perspective better that his attempt to give a final quietus to realism by identifying it with the belief in completely external and independent entities. Beings are one thing and ideas are distinct and separate and never the twain shall meet. How, then, can there be a cognitive relation between them? As is well known, he sought to give an idealistic answer to realistic motivations by making a distinction between the inner meaning of an idea and its external meaning. The external meaning is the fulfillment of the inner meaning. I shall say something about this device later. I have countered it by showing that physical things feed in information about themselves in sensation and that we use such information as evidence in external sense-perception. Thus correspondence between thought and thing is furthered by the use of informational cues. We note how a thing looks, what position it has, how it reacts to other things. Human knowing is an achievement on this operational base. I can, however, quite understand how it was that a cool and capable thinker like Brand Blanshard clung to Royce's scheme. It took me a long time to grasp nature's *from-and-to* technique. As I said above, I circled around it. My first step was to deny the traditional cognitive relation linking subject and object. It seemed to me a bit of myth. In its place, I gradually inserted reference and informed knowledge-claims based on fed-in information.

But I must return to Royce. He started with a stress on cognition and truth. Here he sought to show that error involves truth. It is truth that makes error possible. Error he takes to be essentially an incomplete thought. This was in the idealist tradition and is found in F. H. Bradley. If one gives up a correspondence goal involving increased evidence, then one naturally turns to a higher or completer thought. Royce arrived at an inclusive and even Infinite Thought. This was his first version of God— what is usually called an intellectualist one. For Royce, then, reality is organized experience. His rejection of realism is merely a dialectical defense of this thesis. But now he turns his attention successively to the problem of evil in a theistic setting and to the question of the relation of the Many and the One. This latter question was forced on his attention by Howison and the personal idealists.

Royce saw that, for the naturalist, evil, both physical and moral, is just a feature of the constitution of things and can be understood only in this setting. But he had a responsible God and had, somehow, to integrate evil with Him. It had a role to play in His economy. His answer was that its function was that of a challenge. It was something to be overcome. God's life would be imperfect without it. Hence God chooses to suffer.

But the pluralists were not satisfied. How did this justify evil as experienced by human beings? It was undeniably real. Royce answered in terms of identification. We must realize that we suffer *in* God, that our suffering is an ingredient in His dynamic life.

But this answer brought up the question of the status of the individual. Is he merely a fragment in the whole? As I see it, Howison had reached idealism along other lines, taking the material world to be merely phenomenal. It is the individual who thinks and judges. Royce's abstract, logical ascent does not impress him. How can Selves be free if they are only fragments of a World Mind? Royce answers that the individual is not a mere fragment but a person with a will. Here his voluntarism begins to manifest itself. I am free as a unique embodiment of the Will of the Absolute.

Royce went on his way. The internal and external meanings which he had set up as a substitute for the old notion of correspondence between thought and thing became now two phases of a single purpose. Appreciation blends with description. Within his framework, Royce had a very systematic and ingenious mind. He learned the new logic from Peirce and applied it to the idea of the Infinite as a series. He interpreted Christianity as a Beloved Community and criticized individualism as selfish isolationism. In ethics he stressed what he called loyalty to loyalty, which implies loyalty to my fellows in ever-widening circles.

Needless to say, I struggled with Royce's books, beginning with *The Religious Aspect of Philosophy*. As I look back on it, I can note that I was seeking a different orientation. I thought of knowing more in a scientific setting and was led to explore the realistic import of perceiving. Pragmatism had already begun as an alternative to idealism but I was not satisfied with it. James was brilliant but sketchy and erratic and it seemed to me that Dewey was more a reformer of idealism than one who was striking out on new paths. I shall comment on these two very able men in the next chapter.

It is clear that philosophy combines an internal momentum, dominated by theses with respect to its recognized problems, with the influence upon it of the cultural outlook. The United States was in the nineteenth century still in the climate of the religious view of the world. But this climate was altering, owing to both industrial and scientific developments. By itself, this alteration did not dictate to philosophy's handling of its problems but, rather, led it to reconsider accepted assumptions. Its influence was thus indirect and yet powerful.

The debate in philosophy which ensued took the form of a dialogue about the meaning of truth. Idealism had rested on what was called the coherence theory of truth as exemplified, for example, in Royce's idea that error consists in incompleteness. This was now challenged by the pragmatic theory of truth, formulated somewhat differently by Peirce, James and Dewey. Here the stress was on working within human experience. It is interesting to note that British philosophers did not develop much appreciation for this shift in American thought. They tended to put it at its lowest terms. A revived kind of empiricism played a part here. Russell, for instance, made knowledge by acquaintance primary and sought to make knowledge by description subordinate to it. But in the United States, itself, the realistic movement broke out in full force and drew attention to the nature of perceiving. The new realists were pitted against the critical realists. This dispute had its effect on the question of truth. Some held that a stalemate had developed. I, myself, worked on at the problem, as I said, circling around it trying to get new insights. But, quite understandably, many American philosophers began to look abroad. Europeans took this to be a very natural move in recognition of their cultural priorities. I, myself, came to call it cultural colonialism. It was not that I was opposed to cultural intercourse and communication but I regarded it as a two-way street. I was even inclined to hold that the American development had considerable richness and novelty. But I shall take up this point later.

3

PRAGMATISM:
PEIRCE, JAMES AND DEWEY

I am not one of those who want to oversimplify. But there can be little doubt that pragmatism arose in the United States as a shift of perspective away from the idealism I considered in the previous chapter. The center of gravity of thought, so to speak, had altered.

While, quite rightly, the European tradition was kept in mind, an indigenous element was introduced, the stress on practice and consequences. It is for this reason that pragmatism is regarded in Europe as distinctively American. The temptation—often indulged in—is to identify it with an emphasis on practical results. Theory is, supposedly, largely ignored.

It may well be that James's racy style is partly responsible for this interpretation. He allowed himself to speak of the cash-value of ideas. And it is true that he belonged to the more subjective and psychological wing of pragmatism which stressed personal experience and personal decisions. Yet James had cosmic and metaphysical interests as well.

But, when we turn to Peirce and Dewey, the balance is redressed. Peirce, as we shall see, had a wide base on which to build. He knew mathematics, logic, science and the main currents of philosophical thought. And, in all this, he was no amateur but an expert, as Europeans are gradually finding out. There are indications that a cult of Peirce is developing in England as well as in the United States. Dewey's instrumentalism is also objective in intention and, while it emphasizes the role of ideas, it stresses their testing in all sorts of transactions. In his beginnings, as we shall see, Dewey was linked with the dynamic idealism of Morris but, under the influence of Darwin, swung increasingly to a naturalistic orientation. From abstract reason he shifted to a stress on intelligence and its function. His logic was experimental in cast, as can be seen in his dialogue with Russell. It was not, I take it, that he was opposed to the logic of deduction and consistency but that he wanted to see it in a larger setting, human thought dealing with problems.

I shall examine Peirce first because he had priority. And I shall be

27

deeply concerned with his epistemology. It took me some time to appreciate the likenesses and differences between his *logical realism* and my own *physical realism*. And I am inclined to suspect that many Peirce scholars, not well trained in recent epistemology, hardly, as yet, grasp the different framework involved. As against nominalism, Peirce was defending the cognitive import of concepts and the logic that goes with them. There was a touch of Kant here as well as of Ockham.

The development of philosophy is a step-by-step affair. And I think it took the succeeding realistic movement to sharpen issues as to the import of perceiving as the gateway of cognition and scientific knowledge of the world.

A reminiscence may be in order. I recall that Professor Pap, a brilliant young philosopher, once spoke here on the topic of realism. This was long after the rise of critical realism and the new realism. But I soon found that it was logical realism as against nominalism that he had in mind. It seemed, in fact, that he was scarcely aware of the other usage of the term. In talking with one of the logical positivists, I encountered the same terminological tradition. This is the way things go in philosophy. There are traditions and winds of doctrine and many seem shut into the tradition in which they have been brought up. There is vital need of communication. I may remark here, incidentally, that I have found European philosophers more shut into their traditions than Americans. This is not a matter of virtue of American thinkers but of historical circumstances. They have had to learn and assimilate until it came about that they could strike out on the paths which appealed to them. Such independence was not always welcomed abroad when it occurred. This, I think, happened in the case of pragmatism and, in some measure, with realism. And, then, curiously enough, when what was regarded as a stalemate in the realistic movement occurred—how justifiable remains to be seen—a new kind of colonialism manifested itself in the United States. One soon heard only of analysis *a la* Moore, of Wittgenstein, and of logical positivism. This to be followed by existentialism. I do not say this attitude was universal. There remained many Deweyites and the study of Peirce increased. But I had to work rather alone. I continued to circle around perceiving, evolutionary levels, double knowledge of the mind-brain functioning and humanism. That is the way things go and one must have what has been called intestinal fortitude. I think the situation is somewhat altering and more of an international equilibrium is getting established. But what I call journalistic philosophy still echoes the period of neo-colonialism. Literary critics, whose philosophy is second-hand, mouth the accepted terms. And

I find that many young philosophers in the United States seem to have little knowledge of past developments. In their eyes, one must be analytic, or a logical positivist or a defender of ordinary language. But enough of this parenthesis. Let us get on with our business.

C. S. Peirce

Let me begin by saying that I knew practically nothing about Peirce when I began to work out guiding lines. I was dissatisfied with the framework of idealism and was not convinced that pragmatism had grappled with the issues I found in my course on the *Main Concepts of Science*. Thus I was moving in the direction of realism in an exploratory way. It turned out that others of my generation were doing the same. James Ward's *Naturalism and Agnosticism* served as a *pièce de résistance* for it was more sophisticated than Pearson's *Grammar of Science*. Long afterward I had a chance to talk with him about it, after a game of chess in his home. I was querying the so-called cognitive relation between subject and object, that is, the traditional formula that there is no object without a subject and no subject without an object, a neat little schematism. I had been suggesting that we make things objects through guided reference. This involved directed claims rather than a mysterious relation. I shall have more to say about this later.

While Peirce was absent, Morris, James and Dewey were very much in the forefront. I read Royce but in a very critical mood. His rejection of realism seemed to me based on extreme assumptions of externality and independence, a kind of *tour-de-force*. While I was critical of a specific cognitive relation hooking up thought and thing, I recognized that there had to be some sort of interplay to make reference and knowledge-claims possible. This I now conceive as a from-and-to movement with a biological base. But this is to anticipate.

While attending a summer session at the University of Chicago in 1906 to hear Baldwin, I became acquainted with some graduate students who had notes on Dewey's lectures on experimental logic. These I read with interest with their stress on problems and the ensuing dichotomy between datum and ideatum. Of course we all read the decennial publication of the Chicago School. Much later I had discussions with A. W. Moore. I particularly remember a train-ride back from Madison to Chicago. I tried to explain to him what was bothering me and why I thought his framework was inadequate. He had a keen mind but it is hard to make such contrasts comprehensible. It was not until the rise of the realistic movement that Dewey grappled seriously with the epistemological question. Then he had largely in mind the essence wing of critical realism, as represented by Drake and Santayana.

But, to come back to Peirce, I am led to believe that he did not anticipate this epistemological controversy. He was a big man, I grant, but not a superman. And so we come back to a consideration of his logical realism.

One of the clearest statements of Peirce's outlook is to be found in his review of Berkeley's *Works* in *The North American Review* (1871). I shall quote and comment.

To begin with, he rather dismisses Berkeley's position as of little interest to scientists. Science is concerned with the validity of induction. And the abstract acknowledgment of God, Freedom and Immortality is now seen to have no practical consequences whatever. That is, apart from religious feelings.

Then he comes to the question of truth and immediately diverges from what was to be later James's version. "Human opinion universally tends in the long run to a definite form, which is the truth. Let any human being have enough information and exert enough thought upon any question, and the result will be that he will arrive at a certain definite conclusion, which is the same that any other mind will reach under sufficiently favorable circumstances." And he goes on to illustrate. "The individual may not live to reach the truth; there is a residuum of error in every individual's opinions. No matter; it remains that there is a definite opinion to which the mind of man is, on the whole, and in the long run tending." So far, so good. But Peirce avoids the question of the source of the information and the import of the knowledge-claim, which is truth. Let us see why he does this.

"The theory involves a phenomenalism. But it is the phenomenalism of Kant and not of Hume." Here is the import of his dichotomy between nominalism and logical realism. "It is plain," he holds, "that this view of reality is inevitably realistic; because general conceptions enter into all judgments, and therefore into true opinions. Consequently a thing in the general is as real as in the concrete." It was the essence of Kant's philosophy "to regard the real object as determined by the mind. That was nothing else than to consider every conception and intuition which enters necessarily into the experience of an object, and which is not transitory and accidental, as having objective validity. *In short, it was to regard the reality as the normal product of mental action and not as the incognizable cause of it."* I am not a defender of Humian nominalism. And I shall argue that Russell was wrong in making acquaintance with sensations as the primary kind of knowledge to which knowledge by description is subordinate. But I am persuaded that Peirce has confused validity with truth. I am not defending Kant's things-in-themselves. I think that their assumption was a huge mistake going back at least to Locke. It was to assume that perceiving is not objective in import and that sensations do not give us usable information about external things. As I see it, in perceiving we use the information fed into us by our senses to gain what we regard as *facts about* external things, how they look, where they are, etc. And scientific method takes up from this point. Thus I am not defending *incognizable* things-in-themselves but rejecting them as heartily as does Peirce.

What, then, is truth? It consists of tested statements, achieved very much as Peirce holds, which we regard as giving us knowledge about our world. Does this involve a correspondence thesis? Yes, but in a new formulation. It holds that sensations feed in information about the object and that this is constantly appealed to in what Galileo called the interrogation of nature. Correspondence is thus an achievement implied by knowledge-claims and the method of their verification. It is no wonder that the realistic movement concentrated on sense-perception. I shall have something to say about this in connection with James. Half unconsciously, he started the realistic movement and, I think, misled the new realists.

But a word about the difference between logical realism and physical realism. As a physical realist, I sought to work out the categorial constitution of the world. I took categories to have ontological import. In a way, Peirce did also. But this led me to what I called a new, or evolutionary, materialism. Peirce, on the other hand, is quite definite in his rejection of materialism, which, in part, like the later Whitehead, he identifies with a crude mechanicalism. As he sees it, logical realism frees science from contamination with nominalism, on the one side, and materialism, on the other. Make way for logic! But he always sought to keep logic in touch with epistemology. Not so the logical positivists and I fear many others who graduated from logic to philosophy. I shall not name names. To some extent, the *ordinary language* school represents a protest against this current. But it seemed to me rather open to Russell's jibe that it sought to make philosophy easy. We all believe that we *see* trees. But how we manage to do so is the philosophical question to be worked out in harmony with science.

I have since read several books on Peirce. They are usually carefully done but they seemed to me to lack epistemological insight. Just why was his logical realism truncated?

I have argued that, like Kant, he did not see the functional import of sensations as giving us clues and indications about the world to be coined into facts and used and followed up actively. To call concepts real is not enough. One must understand their rootage and controls. Their role is that of cognitive mediation. I do not think that philosophers have been as ingenious as nature, itself, in these matters.

Kant's unknowable things-in-themselves constituted a disaster which deflected philosophy into sophisticated forms of idealism and phenomenalism. When Peirce talks about *incognizable causes* he is but following this well-beaten path. Ernst Mach did the same. But is it not the very function of sense-organs and brain to translate causal messages from things into factual cues and disclosures?

Morris Cohen's selections in the book, *Chance, Love and Logic*, was my first contact with Peirce's thought. Later I reflected on his prescription as to how to make ideas clear. But is a diamond really hard when it is still in the earth? I agree with Professor Burks that he is a little ambiguous here. And how could he escape being so? Cohen in his own work quite obviously followed Peirce's logical realism. Cohen was a keen and erudite thinker, a realistic rationalist. Perry once asked me where I came from. That is, I suppose, what were my antecedents? I am inclined to think that my very isolation gave me a certain freshness of outlook.

William James

As with my study of Royce, I begin with a quotation from Santayana. I am sorry that I never met James. From all accounts, he was an exceptional personality. I was informed that he read one of my early papers and was puzzled by it. That, at least, was a contact. "The logic of opinions," writes Santayana, "as well as the exact opinions themselves, were not things James saw easily, or traced with pleasure. He liked to take things one by one, rather than to put one and two together. . . . He liked to open the window, and look out for a moment. I think he was glad when the bell rang, and he could be himself again until the next day."

James belonged to the empirical tradition of Mill and Bain and tried to supplement it by recognition of experienced connections and transitions. In his *stream of consciousness*, he was opposed to sensory atomism. I think he would have welcomed *Gestalt* emphasis upon patterns. He was thus instinctively against Bradley's critique of relations as involving an indefinite regress. It was more a psychological rejection than a logical one. I was never impressed by his approach to philosophy in terms of temperament. His "rationalist" was clearly Royce or Bradley. His empiricist was a man, like himself, given to the concrete. But, then, he admitted that something like this divergence existed in art, government and manners. His pragmatism was, supposedly, an attempt to synthesize rationalism and empiricism by doing justice to both concrete fact and theory. But what was the perspective?

It seemed to me that James went at it *wholesale*. I had far more sympathy with Peirce's analytic approach. As nearly as I could make out, one was now to settle traditional problems in terms of practical consequences, and these seemed to include personal satisfactions. If one wanted to be immortal that was so far forth a good reason to believe in it. Is the world material or spiritual? Well, it didn't matter about the past. What had been, had been. But a God would guarantee a future more in accord with human wishes. That, again, was a good reason to be a theist. James used much the same wholesale argument for free-will as against determinism. I could not see that he analyzed either term carefully. Determinism was taken to be a mechanical affair, a kind of pushing *a tergo*. Free-will meant a kind of spontaneity. I may remark that I was led to regard choice as involving a process of more or less deliberate evaluation of anticipated alternatives. That is, I rejected a mere pushing *predetermination*. But I recognized its context in the individual's history and social setting. That is, I recognized its limitations. But I still thought it indicated a certain openness, a kind of locus of novelty in meeting situations. That is, I took the reality of awareness and intelligence at the human level rather seriously. But more about that later when I come to discuss evolutionary materialism. James was very much concerned—as was his time—with a dead-level and impersonal onrush of matter. Much has happened in science—as well as in philosophy—since his time. He was bravely defending a kind of pluralism against both Royce's absolute, monistic idealism and the dead-level motion of matter. He was a kind of Ajax defying the lightning.

Pragmatism, as James saw it, was both a method and a theory of truth.

I'm afraid he rather mixed these two aspects up. Certainly, Peirce objected to James's view of truth as too subjective. In his eyes, it made truth too personal and too much a short-run affair. Purely objective truth, James held, was nowhere to be found. I suppose he had been impressed by Royce's stress on error and incompleteness and his appeal to a transcendent, omniscient Mind. Truth, James held, was attached to ideas. Ideas are made true by their working. They thus *become* true by getting into satisfactory relations with other parts of our experience. This involves corroboration, the fusion of the old with the new, satisfaction, expediency. It is all an immanent affair. We may say of an idea either that it is useful because it is true or true because it is useful. He spoke of assimilation, validation, verification, as essentially synonymous terms. And he did all this with verve. It was obvious that he could see no defensible alternative.

But James had an interesting theory of cognition and to that we turn. It was to lead him on to what he called *radical empiricism*, which he came to regard as basic. It was the point of departure of much of the new realism. What the realists sought to add was a logical framework. This comes out clearly in the arguments of R. B. Perry, a great admirer of James.

Within consciousness, James points to the difference between feelings which do not point beyond themselves and those that do. The latter are usually called ideas and these seem to have a self-transcendent function. But James seeks to show that this function arises within experience in a quite natural way. This is through context. If a feeling, q, follows another q and remembers it, it can be taken to stand for it. Such standing-for is the basis of the only kind of self-transcendence possible. Out of it arise distinctions like those of subject and predicate and the linguistic complications to which they lead. It is all an immanent, transitional affair. There is no jumping out of the envelope of experience.

James now turns to the distinction between percepts and concepts. As he sees it, percepts are essentially matters of direct acquaintance and are primary. Concepts are computational substitutes for them. Of course, there is interplay between them but the line still holds. In the last analysis, perceptual experience both verifies our concepts and gives their full meaning to them.

But James realizes that he is confronted by the challenge of solipsism. I early wrote an article entitled *Whose Experience?* directed at both James and Dewey. I was working toward another kind of transcendence which I came to call referential transcendence which I came to regard as based on the very mechanism underlying the act of perceiving. It involved directed response and the use of sensations as informational about what we are responding to. I shall go into details about this in connection with critical realism. But to return to James.

James holds that he can brush "metaphysical cobwebs" away in a pragmatic fashion. Do we not believe that our *percepts* are possessed by us in common? "Men who *see* each other's bodies sharing the same space, treading the same earth, splashing the same water, etc., will never practically believe in a pluralism of solipsistic worlds." Yes, I would say, but may you not be wrong in your *identification of perceiving with having percepts?* Is this not the psychologist's fallacy?

James was now ready to draw his most general conclusions, those of his radical empiricism. He was led to conclude that reality is an experience-continuum. He fired an opening gun in a paper denying the existence of a Kantian kind of consciousness. Thus he was left with percepts and concepts and mere feelings. There was neither thought-stuff nor thing-stuff. His thesis here was akin to that of the British thinker, Shadworth Hodgson, whom he admired. Things are as they are experienced as.

As I look back on this whole development, I can note the underlying belief that the only alternative to experientialism was Kant's agnostic realism of things-in-themselves. This motivation had operated in idealism and it still held for pragmatism. I call this the "fallacy" of the neglected alternative. But it is not easy to locate and formulate such an alternative. Could perceiving be referentially direct and factually informed? That possibility remained to be explored.

In the meantime, James expounded his radical empiricism. Pure experience divides itself functionally into two groups, the inner and the outer, the psychical and the physical. It is an affair of context. Nothing is basically material or spiritual. Later this was called neutralism and was taken up by Bertrand Russell. It was the origin of his neutral monism. That is the way things go in philosophy. A lead is taken up and developed. It gets prestige and is proclaimed abroad by what I call journalistic philosophy. We shall have occasion to note several such leads and their proclamation.

James was now—and quite rightly—a man of international reputation. He had the gift of vivid exposition. And he proceeded to defend what he called a pluralistic universe in opposition to Royce's monism and absolutism. Incidentally, he wrote many stimulating essays. And so we take leave of him.

John Dewey

I turn now to John Dewey. And, of course, I am going to concentrate on what I regard as fundamentals. Dewey had a wide sweep of interests which ranged from education and ethics to public affairs, from psychology and logic to epistemology and the nature of things. And he was a prolific writer on all these topics. He had his convinced followers and ardent disciples. Ratner and Hook are distinguished examples of this discipleship. Within a certain context it is, I think, fairly justified. If I concentrate on what seem to me weaknesses, this is not to derogate from my recognition of his breadth of vision. He was a liberal when America needed liberalism, as, I believe, it still does. I remember that I used his book, *Liberalism and Social Action,* at one time in my course in social philosophy as a point of departure.

Dewey took his graduate work at Johns Hopkins when both Peirce and Morris were teachers. I have paid my respects to Peirce. A few words about Morris are in order. He was well trained in the Germany of his time. There he came under the influence of Trendelenburg and the neo-Kantians. Thus he moved away from straight Hegelianism in a more voluntaristic direction. He also came in touch with Aristotelian thought. These influences led him to stress mental activity and a kind of experimentalistic approach. In the broad sense, he still belonged to the idealistic tradition. This meant that he was opposed to Cartesian dualism, Kant's things-in-themselves, and the lingering problem of the external world. Dewey, I believe, inherited these assumptions. It has always been my belief that idealism rather sidestepped epistemology on the grounds that it started from false assumptions. It was rather late in his career that Dewey was confronted at Columbia with a rather vigorous realistic movement spearheaded by Woodbridge and Montague. On the whole, this belonged to what was called the new realism. I shall examine its principles in the next chapter. Dewey was also faced by the opposing critical realistic development. And, as we shall see, he replied to both, basing himself on the outlook he had established through the years. Dewey was an able dialectician, that is, a handler of ideas in controversy. And he picked out the weak points in both positions, concentrating on the cognitive presentationalism of the new realists and on the essence doctrine of Drake and Santayana. My withers were not wrung, since I had devoted myself to the role of sensations in the act of perceiving. But I found, here again, that I was rather isolated. I had to go my own way. Yet I would have welcomed relevant criticism and, since I had given the movement its name, I was a little irked. I never quite forgave Montague for his very one-sided story of realism.* Personally, he was a very friendly and charming fellow. But, to come back to Dewey, his fundamental category was *experience*. This was his link with idealism. Let us recall his earlier effort at experimental logic in which he stressed problem-solving and the ensuing dichotomy between datum and ideatum. This was a time-involved operation. Following in the footsteps of G. S. Morris, he emphasized intelligence as against the older appeal to a *constitutive reason*, somehow in control. That is, he had aligned himself with Darwinism and the biological phase in William James's psychology. Later this led Dewey to behaviorism.

The question now was, What would be his answer to the epistemological debate? Since he rejected both the new realism and the essence-wing of critical realism what position lay open to him?

The first principle to which he appealed was that cognition is not something given in a presentational way, as it seemed to be for the new realists. It was, rather, something achieved. Knowledge arises *within* experience and can never be separated from its experiential context. But what, then, is experience? He had first begun with the traditional notion that experience is personal and goes with consciousness, mine and yours. But, as he reflected, he saw that this traditional view led straight to the brain-mind problem. And this was a hard nut to crack. Besides, it suggested that human knowing terminated on states of mind tied in with brain-states. But if this was the primary terminus, how could we possibly know the world outside the body? Why not reject this way of approach?

And it was this that Dewey did. Experience was *redefined* as a term for the interaction of the organism with its environment. Under the influence of Bentley, he was led to make *transactions* his operative term. Nature consists of all sorts of transactions. Out of this came what the Germans call his *Naturphilosphie*. It was, quite naturally, somewhat akin to Peirce's. He speaks of the precarious, uncertain, hazardous nature of the world.

Many wanted to know what he would do with consciousness? I, for one. I remember that Philip Blair Rice tried to pin him down. His answer was, in effect, that consciousness was a small, shifting portion of experience which went with the organism-environment interaction.

*The new realism was a rather doctrinaire movement, much as logical positivism was to be later. See Preston Warren's article in *Philosophy and Phenomenological Research*, Sept. 1955, entitled "The Mote in the Eye of the Critic of Critical Realism."

What, else, could he have said? He had turned his back on the usual view which connected personal consciousness with cerebral activity. That, he said, implied a sub-cortical mind, and that would be a shut-in mind. It is interesting to note that Lovejoy, a critical realist, felt this difficulty and attacked Russell's "under-the-hat" theory of mind. All of them ignored my solution which was, in effect, to take the act of perceiving as resting on directed response and the use therein of sensations as informational guides. Perceiving, in short, does not consist in a mere acquaintance with sensations, which may well be "in" the brain, but the use of them in a directed response, reflected in such terms as looking at, feeling, listening to. I emphasized the use and function of sensations in a from-to circuit. The brain, in this way, acts as an organ of adjustmental behavior. I shall go into all this in a later chapter.

What I wanted to bring out was the strategy Dewey adopted. Like James, he took things to be as they are experienced as, a kind of immediacy. I suppose as with this whole generation, both in the United States and in Europe, he thought the only alternative was the belief in Kant's things-in-themselves. But these, as Peirce said, were incognizables. Thought, knowledge and being were to be interconnected. Now I took physical things to be cognizable in terms of the evidence they feed in through the sense-organs. I stressed referential response and the relevant use of sensations as the point of departure for facts about. I thought that nature had been very ingenious in working out the from-to mechanism of perceiving.

I have tried to do justice to Dewey's strategy when confronted by the realistic movement. This culminated in his cosmological employment of the term experience. All is experience. It cannot be derived from anything more basic. It is the envelope within which we live and move. The role of mind is that of synthesis and redirection. Thus it is a form of naive, or presentational, realism which treats knowledge as a special achievement in its own setting. His "immediate empiricism" is the background of thought. And he holds that things are poignant, beautiful, harsh and comforting in their own right.

But where are atoms, molecules, etc. in all this? As nearly as I can make out, they are regarded as artifacts, "scientific objects," employed for control. I have had some controversy with Sidney Hook on the topic. I give them extra-mental status and am critical of Dewey's immediate empiricism. This leads to a new, non-reductive, evolutionary materialism. To this, Professor Hook is opposed, and quite rightly on his premises. We shall see that Whitehead, also, is opposed to naturalism and materialism.

Well, I have tackled his rather complex epistemology in several places and contrasted it with my own. And so the dialogue goes on. So concludes my rather summary account of pragmatism. I have tried to do justice to Peirce's logical realism, to James's working theory of truth, and to Dewey's instrumentalist stance. I endeavored to show why I was not satisfied with any of them. And yet they were logical moves. There are, as I see it, certain questions that you either solve or you don't. One of these is the nature and reach of perceiving. This point of departure was uppermost in the programs of both the new realists and the critical realists. It is to their debate that I now turn. Some thought that a stalemate ensued; and they turned to Europe for guidance. I had my own momentum and tried to clarify issues as I saw them. There are indications that the tide is again turning in the realistic direction.

A Note on Mead

George Herbert Mead was what Arthur Murphy has called a constructive pragmatist. I had early thought of him chiefly as a social psychologist who stressed the role of the "other." Here he had seemed to me to supplement Cooley's emphasis on the primary group. The self is a reflexive development bound up with the community and it recognizes gestures and attitudes in others and can put itself in their place. This is a functional and objective psychology which is an advance on Hume but it needs careful handling.

I remember meeting Mead at Professor Lloyd's but never knew him personally as I did Ames and A. W. Moore. I catalogued him as belonging to the Chicago School and took him to emphasize Experience and Situations. It was only later with the publication of his works by Murphy, Charles Morris and others that I became fully aware of his stature, which seems now to me to equal Dewey's. Their positions strike me as largely equivalent with much the same strengths and flaws. What they both seemed to me to lack was a stiffened epistemological framework. I think this affected their cosmology.

Since I shall use the method of contrast, I want to point out that as early as my *Critical Realism* (1916) I was trying to break through Cartesian dualism and introduce consciousness to the functioning brain. As Woodbridge Riley saw, I was conceiving consciousness as *extended* in an event-like and operational way.* This implied an enlarged kind of

*Woodbridge Riley, *American Thought from Puritanism to Pragmatism and Beyond*, p. 377.

materialism, one of levels. Sensations seemed to me to be *used* in perceiving. I shall try to contrast this approach with Mead's. Mead was as much given to emphasis on evolutionary ideas as I was. Like Wundt, he started from gesture and proceeded to language. This led to a recognition of the role of signs and symbols, a topic already appearing in Peirce. This line of thought was taken up later by Charles Morris. Semiotics became a slogan. I have often wondered whether Wittgenstein could be fitted into this development. His context seems to have been more British and Continental. In later years, I must confess I got rather tired of hearing of pragmatics, syntactics and semantics, largely, I suppose, because it seemed to me to get in the way of epistemological analysis. As I understood it, Morris sought to fuse logical positivism with his scientific empiricism. That is the way currents move in philosophy.

But let us return to Dewey and Mead. I have long argued that Dewey did not feel the critical importance of epistemology until he came in contact with it at Columbia. Here it was largely in the form of the new realism, that is, presentationalism.

Mead uses the expression, perceptual object. I, instead, speak of perceiving. Perception is defined by Mead as a *"relation* between a highly developed physiological organism and an object, or an environment, in which selection emphasizes certain elements." This seems akin to a kind of selective new realism. I imagine Murphy got his notion of "objective relativism" from such an approach. Perhaps, Pepper developed his "contextualism" similarly. I am told that Mead was influenced in his later years by Whitehead and the philosophy of organism.

Now I had a different momentum which sought to analyze perceiving as a from-and-to operation and claim. I thought of sensations and images as informing this referential act.

However this may be, Mead seems to take the "perceptual object" to be a complex combining external and internal factors. In distance-perception vision is dominant. We then move, if possible, to manipulation. Here primary qualities make their appearance. Then he moves on to valuation. I am puzzled as to the status of the perceptual object in all this. Is it a physical thing or an experience in a situation? He often speaks of *reconstructing* objects, just as Dewey does. I would, myself, speak of reconstructing our idea of objects. There seems to be a continuation of the outlook of objective idealism with greater stress on the organism. The perceptual object appears to be regarded as an organization of the immediate environment with reference to the experiencing organism. Mead goes on to say that *consciousness* is functional and must be located in the objective world rather than in the brain. It belongs to, or is characteristic of, the environment in which we find ourselves. There is in all this, to me, the same kind of straddling one finds in Dewey. If sensations are in the brain, how can we get beyond it? My answer is that we use them in a referential response as guiding and informing. This operation is objective in import.

I find that Mead later made much use of the idea of emergence I developed with Lloyd Morgan and S. Alexander in my *Evolutionary Naturalism* (1921). I find that few Americans recognize my priority. There seems to be here a lack of careful scholarship.

We now come to the crucial topic of the status of "scientific objects." This bothered Dewey, Whitehead and Mead. I was never much troubled since I began with material things. I thought of new techniques and new information as entering the picture, beginning, perhaps, with mass.

The question for Mead was, How do we get to them cognitively? Perceptual objects are features of experience. But, according to science, Mead saw, we never get to scientific objects in this way. As nearly as I can make out, Mead keeps to the primary status of perceptual objects and regards scientific objects as results of hypothetical interpretations or translations of them. They are essentially abstract statements of conditions under which perception occurs. Some such position is still philosophically popular.

I, on the other hand, consider atoms and electrons, etc. as *constituents* of the things we perceive and handle but constituents knowable only as a result of new techniques, such as the electron microscope or the bubble chamber. Knowing is an achievement.

So much for Mead. It does not do justice to his vigor. As I see it, his constructive pragmatism was a half-way house between idealism and physical realism.

4

THE REALISTIC MOVEMENT

I am now going to explore a development in American philosophy which reflected dissatisfaction with both idealism and pragmatism and which sought new foundations. This was the realistic movement. Since I participated in it, I have my own perspective. This is to be allocated to what is called critical realism rather than to the new realism. A few words about this terminology are in order.

The new realists constituted a group in the East who were convinced that idealists and pragmatists had begged a fundamental question about human knowing. They had assumed that knowing makes a difference to the object known. An extreme example of this view was Berkeley's thesis that *to be is to be perceived*. Kant had approached it in stressing construction so that it seemed that, for him, to know is to construct. The new realists rejected this tradition and argued that knowing is of the nature of an external relation, that it makes no difference to the object known. It was quite usual for them to speak in terms of a cognitive relation between knower and known and to assert that this peculiar relation made no difference to the object known. This seemed to involve a presentational view of what knowing is, that is, that the object is open to inspection. This has sometimes been called the searchlight view of knowing. Objects were supposed to stand out as though in an illuminated field.

It is not surprising that special attention was paid to sense-perception. The implication here seemed to be that chairs, tables, trees, etc. somehow were already there in their own right and that consciousness, or awareness, just enveloped them and made them its content. This was sometimes called the relational view of consciousness. Content and object were identical. As R. B. Perry once put it, the idea of a tulip and the tulip were identical. The verbal difference was a matter of context. One can see here the influence of William James.

As Montague, another new realist, put the orientation it was a question of reforming naive, or common-sense, realism. In a way, it was a return to the presentationalism of Thomas Reid. There would be less stress on intuition and more interest in processes and conditions but the result would be much the same.

There was another strain in the new realism, that of *subsistential Platonism.* Universals can subsist when we are not conscious of them. Spaulding developed this angle.

The critical realists sought to reanalyze perceiving to make it direct though, somehow, mediated. As I recall it, they did not put so much stress on the cognitive relation and its externality. I, myself, had early denied the validity of a peculiar cognitive relation and had sought to explore what went on in perceiving. It seemed to me that we had to do with a directed reference and the use of sensation as giving relevant facts about their external controls. That is, I thought of knowing as an achievement resting on mechanisms worked out by nature. I shall say more about this later.

There were differences among the new realists on certain points but a fair unanimity on general principles. It would seem that they agreed with Montague that the only alternative to their kind of presentationalism was the traditional representationalism of Locke, which meant that we first know ideas and then think of them as copies of things. There were long recognized difficulties confronting representationalism of this type; and Montague, in particular, saw no alternative for the critical realists. This was his basic premise in his story of American realism.

Now I had given its name to this critical realism wing of the realist movement. I had long worked on the lines of a direct, though mediated, kind of perceiving and knowing. I had rejected presentationalism and an appeal to a unique cognitive relation. I thought nature had probably been pretty ingenious in the affair. And I shall later show that I was right in this assumption. In any case, I was unable to accept a return to naive, presentational, realism. As I have sometimes put it, I sought to move between presentationalism and representationalism. I wanted directness of reference united with the use of information. Could the act of perceiving combine both of these elements? I thought it could. If so, Montague's argument would fall flat.

Now the critical realists agreed on their rejection of the strategy of the new realism but were divided on their analysis of perceiving. Santayana, Strong and Drake appealed to what they called an *essence* as something at once within the mind and in the object. Here, they held, was something shared. The difficulty was to identify it and to locate it. Santayana fell back on intuition plus what he called animal faith. He held that he could intuit essences as semi-Platonic entities and, while he could not penetrate into the external thing, he could give reasons why the essences were embodied. Strong and Drake took much the same tactic. Later Strong rejected the essence thesis, as he told me in an interview in 1937.

Lovejoy and Pratt appealed to mental intentionalism, somewhat along the lines of the Austrian psychologist and philosopher Brentano. It is the very nature of thoughts to be directed informatively at objects. We must just accept this intentionalism as a mental fact. Thus we have a mediated directedness and avoid Locke's dilemma. Both Lovejoy and Pratt were mind-body dualists.

Now it seemed to me that we could be more explanatory than this and so I continued to explore the mechanism of perceiving. As I gradually saw it, it involved a from-and-to operation. The *from* vector consisted in feeding in messages from the object as a stimulus-control, messages translated by the brain into sensations. Thereupon there was the vector of response directed at the object; and this was informed by the aroused sensations taken as cues and indications. In short, I took the act of perceiving to be externally directed and informed. The point was that sensations were used in this context to tell the percipient about the object, how it looked, where it was, how it felt, etc. Thus they had a role or function to perform. They had what I called cognitive value. As I saw it, this was the way that cognizing began. It led in man to perceptual judgments with the use of words and concepts. In the lower animals, I suppose, the role of sensations is to guide response in largely instinctual ways. There are interesting psycho-physical points here.

As an emergent evolutionist, this analysis of the mechanism of perceiving interests me as showing the operations basic to the rise of human knowing. I spoke now of well-founded knowledge-claims. The old schematism of a cognitive relation seemed to me to have lost its point. Into all this I shall go later. It was obvious that I had to work out a basis for referential transcendence and for controlled correspondence. The new realists avoided these issues by their acceptance of presentationalism but, as we shall see, it was difficult for them to account for error and illusions.

I agree with Professor Schneider that the "story of the emergence of American realism from idealism, evolutionism and experimentalism is not a long one but it is complicated and difficult to state clearly." And I have the impression that neither Montague nor he has given sufficient attention to my formulation of critical realism. The job was to get referential directness along with mediation. What is the role of sensations in the act of perceiving? It seems to me that we do not ordinarily dwell upon them for their own sake—that is, in my terminology, make them terminal—but take them as appearings of the object or as recognized *facts* about them, how things look or feel. These ways of using sensations in the act of perceiving strike me as analogous. When we talk about *appearings* of the object, we are moving from the object to how it manifests itself to our senses. When we talk about observed facts about the object, we are using the manifestations cognitively. We note how a thing looks, feels, etc. We explore it in terms of its appearings. This shift of emphasis goes with the direction of response, that is, toward the object. We are now cognitively deciphering the object in terms of its manifestations. In both cases, the sensations aroused in us are being used. The flaw in traditional empiricism was that sensations were taken as presented entities and their functional role in perceiving was ignored. For instance, Russell builds on what he calls knowledge of acquaintance of sensations as primary entities. G. E. Moore stresses them as sense-data and cannot get beyond them.

In perceiving, I think we have a strong sense of the object as that which we are dealing with, looking at, taking hold of. We learn much about it, recognize it again and again. It is regarded as coordinate with ourselves as percipients and agents. It is within this framework that we take our sensations to be appearings and to have cognitive value. These are, as I see it, new categories to which epistemology must do justice. With them, as a starting-point, that novel activity called human knowing emerges in a quite natural way.

I thought it best to offer my theory of perceiving before I examined the new realism with its rather conventional view. This, we saw, was presentationalism. Things are out there to be inspected. The only alternative to this Montague could think of was Lockean representationalism. That is, that we first perceive ideas and then somehow infer things of which our ideas are copies. I have tried to show that perceiving is directed at objects and that sensations are used in this act as disclosing cognitive facts about the object. I do not see how nature could have worked it out in any other way. At least, I think this is the way nature actually worked it out.

Now I do hold that American thought had by now secured a momentum of its own. It had moved from idealism, to pragmatism, and thence to realism. Thus it had ingredients somewhat different from those dominant in Europe. Schneider points to three: (1) its objectivism and alliance with science, (2) its adjustment to a modified behaviorism, and (3) its anti-idealism. But now, regrettably, the dialogue between the new realists and the critical realists turned out to be largely a stalemate. I am inclined to think that too much stress was laid on the essence wing of critical realism. Probably, Santayana's prestige had something to do with this outcome. And I am quite willing to admit that my own analysis of perceiving was, as yet, not fully clarified. But the indications were already there.

Under these circumstances it is not, perhaps, surprising that attention swung to new developments in Europe. G. E. Moore and his admirers stressed analysis. Speculation was to be frowned on. It was not quite clear as to what was to be analyzed. But it was a good term. Mathematical logic had also come to the front and was regarded by many as an essential tool. And then Wittgenstein and logical positivism took the center of the stage. I continued to work on my own lines. I sometimes allowed myself to speak of neo-colonialism but I knew what had happened. And I was aware that philosophy was being technically enriched. But I was convinced that, sooner or later, epistemology and the analysis of perceiving would come to their own. And I think this now is occurring.

The New Realism and Its Critics

It is generally recognized that realism was in the air in the first two decades of the twentieth century. Besides the "official" new and critical realists, that is, those who cooperated in groups, there were several able thinkers who should be mentioned. Woodbridge at Columbia was one. He took the line of the relational theory of consciousness, that is, that consciousness brings objects together but does not modify them. McGilvary was another. His "perspective realism" was akin to Holt's of the new realism. For McGilvary, consciousness was vision, a relation in which objects stand to the organism. It followed that all perspective appearances have the same status. The next step was what was called objective relativism. We perceive things as they are from a point of view. Whitehead seems to have been influenced by this approach. It was attacked by Lovejoy and even its advocates became skeptical of its validity. It is to be noticed that Woodbridge and McGilvary were presentationalists. D. C. Macintosh should also be mentioned. He wanted to be a direct realist and was opposed to traditional, epistemological dualism of the Locke type but it is a little difficult to make out how he got to things. He sometimes used the language of Reid and Scotch realism. I recall that Macintosh was invited to cooperate with the critical realists but refused.

One could hardly leave out Morris Cohen. I have classified him as coming nearest to Peirce's logical realism.

Let us now turn to "official" new realism. Holt, Perry and Montague were excellent spokesmen. I recall that S. Alexander had a high opinion of Holt's book, *The Concept of Consciousness*. Warren speaks of it as "the first effort at a full-orbed behavioristic theory of knowledge." Consciousness is, for Holt, like a searchlight. Response defines a cross-section of the environment without, which is a neutral manifold. . . . . This neutral cross-section, Holt held, coincides with the list of objects of which we say we are conscious.

I take up Perry next. His approach was rather formal and directed against idealism. In his eyes, idealism rested on what he called the egocentric predicament. That is, it stressed a *relation* called consciousness, or awareness, of a thing to the self or ego, as knower. And it held that this relation was an internal, or modifying, one. But, asks Perry, how can this kind of relation be shown? We can never get to the object out of this relation to make a comparison. That is, we are caught in a predicament. But when we examine it, it reduces either to the redundant inference that all known things are known or to the false inference that all things are known, which is just a begging of the question. Hence we have no right to conclude that knowing is a condition for what is.

Perry goes on to consider three varieties of idealism which he calls, respectively, the creation theory, the formative theory, and the identity theory. The first asserts that the self creates the object. The second, that it forms or organizes it. The third, that the self is the thing. Perry then shows that the egocentric predicament does not justify any of these varieties. Very naturally, idealists held that Perry's list did not exhaust the variety of idealisms.

Because of this formal approach, Perry was led to put a stress on external relations and independence. It is likely that Royce's refutation of realism in terms of complete externality motivated this approach. But he admitted that the realists would have to discover what the self as knower is, what a thing is, and what knowing is.

Perry was criticized by Miss Calkins as ignoring concrete factors like sensible qualities. Are not these ways of experiencing? Pratt argued that it was a drawn battle logically but that idealism had the edge because it stressed experience. Lovejoy brought up memory as showing the role of memory images in one kind of knowing. This was a point he was frequently to make.

I think I should here make my own comment. I have always held that sense-perception inaugurates the framework which is developed by both common sense and science. In perceiving, I hold there is an integrative use of directed response, as in looking and pointing, and the role of aroused sensations as relevant appearings of the object responded to. Such appearings are taken as giving us *facts* about the object perceived, how it looks, where it is, how it feels, etc. There is much learning involved in the development of perceiving. But the essential point is this union of directed reference and sensory information. Together, they explain and naturalize what has been traditionally called transcendence. I think it, likewise, gives a basis for correspondence between thought and thing. It is in this way that human knowing emerges.

At the level of perceiving, what Perry calls the self or knower, is the percipient organism. Here, of course, I am not an extreme behaviorist, like Holt. The thing is the physical object about which we are learning. And knowing, as I see it, is an achievement based on reference and information about. It goes without saying that I never liked the phrase, cogitive relation, as a mysterious entity linking knower and known. It seemed to me, rather, that knowing consisted in a justified referential claim resting on this from-and-to operation. So much for Perry.

Before I pass to Montague, it may be well to comment on a pragmatic theory of *common objects* suggested by C. A. Strong and Dickinson Miller to James. "If my candle goes out when you blow out your candle, why may we not say that we have a candle in common?" James reflected on this and spoke of *natural realism.* Yet he seems to have meant by this that he could see no difficulty in a "numerically identical *content* of two or more minds." That is, James still kept to his thesis that things are as they are experienced as. But it was not far to the new realism.

What is my own theory of common objects? It would be that two people were being stimulated by the same thing and responding perceptually to it. But I see no reason to believe in an overlapping of content. Their responses would be to the same physical object but they would use as a factual basis merely similar sensations. In my sense of the term, they would be perceiving the same object, in this case, the candle.

Montague and Critical Realism

When we turn to Montague's exposition we must keep in mind his belief that there is really no alternative to naive, or presentational, realism. In his eyes, the critical realists were unable to escape from an old dilemma. How could they move from the sensory given to something external? This would have to be inferential. And where is the basis for such an inference? This was a point Berkeley had made long ago and, as I remember, Russell had accepted it and taken the path of logical construction from the given. It seemed to Montague that Santayana with his essences was the only one who had made an attempt to bridge the gap. But even he had landed in skepticism and appealed to animal faith. Well, I had, naturally, been aware of this traditional dilemma. And I think that all the critical realists were. They wanted the external thing to be the direct object of the act of perceiving. As we shall later see, there were three schools of thought represented. Strong, Drake and Santayana had opted for essence as both before the mind and in the object. Lovejoy, Pratt and Rogers had appealed to the intentional role of ideas as about something other than themselves. In their eyes, there was no need for inference. Both Pratt and Lovejoy appealed to an *intentional transcendence* on the part of the mind. I, on the other hand, was concerned to analyze perceiving as an operation resting on a from-and-to movement resulting in (1) external reference and (2) the use of sensations in this context as giving information about their objective controls. That is, the sensations were not simply terminal, as they had been for Locke and Hume, but functional. It was their role to be controlled appearings used to give facts about the object, how it looked, felt, smelt, etc. It is thus that the percipient gets into contact with the outside world. It seemed to me that this analysis gave a natural, biological explanation of the intentional transcendence to which Pratt and Lovejoy appealed. But, then, they were mind-body dualists while I was a monist. Cognitive transcendence, I was led to hold, rested on external reference and the cognitive value of sensory material in this context. Thus human knowing is an achievement.

I have recently noted that Blanshard and Chisholm regard my location of sensations in the brain as a complication which at once distinguishes my theory of perceiving from that of others and makes it more difficult to carry through. Writes Blanshard on page 429 of volume I of *The Nature of Thought*: "Because writing with the mind-body relation more explicitly before him, he seems to me to reveal most candidly the difficulties it entails for the theory of knowledge." On the contrary, I would say, it suggests the way nature worked it out. It is interesting to note how Russell, following physics, got sensational patterns into the brain but could not understand how they were used in perceiving. Both Lovejoy and Dewey attacked the "under-the-hat" theory of mind for much the same reason. But if we recognize—as most neurologists and psychologists do now—that the brain is a behavioral organ, the point to bear in mind is the linkage of sensations with response. Is not their primary role that of guiding response? As I see it, man dwelt on what was implicit in such guidance and raised it to explicitness in perceptual judgment. One passes from signals and cues to delayed responses and the rise of conceptual description.

But let us get back to Montague. Having condemned any kind of representationalism, or mediation, he is left to formulate presentationalism as the only way out. Here he makes much of a supposed cognitive relation. He takes this to be external and to make no difference to the object cognized. This is a form of the searchlight analogy. Montague was less of a behaviorist than were Holt and Perry, however. He speaks of that peculiar self-transcending thing called awareness. Does it not put us in touch with objects either in other places and times or not in space and time at all? As nearly as I can make out, this awareness must be presentational. He then goes on to consider objective relativism in the convergence of rails when you look back from an observation car. Even "pink rats" must be given some kind of locus. Montague admits that these relativistic objects bear a suspicious resemblance to the sense-impressions of Hume, Mill and Avenarius. He now appeals to the principle of asymmetry. We can explain illusions in terms of the veridical and not in the reverse way. He finally appeals to William James's thesis that the same object can be a member of the independent order of existence and, at the same time and with no disruption of identity, be also an object of experience. There would then be no need to accord any physical locus to the unreal objects of illusion and delusion. Montague then acknowledges his divergence from extreme behaviorism and objective relativism. After this, he offers his critique of critical realism as involving an unjustified inference from the given and a merely postulated resemblance. The reader must judge as to whether I have undercut his argument and established a direct, referential realism with the use of sensations as informative.

Let us now look at the reception accorded to the new realism. Lovejoy, DeLaguna, Durant Drake, and Dickinson Miller, among many others, raised questions. DeLaguna was skeptical of Perry's emphasis upon completely external relations. Lovejoy argued that a percept, or idea, could exist when the physical object had already ceased to exist. How, then, could they be identical? D. C. Miller stressed the potentialities in things and did not find them represented in ideas. It was a very searching debate. Drake pointed to fairly obvious differences between ideas and things. The upshot of the discussion was, I think, rejection of pan-objectivism and the searchlight view of knowing. Montague fell back on what he called cerebral implications. He now held that consciousness was a kind of potentiality which could imply the presence of a thing at a space and time where and when it was not. All in all, then, the new realism turned out to be disappointing. Was there an alternative that had not been explored? It was the critical realist's job to reform traditional representationalism, if he could.

I come now to a matter of terminology. Some of the critical realists stressed *epistemological dualism*, Lovejoy in particular. They meant by this that the idea is not the thing. Rather the idea mediates knowledge about the thing. But it was fairly obvious that a departure must be made from the schematism which made the idea a terminal object from which the external object must be inferred. Could not the external object be considered terminal for the act of perceiving? This would give a *direct realism* which was not presentational. How could this be worked out?

Well, I have already indicated my answer. Perceiving would be correlated with (1) response and (2) the use of sensations as sources of information about the thing to which one is responding. The very mechanism of perceiving seemed to fit in with this analysis. When I look at a tree, the tree, itself, both guides my response and feeds in information about itself. I do not ordinarily concentrate attention on the sensation for its own sake but take it as informing me about the external object. I read off, as it were, facts about the object from the sensation considered as an appearing of the object. The sensation, in this setting, is taken as the source of elementary knowledge about something other than itself. Here is the basis of what is called *transcendence*, which turns out to be an achievement resting on directed response and the use of sensations as informative of that to which we are responding. The very mechanism of perceiving with its from-and-to vectors fits in with this analysis. We react towards the very thing which is feeding in information about itself. Here we have what I call a circuit.

It is in this fashion that nature moved to cognition, a remarkable achievement. As we all know, language and concepts were added in close contact with this break-through. As I see it, animals are guided in their responses to environing things by sensory cues. Man is also guided but he adds concepts and descriptions and develops what is called scientific method to the perceptual framework.

The fault in traditional empiricism is that it did not understand the mechanism of perceiving and concentrated on sensations as terminal rather than on their cognitive use and value. Out of this error came the twin mistakes of presentationalism and representationalism.

As I see it, naive realism, which the new realism sought to reform, largely consists in the acceptance of a fusion between perceptual results and presented sensations. Thus, it is *as though* things were just intuited out there. Critical realism involves a recognition of the rather complex operations taking place.

It has interested me to find how much stress both Holt and Perry put on response while, as simple-minded behaviorists, they ignored the use made of sensations as informative. Consciousness as a term for relations among presentables followed. They showed great ingenuity within this framework. It is not always easy to select the best terminology. Epistemological dualism is an expression directed against epistemological monism or presentationalism. I would favor speaking of a mediated, direct realism. The point here, as Professor Warren sees, is the cognitional use of sensations.* This issues in facts about the object perceived.

There were critics of critical realism, of course. Dewey attacked both the new realism and critical realism. The first because of its extension of the cogitive relation into something omnipresent. In the case of critical realism, he concentrated on the essence wing of Drake and Santayana. His own approach was to take knowing as arising within experience in connection with problems. I always thought he had begged some difficult problems about sensations for fear of getting enmeshed with the brain. If sensations are bound up with brain-states, how can you get to the outside world? My answer, of course, is that sensations are used in the setting of response. Lovejoy seems, also, to have feared the "under-the-hat" locus of mind. He attacked Russell, though I had long anticipated Russell on this point. As I indicated, Blanshard had recognized the tie-in of my epistemology with the mind-body question.

The chief criticism of critical realism was on the score of how it accounted for truth. It was often said that the new realists had no place for error and the critical realists could not certify truth. Those who have followed my analysis have, surely, noted that I hold that things feed in information about themselves and that this is being constantly tested. Truth, then, is founded on evidence. To comment on a statement and say that it is true is to endorse it as expressing received information about things. There is no sense in demanding a hypothetical comparison of thing and thought. Things are not Kantian things-in-themselves but knowable objects. This is my version of the correspondence theory of truth.

I fear that it so happened that many considered that the American realistic movement had ended in a stalemate. Accordingly, they were

*See Warren's article in the journal of *Philosophy and Phenomenological Research*, September, 1965.

ready to take up with new fashions, such as symbolic logic, Wittgenstein, logical positivism, existentialism, ordinary language. But it was clear to me that it was my job to clarify all essential points in critical realism. This I have tried to do. In the next chapter I shall try to summarize my outlook under the heading, *Critical Realism, Evolutionary Materialism and Humanism.* This will be a bringing up-to-date of my contribution to the *Contemporary American Philosophy* essays of 1930.

Schneider on Realism

Professor Schneider seems to hold that American philosophers have gotten bravely over epistemological problems and are content to leave them to physiological psychologists. Philosophy, he asserts, has other problems more attractive and general. And then he goes on to quote a remark of Dewey: "We did not solve the problem. We got over it." I agree that he did not solve the problem but rather bypassed it. I am inclined to believe that critical realism at least outlined a solution.

As I see it, then, actual perceiving is a complex and learned affair. While I do think a stimulus pattern is operative, it is supplemented by habits and expectations. Practical perceiving is, accordingly, concerned with the referential object. That is, it is dominated by concern with thing-objects. I very much doubt that there are two, explicit steps taken, namely, a discrimination of a sensory datum and, thereupon, the use of this to decipher facts about the object. Rather does it seem to me that the goal, perceiving an object, is uppermost from the first and anything relevant is used in the way of cues and indications. What, as an epistemologist, I would stress is that cognition is *mediated* by an integration of sensations, images and thoughts as the basis of ascribing features to objects. Such a view seems to me to avoid the presentationalism of the new realism and the dilemmas of Locke and Kant.

While holding this theory of cognition, I am quite ready to listen to the points made by psychologists. One concerns constancy phenomena. It is well established that we tend to see things in a standardized way, coins, for example. Here we have object-habits in operation. Hebb, again, maintains that learning is involved in the recognition of patterns. In his article on Lovejoy, McGill, who is a psychologist as well as a philosopher, has made these points.* It is not at all surprising to me to find that

*McGill, "Epistemological Dualism and Partition," in *Philosophy and Phenomenological Research*, June, 1963.

common beliefs constitute a framework for perceiving. But I cannot see that this fact militates against the role I have assigned to sensations as informative appearings usable as giving facts about their external controls. I grant, however, that this is just a point of departure. Recognition, inference, accumulated knowledge all play into it. But all this presupposes an underlying, cognitive contact with the world as a point of departure. The tragedy of modern philosophy was that it started with introspective subjectivism and found itself unable to get back to the external world. I have but tried to bring out nature's device, which was, essentially, a from-and-to circuit. Following this clue, I have tried to show *how* that remarkable thing, *knowing, emerged.* Step by step, man has built on it and enlarged its possibilities. But, in considering these, I would come to cultural history.

5

CRITICAL REALISM, EVOLUTIONARY
MATERIALISM AND HUMANISM

In 1930, while American thought was in full vigor and moving, on the whole, from idealism to pragmatism and realism, there was published a series of personal statements, by prominent representatives, of their philosophical positions and their justification of them. The fashion for this kind of personal exposition had begun in Germany and spread thence to England. It was, essentially, I think, designed to introduce order into the field. Issues would be brought out in a concrete way.

Now it so happened that I made my contribution to this project and allowed myself the luxury of bringing it under three headings; realism, naturalism, and humanism. Realism stood for my epistemology. Naturalism, for my ontology and cosmology. And humanism, for the domain of valuation. It was thus comprehensive in import.

Looking back at it now, I have become somewhat autobiographical. I think I can note where my realism has been sharpened, where my naturalism has turned in the direction of an evolutionary materialism, and where my humanism has tried to grapple with social and political commitment. Philosophy, as I see it, overarches the human scene in the way of running comment; but gets its credentials from facing up to perennial problems about man and nature. One of these is how we know external things. Another is the locus and mode of working of the human mind. A third is that of the categorial plasticity of nature. In facing up to these issues, philosophy, of course, works with the sciences, physical, biological and social. It has, however, its own momentum and perspective to keep in mind, that is, a combination of interaction and parallelism. It is in this way that a cultural division of labor maintains itself. Thus, I do not apologize for philosophy. It has its work cut out for it.

What I want to do in this chapter, accordingly, is to complete my earlier presentation and, so to speak, bring it up-to-date. It is my intention to use the result as a base from which to judge the course of British thought. I shall then examine Wittgenstein and logical positivism as variations of dramatic intensity. For the time being, attention has shifted in the English-speaking world away from the earlier American dialogue in which I had participated. As I have indicated, there were good reasons for this shift. In part, there had been a feeling of stalemate, well brought out by Professor Schneider in his little booklet on Realism in America. I have the suspicion that my own analysis was rather lost in the shuffle. Then there was the rise of mathematical logic and the belief that it contained basic clues. There was, I think, added a certain increased self-confidence in Britain, going with its absence in the United States. I began to hear more and more of G. E. Moore and analysis. And Wittgenstein was considered an oracle. At about the same time, the Vienna Circle made its mark.

Well, after this confrontation, if I have the endurance, I shall carry on a similar study of Marxism, neo-Thomism and existentialism, thus boxing the compass. I think I know the crucial points to make. Both Marxism and neo-Thomism are concerned with sense-perception and are realistic in intent. I find it harder to locate either the epistemological or the ontological doctrines of existentialism. But I shall do my best. Here it seems to be more an affair of moving from *Angst* to the authentic life. That is, existentialism would seem to be predominantly a *Lebensphilosophie.* Kierkegaard and Nietzsche are the poles between which it vibrates.

Such, then, is the envisaged undertaking.

Critical Realism as Gateway

I am not going to concern myself with history. It is sufficient to recall that modern philosophy with Descartes and Locke as pioneers set up a dualism of mind and matter and then found it difficult to show how the human mind could reach and gain knowledge about the external, material world. Descartes used the method of doubt and decided, to his satisfaction, that thinking involved a self that thought. Rather uncritically, it seemed to later thinkers, he decided that this self was an unextended substance whose very nature, or essence, it was to think consciously and in a purposive manner. Animals, he believed, were automata or complicated machines, an idea which was later reflected back by La Mettrie to humans. But the question which troubled Descartes was how to show that concepts which originated in the mind had import for the external world. There could be no method of comparing the two to show that they agreed. He finally argued that the idea of extension which we possess was clear and distinct and that God—whose existence he sought to prove—would not have allowed us to lapse into error on this crucial point. In extension, then, we know the world. Descartes went on to work out a mathematical physics in terms of inertia and motion. This involved vortices. It was not until Newton that gravitation was appealed to.

The epistemology of Descartes was thus based on intuited concepts held to disclose the framework of the world. It should be added that he believed that the mind-soul was linked with the brain in an interactive way and that the sensations aroused in it had practical rather than theoretical value. What is called *rationalism* developed along these lines. There was little concern with sense-perception.

John Locke, a physician and an admirer of Newton, was more empirically inclined. Ideas, he held, arose through the senses. He added an inner sense to the outer ones to complete the range of experience. But he made *ideas* the objects of thought and found himself facing the problem of justifying the belief that some of these ideas, at least, corresponded to the world of Newtonian physics.

Thus, in both Descartes and Locke, we find that the method of approach led to a hesitant representationalism. It was Berkeley who challenged representationalism and argued for a mentalistic presentationalism. That is, he identified things with a collection of sensations. He, thus, became an immaterialist. Hume followed in his footsteps but in a more skeptical way. In this manner was established what is usually called the empirical tradition. The emphasis was upon sensations and images. This outlook, as we saw, was called nominalism by Peirce, who wanted to emphasize concepts and logic.

One must remember that, in all this development, philosophy believed itself engaged in fundamentals which could not be avoided. Science might ignore them but in the last analysis, they had to be reckoned with. Human knowing had to be explained and fitted into science.

It is known how Hume was followed by Kant with his constructive phenomenalism and gesture in the direction of things-in-themselves. After Kant came idealism in its various forms. We noted how, in the United States, idealism was challenged first by pragmatism and then by realism. It was with realism that the problem of the nature and validity of sense-perception came to the front.

As we saw, the new realists believed that some form of presentationalism, alone, was tenable. They were convinced that representationalism had long been shown to be a blind alley. And they could not conceive of any position in between. But presentationalism was soon shown to involve dilemmas between being and seeming. It was hard to account for illusions and for time-lapses between what is presented and what is believed to be the object intended. And what was presented did not appear to have dispositional properties, such as those assignable to physical things. Later, logical positivism would be confronted by this same difficulty.

But is there not a possibility between presentationalism and representationalism? May not sensations have a function to perform in perceiving, taken as a referential act tied in with response? It was this line of approach which suggested itself to me. Sensations would, then, not be terminal, as presentationalism had always assumed, but would have a role.

With this in mind, I now took a sharp look at what seemed to be occurring in perceiving. Did there not seem to be a from-and-to circuit operating? One vector of this was the stimulus-pattern arriving from the object. But was this not followed by a directional response to the same object? And was not this response informed by the sensations aroused by the stimulus-pattern? If so, it would seem that the role of the aroused sensations was to convey relevant information about the thing being reacted to. In vision, for example, it is as though I looked through the visual field at the object. When I *see* a tree out there, it would seem that I am directionally looking at the tree—I can supplement this by pointing or by walking toward the tree—and deciphering features of it in terms of indications in my sensory field. I could put the situation by saying that I use the sensory datum as informational or as having cognitive value for the percipient with respect to the object. And why not? Is this not the function of the sense-organs, to feed in information about things surrounding the organism?

Let us now examine what seems to take place in sense-perception. After that, we can consider the biological mechanisms involved. Nature has been very ingenious.

When I look at a tree, for example, I locate it and then read off facts about it from the way it appears or manifests itself. That is, I use the sensations aroused in me as appearings. And this would seem to mean that I put the sensation in a context and do not simply stare at it and make it terminal. What, then, stands out is its import for the object. In this setting, then, what I read off can best be categorized as facts about. It is in this way that cognizing begins.

Such is the theory of critical realism as to how cognizing is managed. What is called natural realism is more a statement of results thus obtained than an explication of the operation. I do see a tree out there and I am led to make certain statements about it. But I do not know how this is managed. I may, in default, say that I simply intuit it. But I really don't know what has been going on. Critical realism is, then, a theory of how sense-perception is managed. I may remark that an "ordinary language" approach may call attention to how we use words but, in itself, it does not work out theories. Of course, I do see trees out there and do make perceptual statements about them. It is well to stick to that as against logical positivism—but more is needed.

Let us now turn to the biological mechanisms involved. As I have suggested, there is a circuit from stimulus-complex to directed response with aroused sensations functioning in an informative way to initiate cognizing. I have argued that these are used in this context as a source of deciphered facts about the object of perceiving. In looking at an object we are both receptive and active. This perspective, I think, enables us to move between presentationalism and representationalism of the traditional kinds. And, in so doing, it does, I think, deepen empiricism which tended to limit itself too much to sensations and images rather than stress facts and the concepts founded on them. I have noted this demand for a deepened empiricism in Peirce, A. K. Rogers, Dewey and C. I. Lewis. Some of these spoke only of a thickened experience. I would emphasize an extended cognition linked with recognition of an enduring, external world. As I see it, in being referentially about the world, human knowing is necessarily engaged in working out its categorial structure, spatial, temporal, causal, and dispositional. Kant was at fault in his innatism and his phenomenalism. Otherwise, he made a marked step forward.

Looking backward at the subjectivistic orientation of Descartes and Locke, one can now readily see their mistake. Descartes took dualism for granted and was thrown back on self-knowledge as a starting-point. In this he had not advanced beyond Saint Augustine. To-day we start with the percipient organism and regard the self as developing within it, as a center of control. As I have analyzed perceiving, each percipient is, from the first, engaged with things both in the way of deciphering and in the way of action. There is a problem of an external world only in the sense that we desire to understand how this is managed. Turning to Locke, we quickly note that his causal theory of sense-perception moved inward to ideas but had no feeling for the additional circuit of directed response. Hence, for him, perceiving terminated on ideas and he and his successors had only the option of a supposed inference from them and a postulated correspondence. Berkeley blocked this path. I well remember trying to explain the circuit of reference to Bertrand Russell as an alternative to his scheme of logical construction. That was in 1922. But I had no success. Dewey, as we saw, bypassed the problem by manipulating the term experience. And G. E. Moore's solution in terms of two hands was not a howling success. I shall note that Moore made sense-data terminal when I come to the British scene. Even the neo-Thomists were puzzled by the problem of bringing the *sensible species* to bear on external things. I conclude that a correct analysis of perceiving is strategic in import.

Reading my earlier statement of 1930, I can see how I was approaching my present analysis but had not quite clarified it. I spoke of reference and knowledge-claims and of looking through sensory data at the object. But I do not think that I had quite grasped how we use sensations to decipher facts about their controls. I spoke of logical characters in the content of perception as enabling us to grasp the characteristics of the object. I would put it a little differently now. In the context of perceiving, we concentrate on features of sensory appearings as significant for the object we are perceiving. Accordingly, we begin to *think* the object in these terms. At the linguistic level they become the basis of predicates assigned. The thing is red, square, hard, etc. It is not the sensation, as such, that is stressed but its informative function. The flaw in presentationalism was that it ignored this role and made things out of sensations.

But perceiving is an exploratory activity concerned with things. It involves learning, handling, memory, expectation, and at the human level, predication. And out of such predication and relating arises logic with identification and the need for consistency, enforced by communication. Logic at least has its roots in the emergence of cognition with its use of sensory features as disclosures of what we are responding to.

A few words now on transcendence and truth. It follows from my analysis that transcendence is an achievement resting on the union of directional response and the use therein of cognitional activities. This cooperative union gives percipients their entrance to the world around them. We look at, point to, locate, work out a frame of reference. All the rest is added, step by step. Once the start is made, there is no great mystery. This orientation shifts us from the dualism, subjectivism and introspectionism of Descartes and Locke. But there is no need to go to the other extreme of the pan-objectivism of the new realists. The intra-personal plays its mediating role in the from-and-to circuit.

I have always held that the knowledge-claim is primary and that the idea of truth is subordinate to it. Truth is an endorsement of a knowledge-claim after processes of verification and falsification. Logic and evidence operate in this intermediate stage but lead up to the acceptance, or rejection, of a cognitive claim. As against C. I. Lewis, I would defend this kind of "metaphysical veracity." If the question of correspondence is raised, I would point to the role of sensations as points of cognitive disclosure of objects. That is, objects feed in information about themselves in this fashion. This is the base of verification and falsification and is called evidence. The assumption used in criticism of traditional representationalism that a hypothetical and impossible comparison between knowledge-claim and object must be added involves lack of recognition of how knowledge is achieved. Correspondence is an implication of knowledge; and knowledge requires the use of fed-in information.

This approach, it seems to me, enables us to do justice to the role of logic, evidence and *praxis*, or pragmatism, in discussions about truth. We expect that which is true to work in the long run. Peirce's view of truth as that which is accepted in the long run has point but I would back it by indicating the objective foundations which it presupposes. As I see it, logical realism is best understood in the context of physical realism. I think Pierce built too much on Kant and Schelling. What I have tried to bring out is the from-and-to mechanism involved in perceiving and the emergence, therefrom, of cognizing.

To conclude this section, I would call attention to the need, on the part of philosophy, for continuing interplay with science. I early recognized this need and inaugurated a course on the philosophy of science, called *The Main Concepts of Science*. J. B. Stallo, Youmans and Draper, as Schneider points out, had worked along similar lines. But I recognize that I was more a philosopher than a scientist. That is, I had philosophical problems in mind. It is not surprising then, that I have kept a keen interest in developments in human psychology, animal psychology and even in insect behavior.

I have already referred to McGill's admirable discussion of Lovejoy's epistemological dualism. The indications are that the role of the object dominates perceiving. That is as I would expect. Back of perceiving lie interests and needs. A monkey remembers where a banana was put and is disappointed at a substitute. A kind of stable norm dominates the perception of a coin, etc. I have argued that this directionalism explains the *intentionality* to which Lovejoy appeals. That is, I think he was too much of a dualist.

Natural history intrigues me. I have followed experiments on migrating birds who seem to scan the positions of the stars for orientation. Even the bees are able to communicate information about the location of flowers and even to guide their flight by adjustments to the position of the sun. The brain is, even here, a wonderful organ.

Evolutionary Materialism

When I wrote in 1930, naturalism was a daring enough term. It stood for the self-sufficiency of nature and for the primacy of the space-time-causality framework. Dewey and his followers were stressing scientific method within what they called experience. I, on the other hand, as a physical realist, was more frankly ontological. I took materialism to be a descriptive term opposed to idealism, spiritualism, dualism, etc. Its foundation lay in the recognition of material things in all their variety. These, alone, are denotable and measurable. There are molar things, microscopic things, ultra-microscopic particles, magnetic and gravitational fields. And it would seem that out of this foundation have emerged life and mind.

The philosopher has no competence for adding factual detail. This is the work of the special sciences with their method and techniques. He accepts, therefore, what is held in scientific circles to be the best account. But he keeps up a dialogue on questions that have been raised. What is the nature of human knowing? How penetrative is it? What should we mean by mechanism? by teleology? All this constitutes a kind of debate. A main query is just what materialism *implies*. On the one hand, there is the question of theism. Is nature self-sufficient? This must, of course, be discussed. Then there is the question of the emergence of mind and its status in a material world. This is the contemporary mind-brain issue. William James thought of processes in the brain as involving the collision of atoms. To-day we think of the brain in terms of electro-chemical patterns and use such analogies as scanning and computers. Warren S. McCulloch argues that man's brain has about one trillion computing neurons. These can bring together two million separate biological components all at once. Out of such quantity should come novelty.

Science began with the vast, inorganic world and enlarged horizons. It thought in terms of inertia, momentum, acceleration and gravity. Celestial mechanics dominated thought. Then came chemistry with combining components. We are now in the era of the giant molecules and of genetic codes and genetic pools. The very economy of the cell is being worked out.

And it is astonishing. The brain, itself, is being probed by electrodes and transistors. Centers for this and that are being discovered. The stress is on behavior, something observable. As Bertrand Russell noted, all this fits into a materialistic perspective. But how about awareness, the use of sensations and images as conveying factual information, the rise of symbols and concepts? These operations must, somehow, be naturalized. Surely, at this level, behavior has its internal conditions.

May I, at this point, use the technique of the movies and turn back to the past? It so happened that I had early begun to stress integration and the importance of organization and relations. Newtonian, unilinear causality seemed no longer adequate. How about interplay? I spoke of levels of causality. It was along this line that the notion of what later came to be called emergence arose. In this country, Spaulding, Lovejoy, I and several others began to think along these lines. There was a similar development in England associated with the names of Lloyd Morgan and S. Alexander. Integration meant that the whole is more than an additive sum of parts. Later came the feedback approach of physiology and cybernetics. I suppose my own analysis of perceiving as a from-and-to operation is along this line. Dead-level, or reductive, materialism was becoming a thing of the past.

Now it is the very nature of philosophy to be concerned with the human situation and to try to bring thought and things together. Can this be done within the contours of an evolutionary materialism? I think it can. It is time to grapple with the mind-brain issue. But, first of all, we must seek to be open-minded and to leave old notions of the deadness and inertness of matter behind. We humans are flesh and blood and apprehensive; and our bodies have adjustmental wisdom.

As I see it, then, not dualism but some kind of identity of consciousness with the functioning of the brain is the most promising hypothesis. The linguistic problem is how best to think it. Does epistemology offer any suggestion?

I think it does. Science starts with perceiving external things and adds to it manipulation and instrumental techniques. Hence it is not at all surprising that, when it deals with human beings, it favors external observation, that is, behaviorism. It notes with interest how human beings behave. Not so long ago, the brain was considered a little black box, something in the skull, rather hidden. Of course, it could be dissected by neurologists; but then it was not functioning. Needless to say, much has happened since those days. There are ways now of studying the brain as it functions. But I do want to keep in mind the analysis of perceiving which I contend is basic for science, namely, the use of sensation as disclosing features of the object which controls it. Let us call this *external knowledge*, knowledge from the outside. It can become very detailed and integrated with explanatory concepts, subject to verification and falsification. Nevertheless, it builds on what the senses can disclose. As William James pointed out, somewhat querulously, scientists did not pay much attention to the nature of human knowing. I suppose they left that to the philosophers who, as we saw, did not make much headway.

Now, the point I want to make is that, in introspection, we seem to be participating in what is going on in our brains. Are we not on the inside in some measure? As cultivated, this is a sort of reflex activity, a shift of attention, requiring a new vocabulary.

Now it must not be supposed that we have here a repetition of sense-perception, a sort of inner sense, as Locke would have it. But if we are participating in the brain functioning, I would expect a kind of identity or agreement. And this, I take it, is what the Gestaltists accept, a kind of dynamic identity. Only I would take it more literally than some of the Gestaltists do. In this identity, I think the conscious agent is participating in his cerebral activity. This I call the double-knowledge view. This view feeds into an identity theory. In our consciousness we are on the inside of our brain.

There are linguistic questions to be clarified. First of all, what do we mean by "in" or "inside"? I examined this question in my first book, *Critical Realism* (1916). Clearly, it cannot mean the way one material thing is *in* another, like a pea in a pod. As I see it, it stands for enlargement of content. Our historical tendency has been to regard external knowing as more exhaustive of its object than it can be. What it really gives us is facts about the object—in these days, largely mensurational. But, in the background, people—even scientists—carry over a kind of intuitional naive realism. Hence they easily build up the notion that material systems are identifiable completely with the picture they have in mind. Now I am arguing that sensations, images, symbolic meanings, feelings may emerge as factors in neural activities. As I see it, these factors go with signals, guidance, and the togetherness of awareness. For instance, memory patterns must stand out to be used. Even a solitary wasp recognizes its diggings in this way and so does the honey bee circle around its hive to get its bearings. It is this noting and using of patterns out of which *relational awareness* emerges.

I conclude that we must enlarge our notions of what can be intrinsic to the functioning brain to include sensory *qualia* and their functional use. The first level is that of guidance. Afterwards comes cognition, as in man. The brain lends itself to patterning and this must somehow stand out to be used. Here compresence and awareness emerge. As it is usually put, the brain acts more or less as a whole. Thus I move between the intuitional blankness of naive realism and the other extreme of panpsychism.

I want next to say a few words about the language of agency. As has been frequently pointed out, we do not say the brain perceives or the brain decides. We use the personal pronoun "I." I look at the scene before me. I make up my mind. What, then, is the self? It seems to me a center of control developed genetically and in terms of social communication. It is this center which employs and understands language. It speaks of myself, you and they. When we speak of the brain, it is in terms of external, knowledge about. In point of fact, knowledge that the brain was involved came late. But the brain was functioning in this diversified way all along. I do not see any linguistic dilemma.

I have recently read over my Personal Statement of 1930 and find it to be along the right lines. Much the same holds of the cooperative book, *Philosophy for the Future* of 1949. It was published during the cold war and was not kindly reviewed as a consequence. Since scientists were included, the book had considerable substance. Academic philosophy turned away from realism to positivism and linguistic analysis. I shall say something about these developments in later chapters. I wish now to say something about value-judgments and moral commitments. I think they can be easily fitted into evolutionary materialism at the cultural level. But, before I proceed to this section, I want to make a comment on the so-called *formal materialism* of Thomism. I commend it in that it did not fall into the pit of subjectivism and dualism opened up by Descartes and Locke. But, as I shall later try to show, it kept a rather naive teleology and an outmoded idea of matter. In looking over its idea of perceiving, I found that it emphasized a *cognitive identity* of *sensible species* before the mind and in the object where I had stressed the use of sensations as informed appearings of the controlling thing perceived and thus the point of departure for cognition. In Aristotle in his later years there was a tendency towards naturalism. All in all, then, I recognize the zigzag and checkered career of philosophy. But I do not, like Professor Feuer, wish to cancel it. I hold that basic leads can be found. Perhaps, Americans of my generation had healthy insights, too quickly ignored.

Humanism: Valuations and Commitments

I begin this section with the belief that "immaterialism" has little justification in either theory of knowledge or ontology. The job for philosophy is, accordingly, to work out a new kind of materialism, able to do justice to the human scene. Here we have a unique level of existence which has evolved on this planet and is the culmination of biological and cultural developments. Let us look at its texture. One must be careful in one's semantics. Clichés usually mislead.

The first suggestion I would make is that we look on man in an ecological fashion, that is, in his interplay with his surroundings. It is in this way that he is *within* nature. What stands out is a high degree of intelligence in both thought and action. If my analysis is correct, this is the work of the brain-mind, historically and, therefore, culturally conditioned. At this level of causality, symbols and communication operate. All this rests on, and involves, the capacities of the brain. In accordance with my identity-view I speak of it as the brain-mind. Hence we have a materialism which includes the subjective and which has, so to speak, an inside to it. This outlook breaks with the tradition of epiphenomenalism, associated with much of past materialism. As I see it, both cognition and appraisal rest on the awareness and use of ideas and feelings in a guiding and mediating way. These stand out in cerebral activities as signals and cues and go with relational compresence or awareness. As I view it, new causal categories must be worked out to do justice to this kind of activity. We hear already of scanning, programming and computing. Nature has been very inventive. Let us recall the use of sensations as indicative of features of external controls. Higher levels of cognizing build on this pattern.

But I want now to pass to the study of man as an agent. Here is where the whole individual, now called a person, is in action. I have already argued that the self functions as the center of control. In self-consciousness, attention is focussed on it and various strands of its constitution are recognized. It is clearly an historical growth but it is important to note that it is not an impersonal growth, like that of a plant, but a resultant of a succession of selections and choices from childhood on, susceptible of revision. We ask ourselves at crucial times what it is best to do. We survey our goals, evaluate and orient ourselves. Philosophy has given much attention to these operations, especially in the field of ethics and value-theory. It is to this setting that I now turn. What I shall try to do is to clear up certain issues. I shall ask what is involved in valuations and commitments. It is well to keep in mind the continuity of man with the lower animals as well as his emergent differences.

Agency, in general, rests on drives and needs and on their interplay with surroundings. In this context, learning operates in various ways, modifying the drives, leading to recognition of conditions of success or failure. The animal makes necessary adjustments to satisfy its needs and reach the goals of its drives.

Human beings we see in the social group with its folkways and customs. There are approved ways of behaving and ways condemned. Cultural anthropologists and historians of morality have sought to elicit causes and reasons for such, more or less standardized, conduct. When we use the word, cause, I think we have in mind an operative factor. When we speak of reasons, the context is that of judgment. As I see it, reasons may inform causes. I then do something *because* of my judgment. At this level, we can have rational causation. It is usual now to speak of *good reasons* for conduct (I hope Talcott Parsons would accept this analysis).

It may be well at this point to note a popular *transfer* of the term, materialism, to signify conduct dominated by acquisitive motives, chiefly the possession of material things. It is a very natural transfer. But it must not be confused with the ontological meaning of the term. An ontological materialist may have high social ideals and a love of literature. One must be on one's guard against shifts of meaning.

I want now to consider recent controversies as to the nature and status of values and valuation. The subject is called axiology or the theory of values. In ethical theory, it appears as metaethics which is a concern for precise meanings in morals. What do we mean by right and wrong? By good and bad? By ought? As we should expect, morality has its principles which need clarification. But I am here concerned more with general foundations. I am primarily engaged to show that realism and evolutionary materialism in no manner shut out moral commitment and responsibility. As I see it, we have a high level here of causality tied in with feelings of group identification expressed in attitudes of benevolence and demands for justice.

The theory of value has the task, then, of fitting moral philosophy into natural philosophy. My approach will be to show that value-assignments differ in type from cognitions. What stands out in cognizing is the building up of descriptions of a factual sort on the basis of indications in sensations. Even in measurement there are such guiding indications. Cognition is, accordingly, impersonal and objective in a descriptive way. That is what the term, fact, implies. Valuing, or appraising, on the other hand, concerns itself with the *role* of an object, situation or act in the human economy. What is important is the way the object connects up with feeling and desire. We think of it in this reflexive relation. It is the object we appraise, of course, but for its bearing on our interests. I speak of this as its role.

As we should expect, language developed a corresponding terminology of good, bad, harmful, desirable, etc. So used, these terms had their own kind of objective import. People could agree or dissent. This led to the search for criteria, for reasons upon which they might agree. I like the taste of this apple. Don't you? This policy will have satisfactory results. I not only desire this project but consider it desirable. Judgment comes in with its claims and tests. We make statements about the object and hope for agreement. But it is essential to realize that what we have in mind is the role it plays in the human economy.

In England, Moore and Ross and others wanted to get beyond expressions of desires and mere statistical summaries of attitudes. But I do not think they saw that appraisals had their own logic. I can give reasons why I regard some action as desirable. Its results, in all likelihood. I may prefer one auto to another because of its looks or because of its comfort. The additional point I am making, however, is that I appraise the auto, itself, for reasons given. That people might differ in their preferences is quite understandable. I see no reason to postulate an intrinsic quality of goodness in the object, a quality that can be intuited. It is the way the object connects up with our interests that counts. Criteria emerge from this connection.

I wish to say a few words on alternative views. The British took the path of intuition to get objectivity. I think they were mistaken. Perry, the new realist, defined value as any object of any interest. But I think he was handicapped by his epistemology. He did not do justice to the role of judgments. He saw that interest played a part in the assignment of value to an object but did not appreciate the work of appraisal. D. H. Parker countered by defining value as any interest in any object. But this move seemed to me too subjectivistic. I wanted to understand what we humans are doing in valuation.

As I see it, then, valuation goes on within nature and depends on man's capacity both to know objects and to attend to their role in his economy. Taken in this sense, I see no difficulty in acclimatizing them in the *ecology* of human living.

I turn now briefly to moral commitment and a humanistic way of life. Once we grasp the point that man is an agent and that the self is the center of his control, we can, I hold, understand the rise and nature of imperatives. Morality is a group affair but an affair always in the making. Rules of conduct are set up and more or less imposed. Ought and responsibility are symbols of this situation and I find nothing unnatural about them. But the texture of morality alters as we pass from custom to grappling with new problems in a changing society. "Oughtness" becomes more and more personal in location. It requires the working out of principles and their personal application. In an emergency, like Sartre's resistance situation, the stress on personal commitment may well increase and decision become *staccato*. In the United States, sociologists note the shift from inner-directed man to the conformist, other-directed man.

In the next chapter, I shall consider the British scene, in a rather critical manner. I liked its combination of empiricism and analysis but was convinced that it had missed some foundational cues as to the nature of perceiving and that this had made it more susceptible to positivism and turned it away from naturalism and evolutionary materialism. It is in this ambit that I shall afterwards examine Ayer and Wittgenstein.

6

THE BRITISH SCENE

I turn now to the British scene. During the years before the first World War, there had been considerable, philosophical intercourse with the United States. It is true that American students had chiefly gone to Germany for advanced studies in the field. But that was partly a matter of academic organization. Graduate degrees and Ph.D's had hardly any place in the British World.

At the beginning of the century, Anglo-American idealism was still in the ascendant. Bradley and Bosanquet stood out. I learned later that there were other currents in both Oxford and Cambridge. About these I shall say something later.

Pragmatism reached England largely by way of William James. Bradley had debates with him on the question of truth. It was rather a drawn battle, with Bradley, perhaps, stronger on points of logic. F. C. S. Schiller became the champion at Oxford of a form of pragmatism which he called *Humanism*.

In the meantime, Bertrand Russell and G. E. Moore were coming to the front and would play an increasing role in British thought. I intend to analyze their positions. In a sense, both were realists; but with different emphases. Russell kept, on the whole, nearer to Hume, while Moore made much of common sense.

After the realistic movement in the United States faltered, Russell and Moore came increasingly to the front, Russell as one of the founders of the new logic and Moore as the champion of analysis. In these terms, British philosophy gained prestige. I do not wish to suggest any uniformity of outlook. There was debate and a measure of receptiveness. During this period, American philosophy rather marked time. What stood out was an emphasis on technique, on what may be called intellectual equipment, particularly, in mathematical logic. I could not, myself, note any advance in epistemology. What seemed to occur was a sort of plodding on, with an eye to developments elsewhere. And it so happened that the Vienna Circle was convinced that it had a new approach with its stress on meaning and verification. Naturally, it was listened to. Shortly before this, another Austrian, Wittgenstein, had, with Russell's encouragement, written a *Tractatus* of a cryptic sort in which language and logic were pushed to the front. It is still much commented on. Under these conditions, the importance of language was soon recognized. What is called linguistic philosophy had arrived. Sometimes there was a stress on an "ideal" language and its logic. Lately, a reaction to this in terms of *ordinary language* has come about.

What would be the wise policy of a man of an older generation in the face of all this activity? Surely, to keep his bearings and try to clarify points in his own position, while seeking to understand what was going on. If untenable and inadequate doctrines were advanced, these could be criticized exhaustively. And that was just what happened. I am told, for example, that logical positivism for all its original *élan* has now few followers. May it not be that a critical form of realism may secure attention? Perhaps, it was too hastily discarded.

What I am proposing to do in this chapter is to examine the British scene with an eye on its presuppositions. It will be my thesis that British philosophy, from the time of Berkeley on, did not appreciate the from-and-to circuit in perceiving; and therefore, was blind to the role of sensations as informational about the external world. The result was that it made sensations *terminal* and continued in the traditon of a subjectivistic kind of empiricism. That is, its orientation was at fault. Linguistics, alone, will not correct this error. And I suspect that even the brilliant Wittgenstein followed too closely in the tracks of Russell to be able to avoid it.

A Diversity of Traditions

While I want to concentrate on the present scene in England, I think it advisable to note certain diversities. For instance, there was an Aristotelian tradition at Oxford just as there was one at Columbia in the person of Woodbridge. It is only too easy to oversimplify. Cook Wilson had at least local fame in logic and confronted Bradley. I find it interesting to examine their attitudes to *appearings* and the problem of external things. In a letter to me about my book, *Critical Realism,* (1916) Bradley stated that he saw points in favor of realism but could not see how one got beyond *appearances* to an external world. I understand that Cook Wilson held that appearances are not entities in their own right but the appearings of objects. But I do not find that he carried this suggestion out. How did appearings come about? I turn to Prichard, another distinguished Oxford philosopher, in touch with Cook Wilson and find the following move, namely, that we take our sensations to be physical things. We "see" a colored extension and take it to be a material thing. There is postulated a kind of identification. I suppose this is his explanation of naive realism in which we seem to intuit external things. But I do not find in his writings the base for this dominating belief in material things. I imagine this intrigued Bradley too. But he fell back on the internal principle of coherence and pushed aside many beliefs as incoherent.

These were all very able men. It is clear that certain blockages are operating. Sensations were still regarded as terminal. How, then, could we get to external things? One move was to translate them into *universals* and to make things into complexes of such universals. One could, thereupon, get rid, at the start, of many traditional puzzles, such as the correspondence theory of truth and the idea of substances. A distinguished American philosopher, Brand Blanshard, takes this line. I, on the other hand, take physical things to be knowable and actually to feed in information about themselves. With this approach, I can explain correspondence and the dispositional properties of substances. But this reference to Blanshard here is an aside.

I am not going to apologize for philosophy, as some to-day want to do. I think there are perennial questions which have to be cleared up. It may well be that, once the clue is found, traditional problems will become easier to master. In the previous chapter I suggested that realism and evolutionary materialism might constitute the ensuing framework. I imagine that many people would resent this result. I recall that Gilson, who has his brand of a perennial philosophy, reported his belief that philosophers did not expect, nor look forward to, basic agreements. This may be the case. But with the increasing influence of the sciences, it may retreat. There may arise an accepted, secular philosophy supplementing science on overarching questions.

Russell's Type of Empiricism

With Bertrand Russell we pass to Cambridge University. But here, again there was diversity in the background. James Ward was a personalist, not too different from Bowne and Brightman, in the United States. W. E. Johnson was, in logic, a forerunner of Russell but he was less interested in calculus than in principles. McTaggart went his own way, moving from Hegelianism to a kind of deductive metaphysics.

Russell struck out on paths of his own. He was never afraid to change his mind and shift his position. He was more in touch with American philosophy than were other Englishmen. He was influenced by William James and the neutral monism which resulted. In the background was Hume's type of empiricism, as it was for American new realists. I probed him on several occasions about sense-perceptions and, to put it in my language, he stressed percepts rather than perceiving. I had arrived at the notion that consciousness was intrinsic to cerebral activity, an identity view which I advanced in *Critical Realism*. I had been rather isolated and, once in the twenties, I took the opportunity in conversation to advance this thesis to him. Later he adopted what Lovejoy called the "under-the-hat" theory of mind. I don't suppose he recalled this conversation but his later thinking as exhibited in the book, *Human Knowledge, Its Scope and Limits,* came nearer to critical realism. But, as I saw his causal approach, he got into the brain but did not see how perceiving took up, and used, sensations in the context of response.

It is best to begin with his early book, *The Problems of Philosophy.* Here he had very definite ideas. He stressed what he called knowledge by acquaintance. "Every sensation, according to this view, was itself a cognition and consisted in awareness of what I called the sense-datum." Later he gave up this view, partly under the influence of William James, and concluded that sensations are not in themselves cognitive. The result was what was called neutral monism. This view was akin to American new realism.

But if sensations and images, alone, are given, how can we account for material things? Like Berkeley and others he saw no basis for any inference from sensations to things. And, very naturally, he looked to logic for a guide. Might not material things be logical constructs from sensations and what he called sensibilia? Being well equipped and ingenious, he proceeded to translate material things into these terms. The point to appreciate is that he saw no alternative. Only sensory experience is given; and there is no basis for inference to another realm.

I recall that he had undertaken this kind of logical construction about the time the *Essays in Critical Realism* came out. And he happened to be in Ann Arbor for a lecture. I had the timerity to suggest to him that perceiving rested on *reference* rather than on an impossible kind of inference. But, of course, this suggestion required a different analysis of perceiving from the one he had started out with. As the reader knows, I think of sensations as performing a function within a from-and-to circuit. Among animals, their role is largely that of guidance. And this guidance occurs within the setting of response. Response is usually very quick except when there is no fear and curiosity is aroused. In man, response is often delayed and, moreover, past experience intervenes in the way of habits and concepts. The point I would make is that we use sensations as cues and indications in the setting of dealing with what we regard as things confronting us. Thus perceiving has a context. In this setting we note how things look and how they feel, etc. That is, sensations are dwelt on, not so much for their own sakes, but as informative. The result is the growth of what is usually called natural realism. Language develops in this context. I shall later examine the searching study of ordinary language by Austin. I think he has a point against the sense-datum translations of Price and Ayer. These thinkers seem to identify perception with the awareness of sense-data, here largely following the traditions of Moore and the early Russell. But I do not find in Austin a well-worked-out theory of the mechanism of perceiving. It will, I hope, be recalled that I accounted for the emergence of cognition from the use of sensations as giving factual *appearings* of their external controls. I do not, myself, see how nature could have developed cognition in any other way. At any rate, it seems clear that this is the path it took.

But let us come back to Russell. We saw that, in line with the tradition of British empiricism, he regarded sensations as terminal and not as functional. This way of looking at sensations belonged to the introspective outlook which went back to Descartes and Locke and was climaxed in Hume. It also went with a one-sided causal theory of perception which ignored response. What I call the *circuit approach* recognizes the role of sensations in biological adjustment. This has analogies with recent theories of feedback. An object stimulates me through an impinging stimulus-pattern and I look at it or the case may be that I reach out to it.

Working within the old tradition, Russell makes sensations terminal and identifies them with a primary knowledge, which he calls knowledge by acquaintance. This is to remain his paradigm. Even his logic is adjusted to it. Out of it comes his logical atomism and his notion of a simple, ideal language.

But Russell had a strong, scientific persuasion. Physics was his example of scientific achievement. And so Russell went back to the tradition of sensations as arising in the brain. Patterns could thus be reproduced. He gives many examples of such pattern-reproduction. But he could get out of the brain only by means of postulates, in a semi-Kantian way. As for the brain, itself, could it not consist of percepts? Other observers could, of course, experience only their own percepts. It was this kind of "under-the-hat" theory of mind which Lovejoy attacked and which Dewey tried to avoid by his experiential behaviorism.

It may be well to recall how I get out of the brain in perceiving and in the cognition which develops on its framework until it reaches and describes the stars.

The first point to bear in mind is that sensations do not carry in themselves knowledge of their cerebral locus. It took mankind a long time to learn the importance of the brain. Aristotle had the idea that it was an organ for cooling the blood. Even Hobbes emphasized the heart.

The question is, then, about the use of, say, visual sensations in the whole complex of active perceiving. It is clear that part of that activity consists of the response called "looking at." There can be added to that pointing, reaching for, walking toward. As I see it, seeing has its setting in just such dynamic complexes. In looking at a tree just outside my window, my visual field functions within the looking at, in a guiding and indicative fashion. I would not speak of this as a projection. There is, certainly, no physical projection involved. I prefer to speak of directional reference. And it is undeniable that one of the functions of seeing and hearing is to locate objects. They are not only distance-receptors but locators. It is in connection with such locating that external knowledge is achieved. It is not that one gets literally outside one's brain but that the resources of the brain work with the organism to produce this kind of patterned awareness of our surroundings in which directional reference combines with sensory appearings to give us knowledge about.

As we all know, there is a proprioceptive scheme, analogous to the exteroceptive one, which enables us to locate the sources of pains and aches. The neurologist has some idea of the mechanisms involved. But it seems to me that epistemologists have been somewhat backward. Russell, Lovejoy and Dewey were, certainly, frustrated.

If I am right in my analysis, natural and naive realism are resultants of the mechanisms I have indicated. It is then, *as though* external things were intuited or presented. The new realism built on this and on what was considered the impossibility of representative realism of the Locke type. Critical realism moves between presentative and representative traditions by showing how, in perceiving, sensations are used as informative about the controlling object. We do not, first, start with Russell's knowledge by acquaintance and then seek to infer external things. Nature was cleverer than that.

Had we the space, it might well be of interest to recall how Mill worried over the question of how to deal with our belief in external things. He tried to solve it by the association of ideas, reducing matter, accordingly, to the permanent possibility of sensations. In France, Condillac, Destutt de Tracy and Cabanis worked on the same problem, stressing touch and resistance. We have a double sensory experience when we touch our own bodies. There was point to this; but I think my analysis of the act of perceiving as involving both reference and the use of sensations as informative-about brings out better the base for the emergence of external cognizing.

Russell gave many leads to a new sophistication, such as his theory of proper names and his analysis of definite descriptions. Logical paradoxes came to the front. Some of these were amusing. Take the statement, It was not Homer who wrote the Iliad but a man with the same name. Epimenides, the Cretan, who, though a Cretan, said that *all* Cretans were liars offered food for thought. Modern logic was in the making. It was clearly bound up with the way we thought about the world and it had objective import. Wittgenstein was one of the first to demarcate it.

I cannot leave Russell without remarking how much sympathy I had with his general outlook. I differed from him chiefly in epistemology. He kept a Humean base while I was a physical realist. Of course, this involved a divergence in ontology also. I became an advocate of a new materialism while Russell kept to his neutral monism.

G. E. Moore and Analysis

Though early associated, Moore and Russell differed in temperament and in emphases. Moore kept nearer to common sense. He was skeptical of the extravagances of idealistic metaphysics. There were certain everyday beliefs which he saw no reason to doubt. There was a touch here of Reid and Scotch criticism of Hume.

But he could not escape the problem of sense-perception. His reflections on this point led him to hold that we directly perceive what he called sense-data. It will be recalled that Russell started with acquaintance with sense-data and shifted to sensations under the influence of William James. But Moore stuck to them as primary objects. The problem, then, was to find out their relation to material things. In one of his last essays, called *Visual Sense-Data,* he speaks of the relation R between sense-data and object and declares that no philosopher has explained clearly what this relation R is "where it is not identity."

While I do not believe in entities called sense-data but in events called sensations, the question of the role and status of sensations in perceiving is akin to the problem Moore raises. The problem of what we perceive is, also, relevant. Those who believe in sense-data hold that we directly perceive them. The added question is that of their relation to material things. H. H. Price who has given the question much thought seems to take the position that material things are complexes of sense-data and a localizable occupant. He speaks of the foreground and the background. As I understand him, sense-data are cognizable entities out there. Thus he takes the identity gambit.

Phenomenalists, of course, relinquish the belief in material things and so do not have Moore's problem. This gambit was taken by the logical positivists, as we shall see when we discuss Ayer. Price takes a more moderate position of conditional identity. He is quite aware of problems, such as the stick seemingly bent in water, the change in the looks of an object as we approach it, etc.

Let us now recall our own thesis. It was to the effect that sensations are aroused in us by an external control and that these are used in a response act, directed toward the control, as giving us factual information about it, how it looks, feels, etc. *Moore's R is twofold.* First comes the causal control and then comes the referential use of the sensation as an appearing, or manifestation, to give us indications about the external things. These indications are employed in perceptual judgments and constitute their ground. The relation R is connected with the circuit from, and to, the object. I suspect that Price had not carefully enough studied the biology of perceiving. I am quite sure that Moore did not.

This seems the best place to discuss what is usually called the directness of perceiving. Those who stress sense-data tend to hold that it is these that are directly perceived. I, on the other hand, take the act of perceiving as referentially directed on the external thing and hold to this type of directedness. Sensations play a manifesting role *within* the act of perceiving. Of course, we can shift our attention to them, if we so wish; and it is the case that the traditional, causal theory of perception did so and made them terminal. But, by so doing, it became blind to actual perceiving, and got itself into all sorts of troubles.

But Moore made his mark in his emphasis upon analysis. This was set over against speculation. Now I had always been naturalistic in my outlook and in touch with science so that this contrast did not impress me.

It was later much used by the logical positivists in their attacks on "metaphysics." They, however, were phenomenalists and metaphysics meant for them something unjustifiably transcendent. One must always note contexts. As a materialist, I stressed ontology.

I have never been quite clear as to what Moore was analyzing, beliefs or the use of words. It turned out to be, very often, a sort of translation of a complex sentence into simpler ones. This led insensibly into semantics and linguistics. At times, it seemed a current dogma that philosophers fooled themselves more easily than did the plain man. This was, perhaps, because they grappled with abstract problems and made mistakes. Warning to this effect was salutary.

I want, in concluding this brief study of Moore, to call attention to his theory of value. What Moore desired was to get an objective foundation for ethics. He found this in the term, good. It seemed to him to have objective import. One could always ask of anything else whether it was good. Pleasure is pleasure. But is it a good? That is to ask another question. Moore seems to have thought that goodness was an intuitable and indefinable property. It was quite set apart from what he called natural properties, such as survival value.

Other ethical thinkers, such as Ross, turned their attention to oughtness and obligation as outstanding features of morality. They were convinced that utilitarianism had not done justice to the validity of these demands. This emphasis went back to Kant's rigorism and his appeal to what he had called the categorical imperative. It was not so much the consequences of actions as their alignment with principles of the practical reason that determined their rightness. Ross noted what he called *prima facie* duties and fell back on moral intuitions. This approach to ethics was named deontological because of its stress on duty.

The consequence of Moore's and Ross's stress of goodness and rightness was a revival of interest in the logic of valuation. It was seen to be of a different type than that found in descriptive knowledge. In morals, at least, there was the element of the prescriptive and the imperative. The next step was a careful study of the language of morality. This, I think, accompanied a search into the psychology and logic of both non-moral and moral valuation. I argued that non-moral valuations expressed the recognition of the role the project played in a person's or the group's economy. It rested on an interplay of knowledge and feeling and had a vocabulary of its own. When we say that something is *desirable*, we make a judgment about it with criteria more or less explicit. The claim involved differentiates it from the purely factual of "I desire it." It should not be surprising that the group has come to set up demands and standards with regard to conduct of its members. Moral reflection works within this context, often in a reforming way.

Let us return to Moore. It is clear that he had the ability to raise questions. And there was a personal touch about his thinking which called out respect. I had only one opportunity of discussing points with him. And then it seemed to me that his outlook was a strange blend of phenomenalism and realism. He believed in material things but, as we have seen, was brought up short by sense-data. I tried to explain my view of perceiving as directed at external things and as using indications in sensations in the process. But it was impossible to present this outlook adequately in these circumstances. So we parted amicably. It will be recalled that I had much the same experience with Russell with respect to his use of the term, percepts. Percepts were, in his eyes, terminal experiences. I, on the other hand, wanted to stress perceiving as a complex act, referential in direction and involving claims based on sensory cues and indications. Only in this way, I thought, could we break loose from the subjectivistic perspective dominant in modern philosophy.

A Few Words about Ryle

In recently reading Austin's *Sense and Sensibilia*, I was very much struck by remarks of his indicating his belief that rapid changes were occurring in British thought. When he quoted from Ayer, for example, he noted that the book he was quoting from was several years old. Ayer could not be held to it. He, Austin, was merely using it as a point of departure.

Now I can note a marked shift in Ryle from the analyses of Russell and Moore. He is interested in the development of perceptual language. While children are still in the nursery, the emphasis is on *what* they perceive. Interiorization comes later. It is at this later stage that children begin to talk about the act of perceiving, about the way things look and sound to us. Ryle then goes on to talk about "glimpses" and "looks." These are not entities but episodes in perceiving. "We do not here use 'neat' sensation words but terms in connection with what we are perceiving."

Now I am in hearty agreement with this observation. It fits in with my thesis that sensations are used in their informational function in perceiving. We are all the time using them in this fashion. As we walk toward an object, or away from it, its looks change. Ayer and Price note this point in their defense of sense-data. They call attention to the series of experiences we have, which differ but slightly from one another. Austin complains that Ayer uses here the ambiguous term, perceptions, as denoting the entities involved. These are, for him, the direct, or immediate, objects. Later he is to advocate a sense-datum language as primary.

Now I would not deny that we can concentrate on our visual field, as Price and Ayer maintain. But I would agree with Ryle that we ordinarily speak of the changing looks of the object as we approach or recede. It will make all the difference in the world whether we connect perceiving with looks of things or with sense-data. I, myself, hold that perceiving is an achievement activity aided by using sensations as informative. In this context, it is the external thing that we perceive by means of them.

Ryle seems a little afraid of the bodily location of sensations. If we so locate them, how do we get outside? I have already discussed this problem by stressing the full context in which, for example, the visual field is used. The motor setting of "looking at" dominates. I have sometimes allowed myself to speak of looking through the visual field at external things.

Ryle rightly points out that sense-impressions do not themselves constitute a component of what we perceive. There is no literal projection. But, in using sensations to help to achieve perceiving, it is cognitive relevance of features of the sensation which stands out. For instance, I say this object feels hard. That is, there is an indication in the feeling in this context. It is in this fashion that I spell out qualities in perceiving things. Language and concepts take over from here. It is the tree that I see and whose rough bark I touch. Here we have what Ryle calls sensuous thinking. I sometimes spoke of it as deciphering. As Austin indicates, there is no explicit appeal to what science and the courts call evidence. And there is no overt inference. I am in a position to know there is a telephone in this room, for I have used it.

Should this outlook be called naive realism? I call it critical realism because there is awareness of the complex operations involved in human knowing. I call it direct realism as against the two-stage view of representative realism. Naive realism seems to me to go with the presentationalism of the new realism while I move between it and representationalism.

Price and Broad

Both Price and Broad are meticulous thinkers. Price stresses sense-data and makes them constituents of what he calls the perceptual object. They are entities which can become the objects of a cognitive intuition; and many people's sensa are constituents of the public, perceptual object. Thus he is nearer to naive realism than I am.

C. D. Broad is a careful thinker also. Sensa are constituents of the same perceptual object and he speaks of perceptual acceptance. There is enough Lockean dualism in his outlook to make him distinguish between the epistemological object and the ontological object and it is hard to see how he gets them into cognitive contact.

Broad is interested in the categories, like causality and substance, and speaks of non-perceptual intuition. I, on the other hand, think of categorial meanings as arising within the context of perceptual achievement. I look at an object which I consider as real as myself, handle it, remember it; and so habits and beliefs arise. As I see it, it is in this setting that our notion of things and persons arises. Attitudes and expectations play their part. There is a growth of meanings. I see no justification for the *a priorism* of Kant yet recognize that his emphasis on categories represented an advance on Hume. In his early days, at least, Russell was, like Hume, hostile to categories. Thinghood was, for him, a primitive, metaphysical aberration. I regard this as a mistake of this reductive kind of empiricism. An adequate notion of perceiving gives us cognitive entrance into the world around us. And we learn more and more about it. The dispositional properties of objects are a case in point. Rubber is elastic and sugar dissolves in water. As we shall see in the next chapter, the logical positivist met difficulties here.

I conclude that Broad has not moved far from Locke and is nearer to representative realism than to critical realism. But he has great powers of exposition and is in touch with science.

I want, in conclusion, to say a few words about J. L. Austin, a brilliant Oxford philosopher with a gift for verbal usage. He is a sharp critic of Ayer and Price with their emphasis on sense-data as the primary objects of perception. I am not quite clear as to his own view of perceiving, so that, on this point, I must content myself with questions.

First of all, Austin charges these philosophers with oversimplification. There are many kinds of things perceived, rainbows and pictures on the silver screen as well as material things. And people are not deceived by mirrors. It is not only false but simply absurd to say that such objects as pens and or cigarettes are never directly perceived. This, I take it, is a matter of usage. In his war against the introduction of sense-data, Austin analyzes such terms as looks, seems and appears. At the same time, he rejects such locutions as visual appearances, perceptions, etc. His strategy

is to show that ordinary language has learned to do justice to qualifications demanded by special circumstances.
Now this is just what I should expect. The plain man is not concerned with theories as to what takes place. He is concerned with results expressible in ordinary language, such as looks, appears, seems. That is, he moves from the language of direct perceptions to qualification. Ayer and Price, on the other hand, are convinced that sense-data are the entities we directly perceive and revise language accordingly. In fact, Ayer seeks to move from a language built around sense-data to a secondary language about material things founded on the first one.
As I see it, then, Austin takes his stand on ordinary language and concludes that Price and Ayer are continuing the traditions of Berkeley and Kant, though with more linguistic liberality. I, on the other hand, have sought to show the role of sensations in objective perceiving. Thus I move between Austin and Ayer. I can admire the former's linguistic ingenuity while pointing out what I regard as Ayer's mistake, namely, the taking of sensations as terminal objects, to be called sense-data. That is why Ayer seeks to reduce material-object language to sense-datum language.
One last point. I think that Austin is quite right in holding that I can be empirically certain that I perceive the things around me, this typewriter, this book, etc. I am using the sensations they arouse in me, under favorable conditions. But I would still like to know his ideas on how perceiving is achieved. I have been told in Oxford recently that Austin would have left this job to science. I, on the other hand, would cooperate with men like Lord Brain and Herrick.

7

POSITIVISM, LOGIC
AND LANGUAGE

In a previous chapter, I pointed out how a sort of stalemate has arisen in American thought. Idealism had been confronted by pragmatism which had challenged its assumptions. And then pragmatism in turn had been confronted by the realistic movement, which was divided in its counsels. The resulting impression was to the effect that the new realism and critical realism had cancelled each other out. As I have indicated, I did not agree with this verdict and kept on exploring. But I was in the background and cut no great figure in the debate. Under these conditions, it was not all surprising that attention shifted elsewhere. England first attracted attention in terms of its stress on analysis. This shift went with developments in logic. Logical forms were clarified and the rules of deduction made explicit. And it so happened that this initiated a contrast between the grammar of sentences and the correct logical form. Russell played a pioneer role here and his treatment of definite descriptions set a standard. It was improved upon as time went on but drove home its point. Philosophers should be on their guard against being misled by the vagaries of language. Russell had high hopes that this was a turning point in philosophy. Moore and others seconded him. Common sense was to displace transcendentalism.

But Vienna came forward as another active center deserving of attention. Ernst Mach's influence lingered there and was reenforced by Schlick. Around him gathered mathematicians and scientists, such as Carnap, Waismann, and Neurath. Others, such as Feigl, Zilsel and Hahn, came into the picture to constitute the famous Vienna Circle. It so happened that another group arose in Berlin concerned with the philosophy of science. Reichenbach and Hempl stood out here along with Grelling and Dubislav. I am told that this second group was less inclined to positivism than was the Vienna Circle. However that may be, their emphasis was upon science. In contrast, academic philosophy in Germany was swinging in the direction of existentialism. Of course, one must not generalize too sharply in these matters. Husserl had many followers; and neo-Kantianism was by no means dead.

I understand that the name, logical positivism, was given to the position being worked out in Vienna by Herbert Feigl. The addition of "logical" indicated the role played by the new logic. The epistemological outlook was much like Hume's. The movement was aggressive and self-confident and soon secured much publicity. I was impressed by the number of International Congresses these men could convene. The unity of science was one of their watchwords. Another one was their theory of meaning as tied in with the method of verification. Schlick made much of meaning as central to philosophy.

It so happened that a free lance named Wittgenstein, under the influence of Frege and Russell, had written a short treatise called *Tractatus Logico-Philosophicus*. It was terse and aphoristic and stressed a structural identity, or isomorphism, between language and reality. This seemed to fit in with the positivist's theory of meaning.

It was quite in the cards that metaphysics was to be banished as meaningless. Aside from poetry, which was an expression of feeling, there were only two kinds of meaningful statements, the analytic ones of logic which were tautologies and made no claim to give factual knowledge about the world and the empirical ones of sense-perception and of science. Metaphysical and theological statements were *pseudo* ones and, in the strict sense, meaningless. Naturally, this doctrine created rather a furor. It was, certainly, forthright. Hitherto, naturalistic humanists and atheists had contented themselves with trying to show the invalidity of the traditional arguments for the existence of God. This was a shortcut, indeed. But it depended on its criterion of meaning. This became a battlefield. As we shall see, it passed, from strong verification, to weak verification, to confirmation and thence to semantics and syntax. There was much dispute as to the logical status of the principle. Had it empirical standing? Or was it a postulate?

It is to anticipate, but, as time went on, language was more carefully studied and the verification condition was seen not to hold. It was a sort of *tour de force*. Even Schlick came to admit that the meaning of a sentence goes with the vocabulary and grammar of a language. Testing for truth comes afterwards. And it seems natural to hold that we must know what we are testing. Wittgenstein, himself, who seemed in the *Tractatus* to support the principle, departed from it in his later book, *Philosophical Investigations*, to stress the principle that the meaning of words go with their *use*. There he speaks of language-games and ways of life.

Another aspect of logical positivism was its acceptance of phenomenalism. Here it was opposed to realism. Carnap assumed that the old
controversy between idealism and realism could be bypassed because it
was otiose. There is reason to believe that he knew nothing about the
realistic movement in the United States. As I recall it, he began as a
methodological solipsist concerned to construct the world out of primitive
ideas linked by primitive relations, such as the recognition of similarity.
Much logical ingenuity went to this *Aufbau*. He, however, shifted to
Neurath's stress on sentences as foundational. Here something akin to the
idealist's identification of truth with coherence entered the field.Sentences
could be compared only with other sentences and not with raw experience. Basic sentences were called protocol sentences. These, however, are
not incorrigible. If a new sentence is presented to us, we compare it with
the system we already have. If it fits in we accept it. If it does not, there
are two possibilities. We can either reject it or modify our system.

It is interesting to watch these transformations of outlook. Neurath, as
a sociologist, wanted to avoid any reference to a subjective percipient;
and, accordingly, resorted to a biological or behavioristic approach. Thus
what was called *physicalism* was born.

There were many controversies on moot points. Carnap held that
observation must be stressed if we are to do justice to science. This led him
to assert that protocol sentences could be translated into statements about
states of my body. The body, say C's, is "now seeing red" is equivalent to
the protocol sentence "red, now."

I remember that I tried to follow these disputes. Was physicalism a new
formulation of physical realism? It was certainly different from phenomenalism as I understood it. I shall soon turn to the British thinker, A. J.
Ayer, who kept nearer to the British tradition and talked about sense-data
and their relation to material things, making the former logically prior.

Before I go farther with Carnap's development, it might be well to
make some epistemological contrasts. On the face of it, my experiencing
red is different from what you observe when you see me reacting to a red
stimulus. But Carnap holds that the two statements are logically
equivalent and so have the same meaning. Here enters his adoption of
logical conventions. Any singular proposition can be treated as a protocol
sentence and absorbed into science. It will, I hope, be remembered that I
regard statements about a person's sensation as not the equivalent of
perceptual claims about the external world. In these latter we use
sensations in the context of directed response and achieve statements
about external things. This whole experience may well be in my body but

this fact in no way undercuts the referential claim and its criteria. I can verbalize the claim and you can agree with me. It is that unique achievement which we call knowing. So far as I can make out, the protocol sentences of Neurath and Carnap are, at the best, records of personal experience. There is not attached to them any claim to know an object by means of them. From this flows their coherence theory of truth. It is, also, the basis of their phenomenalism. Over against this immanentism is put that horrid thing called metaphysics, which is regarded as speculative and unempirical. But, as a realistic empiricist, I arrive at knowledge about the material world of common sense and of science. If this be metaphysics, make the most of it. I prefer to call it ontology, a concern with what is.

I have the impression that Carnap talked things over with people like Neurath and Popper, when he came to a difficulty. The question was often one of what he called tolerance. How are words to be used? I do not find in him any grappling with epistemology. His training was not along that line. Now I am one of those who take epistemology seriously and feel a certain competence in it. It will be recalled that I advocated a return to the correspondence theory on the grounds that objects feed in information about themselves in sense-perception. As I understand it, the logical positivists took protocol sentences as terminal in a presentational sort of way.

In many ways, the high point of Carnap's thought is his book, *The Logical Syntax of Language*. Philosophy is here regarded as a branch of logic which he calls the logic of science. It cannot contain information about transcendent entities since all sentences purporting to be about such entities are senseless. Most of the propositions of traditional philosophy express feelings, for example, ethics.

Carnap is thus left with three classes of sentences: syntactical sentences, object sentences and pseudo-object sentences. Philosophers are inclined to speak in terms of object sentences and use thing-words when they should be talking syntactically. To say that a lecture was about Babylon may be misleading. It should be reformulated to the effect that the lecture contained the word Babylon. The material mode of speaking is replaced by the formal mode. If these distinctions are recognized, many disputes will vanish.

One can have admiration for Carnap's logical and linguistic ingenuity and yet wonder about its importance. It seems to me that a clearer epistemology would also help. Babylon seems to me a name-word used in speaking about a city which once existed in Mesopotamia. It is, of course, names which have meaning and not things. This sort of linguistic house-cleaning is made much of by Russell as well. It may be that I have absorbed it but I find that I had no tendency to reify round squares and mermaids. Perhaps, my physical realism acted as a safeguard.

A Few Words on Wittgenstein

One of the difficulties facing a serious philosopher is that he must keep his eyes on so many subjects. He must recognize the fruits of division of labor and yet try to appreciate what is going on. On the one hand, he must be critical of many moves in the past, such as a deductive approach to what is, which have shown themselves to be mistaken. On the other hand, he must have a keen eye for genuine puzzles and problems. I, myself, concentrated on the nature of human knowing, on the status of value in the world, and on the traditional mind-body problem. I did not think that philosophy just by itself could solve these problems. The increase of knowledge would help. But I thought that philosophy could make a cooperative contribution by what has come to be called categorial analysis. Philosophy usually had a long historical perspective in these matters. It could keep its eye on the nature of the puzzle. In short, philosophy never meant to me uncontrolled speculation about a supposed transcendental realm, as positivists always assume. I was quite early naturalistic and even materialistic in my outlook. I just wanted to fit things together in an intelligible way.

Turning now to Wittgenstein, I take it for granted that he made definite contributions to formal logic—though some of these had been anticipated—in his truth-tables, his view of tautologies and contradictions and his treatment of logical constants, such as *and*, *or* and *not*. "It is a characteristic mark of logical propositions," he writes, "that we perceive in the symbol itself that they are true." But tautologies and contradictions are without sense because they do not picture the world.

It is to this picturing of the world to which we must turn for knowledge about. Here we come to Wittgenstein's ontology and its reflection in language. The world consists, he asserts, of atomic facts. A fact is what is the case. It seems to me that a "fact" is knowledge of what is the case. Such facts involve connections between objects. Take the formula, ARB, for instance. It would stand for objects and their connection. There would thus be an isomorphism between signs and what is signified.

But how is this achieved? It will be recalled that Carnap and Neurath were puzzled about the status of protocol sentences and their relation to what is experienced. This led them to make sentences basic and to resort to a coherence theory of truth. As nearly as I can make out, Wittgenstein assumes an ostensive naming. Both signs and objects are presented and the correspondence between them can be *shown*.

There is a certain virginity of mind here. It will be recalled how much theory of knowledge had been exercised in the past on the nature of sense-perception. I was led to maintain that sensations are sources of information about objects and are so used in perceiving. Wittgenstein ignores this puzzle and builds on the fact of achieved knowledge. There is the tradition that this idea of picturing came to him from observing a model in miniature of a motor-car accident. The model seemed to him to function like a propositional sign. One could just see the correspondence. That is, there stood out the agreement in structure. This was a comparison *within* knowledge. Now while I have a correspondence theory of truth in that I think that the external object feeds in information about itself which is used in perceptual judgment, I do not resort to comparison between the object and the achieved thought of it. As I see it, what Wittgenstein did was to institute a comparison between the external object, *as known,* and the model, also as known.

Reflecting on this correlation, Wittgenstein as a logician—and not as an epistemologist—puts names in one to one correspondence with objects. But, of course, the objects dominate the situation. "In order to tell whether a picture is true or false," he writes, "we must compare it with reality." There are no pictures which are true *a priori.*

As I see it, then, Wittgenstein's outlook is near to that of the naive realist. There are the things out there and here are our symbols. An agreement in structure can be noted with the external objects the standard. I think his aphorisms all follow. He is not yet aware of the flexibility of language as a human instrument. It was as though he regarded propositions as fixed factors like maps and charts. The idea of meta-languages, of talk about a first-order language, had not yet arrived, though Russell hinted at it. A proposition taken to be like a map does not talk about itself. If we apprehend it, it shows its structure.

We have, then, in the *Tractatus,* a kind of virgin thinking of an acute mind, not too much encumbered by philosophical puzzles. He regards philosophy and metaphysics as rather misleading obfuscations. And so he presses ahead with his schematism. What is a thought? It is a logical picture of a fact. The totality of true thought is a picture of the world. It is within this universe of discourse that he moves. On the one side, he makes contributions to the set-up of logic. On the other, he allows himself to make remarks about feeling as somehow additional. This is his so-called mystical side.

It is not surprising that Wittgenstein aroused both admiration and controversy. The doctrine seemed so clear-cut. Logic and knowledge were at last united. But it was quickly noted that some of his remarks pushed things to extremes. Granted that a proposition did not comment on itself but was of cognitive value by reason of its structure, did it follow that another proposition could not comment on it? The *Tractatus*, itself, seemed to be a series of such comments. As Russell put it, Mr. Wittgenstein manages to say a great deal about what cannot be said. As I have indicated, the meta-language development handled the situation.

But there was, also, the mystical side. What can be done about feeling? Is there anything left over which cannot be dealt with by propositional thought? Does science exhaust the world? Value appears to be left out. And now we have some musings, "If there is any value that does have value, it must lie outside the whole sphere of what happens and is the case. For all that happens and is the case is accidental. It is clear that ethics cannot be put into words." Here we come upon Wittgenstein philosophizing. Carnap came on the same problem and regarded ethical statements as expression of feeling or commands.

As I indicated, I regard value statements as resting on the recognition of the role of objectives in the human economy. They are not descriptive but evaluative and good reasons can be given to justify them.

I pass now very briefly to the book, *Philosophical Investigations*. Here the use of words is emphasized. Such uses involve patterns of procedures. And such patterns can be spoken of as games with rules. The status of such rules must then be considered. Does the speaker conform to such rules as learned patterns of behavior which have socially arisen? Or must he obey them as explicit demands? It is questions such as these that are now discussed.

As nearly as I can make out, Wittgenstein enlarged his approach from naming to all sorts of linguistic activities as ways of life. He takes in exclamation, attitudes, mental processes, such as wishing, intending, understanding, and so on; and he raises questions as to their applicability. I found his treatment of the expression, I understand, particularly interesting. It is similar to an exclamation. But it goes a little bit farther as a claim which demands justification. If I cannot carry on in accordance with the claim, I and others may decide that I did not understand.

There is freshness and suggestiveness about his handling of words. He notes similarities and differences; and so he arrives at what he calls families. From this vantage point he goes back to qualify the simplicities of the *Tractatus*. His thesis now is that language is self-sufficient. The philosopher should not try to interfere with it but follow its indications. Hence the advice of Wittgenstein to philosophers is that they should seek to clarify usage and not invent artificial problems.

Now my reaction to this advice is to look back on the rise of such traditional problems as the mind-body problem and the problem of the nature of perceiving in an historical, cultural way. Has language dealt adequately with them?

I fear not. Why should we expect it to have done so? Language goes with current concepts. In Locke's and Berkeley's time, it spoke the language of ideas. Let us admit that ordinary language also spoke of seeing trees and tulips. And Berkeley made much of his supposed agreement with common sense. But there was a genuine puzzle here. What is involved in seeing these objects?

As I understand his emphasis, Wittgenstein sets the empirical problems of science over against problems arising from mistaking the logic of language. Now I think this is too sharp a dichotomy. It was my experience, as it was that of William James, that science tends to avoid such a problem as that of the nature of human knowing. Or, perhaps, it postpones it for the time being. As has been indicated, I take perceptual knowing as resting on the use of sensations as informational about the objects to which we are responding. Out of this emerges the act of perceiving as cognitional in import. There is nothing in this analysis which conflicts with science; and I have learned much from psychology about the learning dimension of perceiving. And I would hope that there is nothing in my analysis which will be found to be unscientific. There has been just a division of labor, due to the fact that philosophy early raised the question of knowing while science began with the inorganic world and worked upward.

For such reasons, I reject the sharp contrast Wittgenstein has in mind. I think he was biassed by the tradition of positivism to the effect that philosophy was otiose. And yet I have read about incidents which showed that he was, himself, puzzled about traditional problems. How could the mind get to outer things? Just the kind of problem I met by showing that transcendence was an achievement resting on fed-in information and directed response. I would recall, also, the difficulties Neurath and Carnap met with in connecting protocol sentences with observations. I was always impressed with what seemed to me the rather brazen ingenuity of Carnap in these matters. In each instance, it would seem he saw no alternative. Just what are thing-words about? What positivism and pragmatism had in common, it seemed to me, was a disregard of epistemology. The reader must give his own verdict on this. It certainly has seemed to me that positivists and pragmatists have entertained strange notions of realism.

Introspective Language

At the turn of the century, philosophy was still bothered by the tradition of Cartesian dualism. This expressed itself in the assumption that each person was shut into his own ideas. How, then, could he know the existence of other minds? There was an accompanying problem of the so-called mind-body relation for each individual. It was believed that there were two substances of quite different natures involved in each person's economy or, at least, as J. B. Pratt put it, two processes. These beliefs led to linguistic puzzles. How, for instance, can we talk, in an understanding way, about private sensations? Wittgenstein raised the question here of the use of terms like *know* and *assert*. In what sense do I *know* that I have a pain? Ordinarily, such claims are corrigible. We seem to have to do here with inspections in which the object is given. But how can we communicate the results?

Now, it seems to me the right procedure is to start afresh and, if possible, to avoid artificial problems.

It may be recalled that Ryle pointed out that children first stress the external object perceived, that is, the achievement of the act of perceiving and only later pay attention to conditioning factors like looks and distances. Now it has been the job of theory of knowledge to concentrate on the question of how knowledge is achieved. The critical realist argues that it involves a from-and-to operation leading to the use of sensations as sources of facts about the external object, controlling them in the percipient. If so, we have direct, though mediated, knowledge about our surroundings. And it would seem that what we may call public language develops in this context. Words and concepts grow up together. People name, describe, exclaim, approve, etc. And they understand one another so long as they speak the same language. Vocabulary and syntax grow up together. This is, of course, a remarkable development; and it is well that both philosophy and science are studying it. Now it is not at all strange that words for pain and feeling and sensations should also appear. Whatever attracts attention can be talked about.

It is only later, in the age of reflection, that sophisticated questions will be raised. The locution, "I have a pain," or, "I don't feel well," will at first suffice. These locutions are backed up by behavior and it is likely that their application is learned in this setting. Nevertheless, a stage arises when it is realized that what is called consciousness mediates all these operations. In external perceiving, visual looks, sounds and touch-sensations convey information which is used in naming and describing. It is not that the sensations are literally projected but that they indicate facts about their controls. What is subjective has in this fashion objective import.

But human beings are inevitably interested in themselves as well as in the world around them. Nature has seen to it, through the proprioceptive system of nerves, that they learn about the location of pains and feelings. The locution, "I feel pain in my hand," is thus informative of some-thing unpleasant happening there. This kind of talk inevitably arises and is understood. We have here another kind of information used. It is information about conditions in the body. And it is mediated by pains and feelings.

Now I would rather call this sort of information personal rather than private. It is about the economy of my body. I can convey this information to others and they can reciprocate.

But what is beginning to stand out to the kind of reflection called philosophy is that all knowing, as against the innate behavior of, say, a spider weaving its web, is mediated by sensations and feelings. And these are always personal. Visual sensations are as personal as pains and pleasures. What begins to stand out is the role of symbols. These are impersonal and learned. It is the passage from "I feel a pain" to "Something is wrong with my hand," "Something is hurting me," that is epistemologically important. Wittgenstein is apparently bothered by the use of the word *know* here. Does it not always imply an assertion, criteria and the possibility of error? But when we turn our attention to seeing in the sense of perceiving, we can distinguish between awareness of visual sensations and the knowledge-claim based on them. As I see it, in the case of localized pain, the sensory datum stands out as a *warning*. There is less chance of error here but it is not negligible. Wittgenstein admits introspective talk but wants to clarify its logic. I, myself, see no conflict between inspection, or acquaintance, and functional, cognitive role. And the latter clearly varies from the distance-receptors to the proprioceptive situation.

I want now to make some remarks on "introspective psychology." As is well known, behaviorism arose as a protest against the tendency to subjectivism in traditional psychology. It wanted to look at the organism from the outside. It thought that conditioned reflexes were the key; and it was wary of the thing called consciousness. At the same time, brain research had not got very far. One spoke of the little black box.

Much has happened since then. *Gestalt* psychology has worked in terms of isomorphism between physiological and mental processes. The next step was, of course, to assert identity. But, at this point, language had to be clarified. Suppose we no longer talk in a Cartesian way about two substances or processes.

Ryle has his suggestions here. Do we not talk about dispositions and tendencies, such as vanity or stubbornness? These are lawlike statements which explain actions. If a man is vain, we can understand his behavior in terms of this disposition. It is akin to saying that salt dissolves in water because it is soluble.

But there is still the question of locating conscious states in the organism, mine or another's, and of giving them a function.

One tradition has it that, in my own case, I merely correlate consciousness with knowledge about the structure of my organism and then argue from a similar structure in another's organism to his possession of consciousness. This is the so-called argument from analogy. But it seems to me that we can go deeper than this. In our own economy, do not visual sensations function as guides to our action? And do not pains and pleasures act as signals? It would seem that we have a level of causality here involving the compresence we call awareness. When we work along this line, we can regard the self as a center of control.

But if we think of ourselves along these lines, is it not natural to think of others along the same lines? We have simply rejected Cartesian dualism. And we find that a person can talk with another about his sensations and feelings despite their existential locus. Talking about has its tests and conditions but these can be realized. They certainly do not involve a literal, common inspection of the referents. I conclude that communication does not conflict with existential separateness. In all this I am not so much an interactionalist as an emergentist. The way in which visual sensations are used to give cognition of external things offers a paradigm. But, as Professor Ryle shows, we must be careful in our use of language.

Comment on Ayer's Phenomenalism

It will be recalled that I thought that Austin had it a little better than Ayer in his account of perceiving but that he did not fully appreciate the role of sensation in the operation. So I want to examine Ayer's phenomenalism and its logic.

Ayer's position is that only sense-data are observable while I hold that we observe material things through, and by means of, indications in our sensations. And I also hold that the act of perceiving is referentially directed towards the thing perceived.

Ayer, it would seem, holds that the sense-datum language is primary because it gives evidence. This evidence is used to establish the logical construction of language about material things. This is his linguistic approach which goes back to Russell. And Ayer goes into great detail as to how we arrive at the notion of a material world. Yet this material world is never, strictly speaking, observable. It can, however, be talked about. He even argues that we can rightly speak of things existing when not perceived. This would signify that certain sense-contents would occur if certain conditions were fulfilled. Some sense-contents, again, have predictive value for other sense-contents.

Now the critical realist emphasizes learning about the material world. The first stage is that of using information from the various senses in order to achieve the thought of material things as having size, shape, weight, resistance, internal structure. They are regarded as coordinate with the percipient's body and with that of his fellows. It is not that we project our sensations on them but that we assign characteristics to them. At the level of natural realism, we do this rather naively as from the passage from a color sensation to a color quality. Later we puzzle over this assignment. We can differentiate between things in this fashion; but we later learn what has taken place.

At the stage of natural realism we arrive at the notion of things as external and independent and massive. We walk towards them and they are public. We account for the different way in which they look by distance and atmospheric conditions. This, as I see it, is the setting of our learning. We regard ourselves as observing the things in terms of sensory indications. These give *facts* about the objects. As I understand Ayer, he regards observation as inspection of data, while I identify it with, say, looking at, and the use in this activity of sensations as disclosing the object. That is, he makes sense-data terminal in observing while I regard observing as a mediated activity. Science now enters in with measurement and experimentation. Mass and acceleration come to the front. This approach gives us new facts about bodies. That is the way they behave. Chemistry arose as an improvement on the beliefs and techniques of alchemy. The idea of elements came to the front. In this development, observation was always directed at the material being handled. The balance gave indications. And so on from stage to stage of science. Phenomenalism, as I see it, keeps sense-contents in the foreground, while realism stresses their cognitive import. With this perspective, the scientific conception of the world and evolutionary materialism become options.

I have the impression that the positivists were fighting what they called metaphysics and speculation about a transcendent realm. It has interested me to find out what scandalized them. Carnap had in mind, apparently, the sort of utterances Heidegger indulged in. But how about realism and naturalism as philosophical positions? They were wide-spread in the United States of my time. But the Europeans paid little attention to them. Ayer is interesting in this connection decause he tells us what his idea of metaphysics was. It consisted of *a priori* propositions about the world. But, he argued, all such propositions are tautolgies or analytic. As for empirical propositions, their meaning is the manner of their verification. Even if we drop this theory of meaning, empirical propositions need verification. There are no self-validating intuitions.

It is obvious that the critical realist does not support this transcendental kind of metaphysics. That is one reason why I have, myself, preferred to speak of ontology or the theory of *what is*.

Blanshard's Idealism

And now I am going to examine various contending movements, such as dialectical materialism, neo-Thomism and existentialism. But, before I do so, it may be wise to look at the foundations of idealism as represented by a very able thinker opposed to positivism and pragmatism. I shall argue that his theory of knowledge is at fault.

Blanshard takes a particular—what the realist would call a thing—to be a pattern of characteristics and nothing more. There is, as he would express it, nothing more there, no "it." I, on the other hand, would hold that, in perceiving, we think of an object in terms of facts about it, as of a certain size, shape, weight, color, etc. These facts exhibit the object and make it thinkable. It is not an unthinkable it. This is another way of saying that descriptions describe and categorial meanings, such as thinghood, arise in a behavioral setting.

In essentials, this is the basis of a correct formulation of the correspondence theory of truth. In perceiving, information is fed to the percipient and he uses it in describing the object perceived. There is no need of a supplementary comparison between thought and object, an impossible undertaking, in any case. The correspondence theory merely reflects the way in which knowledge is achieved.

But, as I see it, the idealist ignores this operation and falls back on a coherence theory in which universals are terminal. At the most, there is an internal movement from the incomplete to the complete, from Royce's internal meaning to his outer meaning.

The debate here is purely of the philosophical type. Science proceeds to discover molecules, atoms and particles and to measure energies. In the realist's view these are essentially as the scientist conceives them. They are entities which make up the physical world in discoverable ways. The idealist sets up his translation of them in terms of coherent universals. Back of this translation lies, as I see it, a wrong analysis of perceiving.

Idealism has much in common with phenomenalism. The phenomenalist takes up his story with sense-data as primary and evidential and resorts to logical and linguistic ingenuity to talk about material things. The modern idealist is a rationalist who thinks in terms of universals. Particulars are, for him, nothing but patterns of these realities. Neither approach seems to me able to do justice to our realistic beliefs and conceptions. And this flaw, I hold, stems from an inadequate view of what is involved in perceiving.

There are other phenomenalists—Stace, for example—but I cannot find in their writings any particularly novel lead. It is of interest, however, to note that Stace moved from Hegelian idealism to phenomenalism. I doubt that he studied carefully the American realistic movement. In considering a man's certitudes, his intellectual history must be scanned. I can understand why Stace is more receptive to Whitehead's theses then I am. But enough on that topic.

8

INTERSECTING
DIALECTICAL MATERIALISM

In the next three chapters, I shall concern myself with contemporary philosophical positions which combine an ideological ingredient with philosophical analysis. These are, respectively, dialectical materialism, neo-Thomism and existentialism. I mean here by an ideological ingredient a *parti pris*, or emphasis, what has come to be called a commitment. Dialectical materialism was committed to socialism and communism. This was its center of gravity. Neo-Thomism was dominated by the assumptions of Christian theism and sought in Aristotelianism its epistemology and its ontological categories. Religious existentialism, at least, sought to develop the subjective dimension of experience and bypass the objective world of science. Other forms of existentialism took their departure from Husserl or from Kant but concerned themselves with human *Existenz* and its place in the world.

I have been very much intrigued by a certain cultural discontinuity in philosophy. English and American thinkers stress empiricism, modern logic and, in some measure, science. Neo-Thomists are convinced that Descartes led modern philosophy astray into sophisticated forms of subjectivism and want to return to their form of realism and their ontology of form and matter. The dialectical materialists stress science, it is true, but want to supplement it by appeal to dialectical principles. The role of these is sometimes obscure. Engels speaks of both objective dialectics and subjective dialectics, the latter being a reflection of the former. The minimum meaning is an emphasis on change through opposition and conflict. Much is made of a contrast with a static metaphysics. In an interesting passage Engels in his book, *Dialectics of Nature*, states that "it is the merit of Marx that, in contrast to the peevish, arrogant epigone, he was the first to have brought to the fore again the forgotten dialectical method."* The stress here is on Marx's political economy. It almost seems as though Marx moved back from historical materialism in society to a dialectic of nature.

---
*(Moscow: Foreign Language Publishing House), p. 65.

In this chapter I shall compare my own type of evolutionary materialism with dialectical materialism, as I understand it. The term, itself, was,
I understand, first used by Plekhanov in 1891 in an essay on Hegel. It
took on in Marxist circles. It served as a contrast to what was usually
called vulgar, mechanical materialism. I can appreciate the need of an
adjective to qualify materialism since this term had long been used in a
hostile way. One spoke of a materialistic age or of ethical materialism. In
the strict sense, one should speak of ontological materialism in contrast to
idealism or dualism. The status of life, mind and values within the
framework of ontological materialism is a problem to be worked out. In
these days, one speaks of emergent, or evolutionary, materialism. But
popular polemics ignores these finer points. It just does not like
materialism.

The Development of Dialectical Materialism

I shall argue that there were two stages, at least, in the development of
dialectical materialism. The first occurred when Marx and Engels turned
Hegelian idealism downside up. For Hegel, the Idea is associated with a
cosmic mind. Marx, on the contrary, regarded the Idea as nothing but the
material world reflected by the human mind and translated into forms of
thought. He was encouraged to take this stand by the writings of
Feuerbach. There is, as I see it, no sharp development of epistemology
involved. But the consequences are clear. The brain must be the organ of
mind and we must somehow perceive material things. As against
Feuerbach, Marx wanted to stress history and human activity. I shall say
something about this in connection with Marx's famous *Theses on
Feuerbach*.

The second stage comes with Lenin and his polemic against what he
calls *empirio-criticism*. This was a form of positivism, associated with
Mach and Avenarius, which was influencing many Marxists at the time.
Out of this came the "reflection theory" of sense-perception. Epistemology was now to the fore.

Those who have followed my own epistemological analysis can see that
I stress the use of sensations in a referential act of perceiving directed at an
external object. The weakness of the "reflection theory" is that it tends to
make sensations epistemologically terminal and this comes near to
Locke's representational realism. Of course, Lenin is convinced that
things are primary, as common sense holds. But he does not quite succeed

in so analyzing perceiving as to bring this out. But Lenin's book is quite a *tour-de-force* and shows extended reading and reflection.

So much in the way of an introduction to this chapter. I shall now proceed to develop my own evolutionary materialism on the basis of my realistic epistemology. I shall first show how the common-sense view of things arises and then explain the development of the scientific outlook with its atoms, electro-magnetic fields, energies, giant molecules, replication of nucleic acids, evolution of living things, the brain-mind, etc. In this ontological context, I shall try to do justice to the characteristics of human living. That is, I shall seek to give a setting for human thought, descriptive and evaluative. After this has been done, I shall make some comments on dialectical materialism. Taken in its historical setting, I do not think it shows up so badly as against idealism, pragmatism, logical positivism and ordinary language. I must leave it to the Marxists to tell us how they employ the term, dialectical. But I note that it is a term more frequently used on the continent than in English-speaking countries. This, as the "ordinary language" people would say, is a matter of usage. I find that the existentialists speak of negation in a quite dialectical manner. But, of course, they are not materialists.

First, then, as to common-sense realism. It is important to realize that immaterialism of the Berkeley type was a sophisticated product based on a reduction of perceiving to having sensations. Berkeley saw a weakness in Locke's representative realism, namely, the difficulty Locke had of passing from ideas to things. He was also motivated by Newtonian physics which emphasized a kind of matter which seemed to him abstract and divorced from perception. Berkeley's immaterialism led to positivism and phenomenalism. These have been very important moves in modern philosophy up to the present. In my own critical realism, I sought to return to what seemed to me a more adequate analysis of perceiving which stressed both the referential moment in perceiving and the informational use of sensations as leading to factual cognition of objects. There is, in perceiving, much recognition, learning and exploring.

The other line in modern thought which led to an idealistic version of immaterialism was the shift from Kant to Hegel. Kant had been an agnostic realist who regarded the sense-manifold as caused by unknowable things-in-themselves. Fichte and, after him, Hegel had rejected such things-in-themselves and set up a Self as primary. Hegel postulated the Idea as supreme and worked out a new kind of logic which moved from abstract being through nothingness to becoming and thence up the dialectical ladder. This kind of idealism is called panlogism. It was not only Marx but also Kierkegaard who reacted against it. As we have noted, Marx turned back to a kind of materialistic naturalism without too much concern for epistemology. Here Feuerbach acted as a catalyst. As we have pointed out, Lenin had later to meet the objections of Machian positivism. He did so in terms of the "reflection theory" of sensation. I have tried to show that this approach is incomplete and does not do justice to the complex act of perceiving.

I want now to go back to the historical development of modern science. I shall endeavor to show that it was always realistic in intent but, as it became more complex, was immersed in epistemological problems and was often puzzled. I think it was unfortunate that philosophy tended to mislead it because of its own path. That is, philosophy was weighted in the direction of positivism and idealism.

To begin with, the Aristotelian outlook had dominated the later Middle Ages. This was a qualitative realism with a geocentric cosmology and teleological notions of causality. I need not go into details for they are so well known. The Achilles heel turned out to be the theory of motion. Aristotle had no idea of mass, inertia and momentum. With the introduction of these concepts and techniques for measurement, the whole idea of the physical world altered. This was added knowledge about the things we perceive.

The next stage was the revival of atomism. In the Ancient World, atomism had been largely speculative though there had been supporting indications in evaporation and the wearing away of stone and wood. It was probably in chemistry that new indications of atomism were found in combining proportions. Epistemologically I can see no difficulty in all this. Atoms are parts of things we can perceive and, presumably, if conditions for perceiving were achieved, could be perceived. These are now approximated. In these days of atom-fission, there is little doubt of their reality. One must, of course, give up naive ideas of perceiving. The stress should be on factual knowledge-about. Perceiving passes into tested ideas about. With new techniques there is much stress on what Eddington called pointer-readings. But I see no good reasons to draw idealistic conclusions. Even the ultra-microscopic develops within the framework of the macroscopic.

The Ups and Downs of Dialectical Materialism

This would seem to be the place for a few words on the ups and downs of ontological materialism. In his *Introduction* to Lange's famous book on the subject, Bertrand Russell remarks that materialism has had a curious history. "Arising almost at the beginning of Greek philosophy, it has persisted down to our own time, in spite of the fact that very few eminent philosophers have advocated it." He even speaks of the contempt poured on it by most professors of metaphysics. He, himself, takes his stand on what he calls neutral monism, a type of empiricism developed around William James and not too far from Machism. I think we should bear in mind what I have said about the immaterialistic and idealistic stances taken by philosophy. I do not think that materialism has been so much refuted as rejected out of hand. I am going to argue for a new deal. Certainly, it involves a realistic epistemology and, after that, it must face up to life and mind and values. It cannot be a reductive, dead-level affair. But, if it can be carried through, it has much to be said in its favor. Certainly, it fits in more with modern science than does transcendental idealism.

It strikes me that its chief competitor these days is some form of pan-psychism. For that reason, I shall later examine Whitehead's construction. Of course, Leibnitz began this strategy. It was in this way that he moved away from materialism to his theism and his preestablished harmony. Had he given as much effort to a reconstruction of materialism it would, I think, have been better. But I am inclined to believe from my own experience that this could come only slowly and as a consequence of advances in science, such as the theory of evolution and a greater stress on patterns and relations.

One should, of course, begin with Democritus. He was of Ionian stock and naturalistic in his outlook. In the broad sense, he was a physicist, concerned with *physis* or nature. He seems to have followed Leucippus in breaking down the monism of Parmenides into a pluralism of atoms and the void. In this way he could account for change. The atoms were conceived abstractly and as simply as possible. To-day, as we all know, we have much tested knowledge of their constitution and the way they connect up with one another. Some elements are, apparently, cooked up in the stars.

Democritus laid stress on what he called the fire-atoms which made up the soul. He seems to have thought there were ordered movements in these atoms and connected these with reason. The moral goal should be serenity and mastery of desires. Epicurus took over from here.

It is not at all surprising to find that Plato and Aristotle appealed to a soul of quite another type. Socrates had given the lead when he stressed reason and purpose as the fulcrum of action. But how do these get leverage on the body? This turned out to be a blind alley. As I see it, we are only beginning to understand the higher cerebral processes involved in thinking and decision. I shall speak of levels of causality and defend an identity view with double knowledge of the brain-mind, knowledge from outside (neurological knowledge) and knowledge from the inside (introspective knowledge). We think of ourselves to-day as working out of Cartesian dualism. The Aristotelian approach, as we shall see in the next chapter, has quite a different texture whose foundations were destroyed by the new physics. Purpose and teleology are now regarded as local achievements having complex conditions.

I pass to Lucretius. There is much in his poem that deserves study. I wish merely to call attention to his recognition that sensations would seem to go with combinations of atoms rather than being the qualities of individual atoms by themselves. This is the basic question of novelty, of how the sentient arises from the non-sentient. A principle of integration seems to be at work. Can wholes have properties which parts by themselves do not have? As we shall see, panpsychism stresses the primacy of sentiency. I would not go that far but I certainly would not accept the Cartesian tradition of inertness and alienness. Activity and being go together, so far as our evidence reaches. Is feeling a quality dimly emergent with life activities? Does an appeal to potentialities carry us farther? These are interesting questions. Nerve cells seem to be resonators and repeaters. And they seem to act in patterns. We are far from the older type of atomism. Chemical compounds share some of their electrons in a new pattern. And in the formation of giant molecules there are even codes.

But I must be brief. And so I turn to Hobbes. We find him stressing motion and using a vocabulary tending to identify internal motions in the organism with sensations and images. Endeavor was one of his key terms. There was ambiguity here since many of the terms he used had both physical and mental overtones. He was aware of the importance of sensations but did not isolate them from bodily operations in the way that Locke later did. At his time, philosophy and science were hardly distinguishable. One can say that Hobbes's philosophy was immersed in his physics.

And yet there was one emphasis in Hobbes which should not be neglected, and that was the stress on words and speech. Man differs from the animals in his use of words as conventional signs. Here categories appear which are not to be found in physics, such as decision and use. In speech, words are joined together by the decisions of men to stand for a train of conceptions of things which are objects of thought. He puts stress on definition and the correct use of words. Speech is essential to reasoning. Words are a wise man's counters. Here there was a recognition of meaning and purpose. But, as a mechanist, Hobbes also wanted a causal explanation of signs. In some measure, he could do this for animals. But human discourse had a different setting. This remained a challenge to his type of materialism. If modern behaviorism is a type of materialism, as Russell suggests, it at least acknowledges complicated types of conditioning. Words act as symbols, that is, as substitutes for perceived things; and a whole new area of activity opens up. It would seem that language involves a new level of cerebral activities. And these go with group cooperation. I am not surprised that recent philosophy has laid so much stress on language and what it involves. I would only argue that it should be supplemented by a basic realism.

I turn next to Locke. Like Descartes, he favored dualism in ontology. Ideas are the objects of the understanding. And Locke could not see how they could be integrated with cerebral activity. The farthest he goes is to suggest that God could have given matter the power to think, a suggestion often referred to by materialists. But the emphasis in Locke was toward a kind of transparent empiricism. Ideas are given and we seem unable to transcend them. While we tend to believe in an external material world, it is difficult to see how knowledge of it can be attained. This is the barrier set to representative realism, as it is called.

By this time, philosophy had become differentiated from science. Each went on its own path and intersected only now and then when some thinker, or group of thinkers, sought to integrate them. I have in mind a man like La Mettrie or Cabanis, both medical men, or the group in Germany in the middle of the nineteenth century, consisting of Vogt, Moleschott, and Buchner. From the point of view of technical philosophy, these men were essentially amateurs. As a matter of fact, they were rather careless in their expressions. Philosophy was entrenched behind Hume, Kant and Hegel. It saw many difficulties in epistemology, the mind-body problem, and the foundations of morality. In some measure, too, there was a background of dislike of what was regarded as reductive simplicities. Much had to happen before a new orientation was possible. As I look back on this situation, I would suggest that the theory of evolution played an important role. So did the rise of the social sciences which helped to knit man's life to biology while recognizing novelties. So did the increase of secularism. All this, I think, affected philosophy and made possible new lines of thought. Something of this came out in my study of developments in American philosophy from idealism, through pragmatism, to realism.

I should, in this connection, like to refer to the divergent paths taken by Huxley and Tyndall, both distinguished scientists of the nineteenth century in England. It seems that Tyndall had read Lange's *History of Materialism* and was inclined to speculate along materialistic lines as in his famous Belfast Address. Huxley, on the other hand, was much influenced by Hume's positivism and in the controversies of the times took an agnostic position. I think their differences were rather typical of the period. There were leads but no clear-cut principles.

I note that Lenin refers to James Ward. I remember playing a good game of chess with him in 1922 when he was eighty. I was in Cambridge at his invitation. He had written a book, called *Naturalism and Agnosticism*, which analyzed the situation indicated above and took the path of panpsychism. There was no subject without an object and no object without a subject. Sentiency was the only sample of reality we had to go on. We shall find much the same perspective in Whitehead.

Now Ralph Barton Perry and I had been working in epistemology and both of us were skeptical of these dicta of Ward's. Perry was in favor of externality and independence and this led him to a combination of behaviorism and presentationalism. Such was the new realism. To put sensations *in* the brain was, in his opinion, a halfway house to Locke's representationalism. Dewey had much the same fear of such a location and moved to his form of behaviorism. If the mind focussed on sensations in the brain, this would give it a subjective slant which it would be difficult to correct. Better to locate sensations as discriminations in behavioral experience. Dewey exercised much ingenuity in defending this perspective. I, on the other hand, thought of another possibility. Suppose perceiving was a directional act guided by sensations and involving a from-and-to circuit, then sensations would be put to use in this referential context and give rise to informational facts about the thing we are responding to. Sensations would not, then, be terminal objects of a subjectively focussed mind but sources of information about external objects. Thus cognition would emerge. In this way, man could achieve knowledge about his world, as he apparently did in the sciences.

The outcome of this approach was the development of an evolutionary type of materialism which stressed levels of organization and of operative activity in nature. This type of materialism was non-reductive and recognized the emergence of novelty. There were, of course, critical points for it to handle. The first was the nature of life. The second was the integration of thinking with the functioning of the brain. I can speak of these only cursorily here.

When I began my thinking about the origin and nature of life, the choice was between vitalism and mechanism. Vitalism was dualistic in import and had no clear theories as to the nature of the life-force. Somehow, it was supposed to be directive. Driesch and Bergson were the outstanding representatives of the vitalistic move. It was, in part, a protest against the almost equal vagueness of the mechanists. How much has happened of late? We hear now of giant molecules, of the helix organization of D.N.A. and the role of R.N.A. in synthesizing proteins. The cell is a sort of chemical factory. And there is both speculation and experimentation concerning a chemical evolution preceding the biological one.

In a quite factual way we can now speak of living matter in terms of organization. The precision of coded processes is extraordinary. We are far from the fire atoms of Democritus or the atomic motions of Hobbes. And yet we can see a continuity of outlook.

It is the brain to which we now turn. This is an organ of guided behavior. The chemical precision of the cell becomes subordinate to the reception of informative messages and learned responses to them. The passage from the sensory to the motor equipment is basic. Neurological knowledge is increasing. But there remain age-old questions of the location and role of what we call consciousness or awareness. The sophisticated materialist, it seems to me, must take an identity view and locate consciousness as involved in cerebral operations. Here each individual participates in these operations. My own view is that signals require the compresence of awareness as does recognition of pattern. As I see it, this kind of activity is causal but consists of a guided kind of causality. I have argued that cognition emerges in the use of information contained in sensations. Cognition thus has a natural base. With this as a start, thinking proceeds. I see no reason to be dualistic about it. Much of it involves the use of verbal symbols. Here learning and conditioning operate. One reason for puzzling is that scientific thought is dominated by a perspective of a descriptive and impersonal texture and it is difficult for it to assimilate the kind of knowledge introspection adds. Yet I think this must be done. What we have are educated brains, brains able to take account of cues and symbols. And this taking account of seems to me to involve the kind of togetherness exhibited by awareness. But I assume that such awareness has its cerebral conditions. Out of this arises recognition of means and ends and of goals in sight. Though the brain is the organ of thought, language develops with no reference to it but to the self as a center of control. The symbol here is the personal pronoun "I." I see no linguistic difficulties in this situation.

It must be acknowledged that factual knowledge about our world is a great achievement but it is a mediated one through information received. It is not an affair of direct intuition. As we examine this knowledge it turns out to be knowledge about structure and processes made as detailed as possible and quantitative. The chemist can synthesize substances and find that they perform in the same way as substances found in nature. Already, in the nineteenth century, Engels made much of this accomplishment as a proof of realism. It has gone much farther in our own day; and I marvel at what is being done.

But it is still the case that human knowledge does not reach the kind of presentational awareness of matter and energy that naive realism encourages people to dream of. This does not mean, however, that material things are the unknowable things-in-themselves that the Kantian tradition postulated. Nor does it mean that they are phenomenal merely.

Panpsychism as an Alternative

I turn now to consider briefly the move, called panpsychism, taken as an alternative to ontological materialism. It is quite an old story. As I have already pointed out, we find it in Leibnitz and later in Clifford, Paulsen, C. A. Strong, Durant Drake, C. S. Peirce and A. N. Whitehead.

The argument is, essentially, that the sentiency we experience in consciousness is the sole sample of reality we have and that, apart from it, reality becomes vacuous.

I pointed out that Peirce rejects materialism because he identifies it with mechanical necessity whereas he is a defender of chance and choice. Evolutionary materialism stresses novelty and levels of causality. At the human level, choice in the light of consequences seems to me undeniable and to fit in with the very role of mind as furthering adjustment. Qualifications must, of course, be added to do justice to conditions and the impulsive power of drives. I cannot go as far as Sartre and make freedom an absolute. I shall discuss this in the later chapter devoted to existentialism. Here I am only concerned with Peirce's objection to materialism on the grounds that it implies rigid necessitarianism. I think that objection is dated.

But the epistemological basis of Peirce's panpsychism comes from his Kantianism. That is, he identifies reality with what is logically constructed and sets this over against any *incognizable* cause. It is, however, a little unclear as to what he means by objective validity.

I pass now to the sort of panpsychism which is defined by Strong and Drake. The first stage of this rested on a kind of agnosticism to be supplemented by the assumption of a mind-stuff. The final stage was more novel. Subjective sentiency, under biological conditions, gave rise to a consciousness of *essences*, such as roundness. These essences did not have a mental status like sentiency. Their role was to mediate knowledge. Drake, here, had an outlook like Santayana. In science, essences mediated knowledge of structure and relations but never attained a vision of matter itself. Why not, then, take sentiency as a sample of the stuff of reality? It would be an instance of mind-stuff.

Now I do think there is a background of bodily feeling and sensed attitude in perceiving. But I hold that perceiving, as such, makes use of sensations as informative signals and cues in terms of which cognitive facts about the perceived object can be deciphered. In this context, recognition and concepts are developed; and we pass to symbols and descriptive references. In short, I see no good reason to postulate essences. As nearly as I remember, they were set up to avoid the framework of representative realism. Essences were at once before the mind and in the object. I put in their place the directed use of sensory cues and concepts founded on them, holding that sensations are not terminal objects of a primary knowledge but, rather factors having a disclosing function. In this way, I move *between* presentationalism and representationalism.

From Drake, one can move to Whitehead, though Drake is far nearer the naturalistic outlook of materialism than is Whitehead. In many ways, Whitehead is nearer to the idealism of F. H. Bradley. He is more Platonic than Bradley.

As nearly as I can make out, Whitehead identifies perceiving with the presentational rise of *percepta*. These consist of "eternal objects," or essences, actively apprehended in an affective *form* of feeling. These percepta are passed on from one concrescent occasion to another because they have a kind of objective immortality. Ultimately, we are led on to God as their source.

It should be clear that I stress the causal rise of percepta as events and point to their function as disclosing external things. Whitehead seems to think that his concrescent monadism is the only alternative to phenomenalistic positivism. Whitehead is not a realist in my sense but rather a reformed subjectivist. I do not deny his ingenuity but regard much of it as ill placed. His notion of materialism as involving a vacuous actuality is foreshadowed in Bradley who could not see how we could get beyond appearances. It is, then, a question of either . . . or. Either something like experiencing or nothing. But I do not think that knowing is identifiable with experiencing. It presupposes something to be known, something which exists in its own right. What we gain are facts about it. I cannot see that this situation makes the object vacuous. It is only so if we set up a subjective standard. As the reader already knows, I regard sensations and thoughts as intrinsic to brain-states and sustained by them. Thus, I am not astonished by this level of brain activity in which it reaches awareness and self-direction in the complexities of life. The tradition of dualism seems to me rather absurd since it really acknowledges this isomorphism of process. Our double-knowledge of the brain, participative and external, involves linguistic problems which are only gradually being ironed out. And it is not uncommon to hear it said that the brain thinks. Yet it must also be recognized that we are, as selves, thinking with, and in, the brain.

At long last, I come now to the dialectical materialism which my own materialism intersects. It had a considerably different history. This was largely apart from academic auspices. Even Lange, as Engels rather bitterly remarks, ignored it.

As I have already indicated, there were two stages in its development, that of Marx and Engels and that of Lenin. The first expressed a swing away from the abstract constructions of Hegel under the influence of Feuerbach. I shall go into this in some detail. The second represents the struggle with Machian positivism, something analogous to what has occurred in these days in the debate over logical positivism. Here I shall endeavor to supplement Lenin's move. Let it be understood that I am not here taking up the complications of historical materialism. These I have considered in an unpublished manuscript on political and social philosophy. Here I am concerned primarily with epistemology and ontology.

But, before I go into these matters, I want to say a few words about the term, dialectic.

There is a minimum meaning to this and a maximum meaning. I prefer the minimum meaning. This lies between logic and concern for the texture of thinking and the texture of nature. Engels speak of subjective dialectics and objective dialectics. The latter builds on the difference between an outlook which stresses fixed things and repetition in nature and an outlook which emphasizes process and novelty. The former concerns itself with the role of conflict and negation in our thinking. I have the impression that the Marxists, to-day at least, do not want to confuse formal logic and dialectics. They are concerned to reject what they regard as a bias in the direction of harmony and oversimplification. There are terminological difficulties here. For instance, the term, contradiction, is used in an extended way for opposing tendencies. I note that Lenin stresses the point that the world is the seat of dynamic interconnections. Now, as I have reflected on this terminology, I sought to translate some of it into terms more native to my own traditions. There would seem to be no need for dispute about formal, deductive logic. Nor should there be disagreement about the nature of scientific method. This should be taken as apolitical. There was some backsliding here since the Soviets wanted to stress the environment rather than heredity. And, for a time, Lysenko got the ear of Stalin. That was unfortunate. But I think that Marxists now recognize the validity of scientific method. The area of dialectics would seem to be that of the texture of thinking, on the one hand, and of the categorial texture of nature, on the other. Surely, we can all agree that it is a restless universe.

I have the impression that, while Marx plunged ever more deeply into economics and sociology, Engels followed the growth of the sciences and sought to work out certain principles which fitted into his materialistic revision of Hegel. He regarded these as empirical generalizations. He held that quantity changed into quality. I note that Soviet philosophers feel it to be their duty to study the conditions of any such change in detail. I had always stressed the importance of organization and noted the role of energy in building up organization. This comes out clearly these days in the chemistry of giant molecules, so essential to life. I could see some point in his principle of the unity of opposites as in magnetism. But I found it harder to locate in facts his negation of negation. Though Engels attacked the *Naturphilosophie* of his time, I could not but feel that he had a touch of it. That would be quite understandable; and since dialectical material-ism puts much stress on time and history, it should recognize the limitations of historical periods. After all, Marx and Engels regarded themselves as revolutionaries who recognized no fixed stopping point for change. I know, of course, that there is a problem here for their social theory. What succeeds the achievement of a classless society? Well, problems would still arise.

So much, then, for dialectic. It is, of course, an old term for dialogue and debate. And it once meant the same as logic. It is much more used on the Continent than in England and the United States. I find examples of it among the existentialists, especially the use of negation. And Hegel is there still much alive. Merleau-Ponty's book on *Adventure de la Dialectique* is worth reading, in this connection.

I turn now to consider the role played by Feuerbach in the rise of dialectical materialism. Engels is very explicit about it and Marx indicates where he goes beyond Feuerbach. Feuerbach returns to sensible particulars, to *ceci* as against universals. That is, he moves in the direction of empiricism. He believes that perceiving "permits us to enter into communication with the exterior of things" but stresses sensations and feelings as enabling us to enter into the interior of human beings, into what he calls spirit. This leads him to stress love and the union of the "I" and the "thou." It is all rather vague, analytically speaking, but the direction of his thought is evident.

At this point, he takes up Hegel's stress on alienation and applies it to religion. Man sets up God and another world as a projection of his own conflicts. This is the base of his anthropological humanism. I must confess that I find this move sounder than that of Kierkegaard, who sets the eternal over against the temporal. But Kierkegaard was more dramatic in exposition than Feuerbach. I have long learned to discount fashions in these matters. One reason, I suppose, was that I had reached a pretty definite framework. One is constantly beset by what I call journalistic philosophy. Logical positivism, or therapeutic positivism, or Kierkegaard, or Nietzsche are taken up and extolled. I think the trained philosopher must keep his eye on basic problems, such as perceiving, the mind-body situation, evolution, the nature of value-judgments. And he must see these in the light of growing knowledge. I was, fortunately, pretty well trained in biology, psychology, history and sociology and so had perspective. I could hardly think of going back to Hume or Kant or Hegel but did, indeed, attempt to understand them in relation to their times.

But, to return to Feuerbach, from humanism he passed to a kind of physiological materialism. The maxim, a man is what he eats, expressed this, just as Cabanis had earlier remarked that the brain secretes thought as the liver secretes bile. But such dicta were more expressions of frustration than advances. It is only in our days that some notion of the mode of working of the brain is arising. And I do think a better epistemology helps. I would emphasize the double-knowledge approach.

Marx and Engels were now ready to turn Hegelianism upside down and to deny the identity of thought and being. That is, in essentials, they had become realists. But their chief interest was in society and history. It had to be an historically orientated materialism. The old materialism accepted ready-made things and repetition. The stress should be on process and development. I take this to be the minimum meaning they assigned to the term, dialectic. But it is up to the Marxists to explain their usage.

Let us look at Marx's *Theses on Feuerbach* (1845). In the first thesis, Marx criticizes Feuerbach's neglect of human activity. That is, he thinks he pays too much attention to external things. He does not stress sufficiently praxis and revolution. In the second thesis, Marx connects objective truth with practice. This is often regarded as a pragmatic touch. I would myself accept the importance of the general connection of technology with pure science but would also emphasize the testing of hypotheses in science itself. In the third thesis, Marx stresses the point that the educator must himself be educated, that is, that the environment is not enough.

In the fourth thesis, Marx points out that the recognition of human alienation in religion is not enough. One must seek to better man's lot and thus remove the causes of alienation; Feuerbach is too passive. In the fifth, Marx recognizes Feuerbach's turn toward empiricism and away from Hegel's panlogism. But I am not clear as to what Marx means by practical sensory activities. It probably connects up with his emphasis on *praxis*. I would emphasize perceiving and its link with conduct and the rise of science and technology. In the sixth thesis, Marx rightly objects to Feuerbach's neglect of social history and his concentration on an abstraction called humanity. And in the next thesis he turns to what we would call social psychology to explain religious feeling. People do not understand why they think and feel as they do. In the ninth thesis, Marx suggests that past materialism has had the setting of the single individual in bourgeois society. And, in the tenth, indicates his desire to enlarge its scope to human society in the large. I think this is being done by the social sciences, although the life of the individual must likewise be cleared up in terms of biology and psychology. In the eleventh thesis, we have the famous demand to change the world. Theory should lead to action. It was on this that Marx concentrated.

Now, as we have seen in his *Dialectics of Nature*, Engels read voraciously in the science of his time. But I cannot see that he devoted as much energy to developments in philosophy. He did not like the positivism of Duhring; and expressed himself in no uncertain terms. But as I, myself, look back on nineteenth-century philosophy I find it rather stagnant. In Germany, it tended to end up in neo-Kantianism. In England, as we have seen, in a mixture of positivism and idealism. I am inclined to think that it needed developments in the sciences to stimulate it. And this impact, I believe, came most sharply in the United States of my generation.

Lenin and Epistemology

I turn next to Lenin and his foray into philosophy. He had his motivations in the vacillations of many Marxists. It was the period of revisionism in Germany and of the impact of Mach and Avenarius along positivistic lines. Now I was in Germany about the same time. I recall that a young Oxford philosopher, just leaving Heidelberg, in 1909, advised me to read Avenarius, which I did. Those who have taken the trouble to read my first book, *Critical Realism*, will remember that I devoted space to Mach, Avenarius and Pearson. They did not satisfy my realistic dispositions. I did not believe that things could be identified with sensations. Sensations might well be sources of information but science stressed techniques of measurement of bodies. I did not read Lenin's book until the twenties. But I was prepared to sympathize with his protests. I felt, however, that he had not quite got the answer to the mechanism of perceiving. He wrote in terms of the reflection theory. But this left open the question of which comes first, in epistemology, the reflections or the external things. As I read Lenin, he starts from things and moves to sensations as reflecting them. But, as his critics argue, he does not explain how he gets to things in the first place. They insist that he makes sensations cognitively prior and that this lands him in something like Locke's representationalism. To quote Passmore, "Berkeley's criticism has to be answered that, if matter is not itself a sensation but only that which gives rise to sensation, we can have no evidence that there is such a thing. Berkeley, Engels admits, is hard to beat by mere argumentation."* My reorientation is basic here.

But if we take perceiving to be an operation which does not terminate on sensations but uses them in its deciphering of the things to which it is responding, we have another situation. We move *between* presentationalism and representationalism. Sensations become factors used in referential perceiving. In this setting we start from the act of perceiving things and afterwards shift our attention to sensations. That is, we first use our sensations as informational about objects and afterwards recognize sensations and the role they play. We conclude that we could not just intuit things and so start from them in that way. And so we realize the disclosing role sensations play. I speak of this as the from-to-circuit. It is in this fashion that I answer Berkeley.

I conclude, accordingly, that Lenin was nearer right than the positivists. The epistemological road to materialism is open. But materialism,

*Passmore, *A Hundred Years of Philosophy*, p. 45.

itself, needs clarification. It can no longer be reductive but must recognize levels in nature and do justice to what is unique in man, his ability to use language both descriptively and valuatively. Attention thus focusses on the brain as an organ of both thought and action. It is at least one of the merits of ontological materialism that it indicates a perspective in line with science. Much needs to be done both factually and in the way of thought-habits. I, myself, welcome this intersection of the secular philosophy of the West with what is often called *diamat*. It is to be hoped that differences of approach and of terminology can, as the saying is, be ironed out. It was with some such idea in mind that I helped to edit a cooperative volume entitled *Philosophy for the Future: The Quest of Modern Materialism*. We asked Soviet philosophers to make their contribution but they did not see their way to do so. And then the *cold war* intervened. It was our belief that pragmatic naturalism was in the right direction but a little too vague on fundamentals. Did Messrs Dewey and Hook really believe in the existential status of matter or was it a working concept in what they called Experience?

In the next chapter I shall examine neo-Thomism and its affiliations. Here we have what is sometimes called *formal materialism*. Quite rightly, the opening emphasis is on epistemology. Here lines are laid down which I would challenge but which I respect. An ontology ensues whose texture is Aristotelian and which is sometimes called *hylomorphism*. It will be my purpose to bring out, as sharply as possible, differences in both epistemology and ontology. The reader can then make his choice.

9

THOMISM AND
EVOLUTIONARY NATURALISM

Foundational philosophy has two main components, epistemology and ontology. As I see it, logic and scientific method play into these and both affect them and are affected by them. What ensues is a development of perspective. The question often is whether we begin with "words and things" or with "words and sense-data." As a realist, I favor beginning with things. But we don't just apprehend things. There are operations involved.

The reader will have noted that I call myself a critical realist in epistemology and an evolutionary materialist in ontology. These are terms which are illuminated both by analysis and by contrast. Thus I call myself a nominalist in that I reject essences as universals in things, in this, perhaps, belonging to the move of Ockham. But I would combine naming and reference with conceptual knowledge-claims. While I stress concepts I think of their cognitive function and so cannot quite call myself a conceptualist. The thing to do, as I see it, is to trace out the leads in knowledge-claims beginning with perceiving. Human knowing is quite a complex achievement.

I would hold, then, I am neither an *essentialist* of the Platonic-Aristotelian tradition nor a psychological nominalist of the Berkeley-Hume approach. As I see it, we make use of sensations and images as information-bearing and pass on to symbols and their meanings. In this way, we make statements about things and, at the same time, develop our thought of them. My own thinking has led me to accept as valid the atomic theory of the constitution of physical objects and to endeavor to harmonize it with a realistic view of perceiving. There is quite a problem here. On the one hand, our common-sense thinking leads to an emphasis upon looks, behavior and dispositions. It reflects what we have learned about objects and our expectations. On the other hand, science has sought to *explain* all this and more too in terms of constituents and laws. It started with an emphasis on measurement and proceeded to achieve the notion of inertia and mass. These gave the thought of material things a new complexion, a kind of independence and self-sufficiency. Scientists began to interrogate nature and to read its answers in terms of relevant observations. This was a slow process and went on from generation to generation.

The first big breakthrough was in astronomy and physics. After that came chemistry. Then came biology. Science had now become a manifold endeavor. In our day, physics vies with bio-chemistry, that is, with large molecules, enzymes, proteins and nucleic acids. It is really astonishing what is being done.

I shall shortly turn to consider the Aristotelian outlook. This man tried to give an *aperçu* of the whole of nature in a kind of closed system. It was essentially a qualitative approach and he worked out his ontology and cosmology in terms of specific categories. These are of interest to us in this chapter because they were taken up by Saint Thomas and put in a theistic, creationistic frame. This constitutes an intellectual tradition of its own. It is now often called neo-Thomism, though Maritain, one of its ablest representatives, simply calls it Thomism without any prefix.*

Now philosophy has a certain autonomy. Secular philosophy moved from Descartes through Locke, Hume, Kant to present winds of doctrine. Some of these I have already considered. In my own day, realism of a novel type struggled with idealism, pragmatism and positivism. What such Thomists as Maritain and Gilson sought to offer was a return to Aristotelian realism as opposed to the secular traditions in philosophy and science they found around them. They were able men and good expositors. It constituted a challenge.

Epistemology and Ontology

Since I am defending realism and materialism and adding to it a naturalistic kind of humanism, I thought it well to study Thomism. I cannot say I am an expert in it. But I have sought to understand critical points in epistemology and ontology. It so happens that Maritain and Wetter, the critic of dialectical materialism, both speak of themselves as critical realists. This intrigues me. I shall later take up Maritain's theory of knowledge in some detail. Speaking in general terms, I would say that he follows Aristotle in a kind of cognitional identity between subject and object whereas I stress the mechanisms which lead to signals, cues and some measure of information transfer, all of which support cognitive

*Maritain, *Existence and the Existent*, Introduction.

claims. The pressures then move on to exploration, suggesting and testing. There is a good deal of interaction between the percipient organism and the external object. And thus we come to live in a world of things, more or less adequately perceived. We run our hands over things to get their shape and contour. Aristotle stressed touch. He could not anticipate the present use of vision with instruments.

Maritain

Long ago, before Maritain made his home in the United States, I entertained him and took the opportunity to ask him some questions to try to bring out his knowledge of American movements in philosophy. I was not very successful and concluded that, like most other Europeans, he had not given much attention to them. I was particularly interested because, like him, I had reacted against Bergsonism in the direction of realism, a sort of scientific realism, such as I have outlined. I may remark, in this connection, that I found Ayer and Carnap to have much the same ignorance of American movements. In this regard, philosophy differs from science, which is international in method. Perspectives and assumptions stand out in philosophy. And it takes longer to test these.

As I read Maritain now, he recognizes that American thought had moved away from idealism and subjectivism. As we shall see, one of his watersheds is Cartesianism. Like Aristotle, before him, he emphasizes "perceptible objects." These are primary and observable. As I see it, he is a critical realist in the sense that he tries to make explicit what he regards as implicit in Saint Thomas. As Copleston points out, epistemology was not, in Medieval Times, an emphasized division of philosophy. It came to the front after Descartes with Locke, Berkeley, Hume and Kant. Even Hobbes does not quite feel the problems implicit in his own stress on phantasms.

Gilson is, in certain ways, more conservative than Maritain. He is primarily an historian. He tends to hold that the whole problem of an external world, so much discussed in secular, modern philosophy is artificial. There is something wrong about the starting-point. But, of course, one is still left with the question of the nature and mechanism of perceiving. How do we perceive this external world we accept? That is the problem. As we have noted, Dewey was led to take much the same attitude as Gilson but worked out a behavioristic experientialism instead of the direct realism of perceptible objects of Maritain and Gilson. But it is important to note that neither Dewey nor Hook, his best interpreter, accepted matter and materialism. This is an important point. In what sense do we cognize matter? As we shall find out, Aristotle postulated an unknowable *hylé* as correlative to his forms. In this he went beyond Plato. If, then, Maritain and Gilson accept external perceptible things, it is with this scheme in mind.

But this *hylé* is quite different from matter as we understand it to-day. The question goes back in part to Aristotle and his divergence from Democritus. But let us remember that the atoms of Democritus were a speculative expression of a pluralistic protest against the ontology of Parmenides. Atomism has a different background now. But it must not be forgotten that Democritus, Epicurus and Lucretius sought to bring out empirical arguments in its favor, like the wearing away of stone and the evaporation of water.

I think that we must, from the epistemological side, clarify the reach and cognitive claims of perceiving. I shall try to bring out just how I differ from Maritain on basic points. Both of us are direct realists but I stress the role of sensations, images and concepts as informative while Maritain, like Aristotle, claims a literal transmission of forms or qualities. His perceptible objects are, quite literally, as they are perceived. And perceiving depends on the transmission of forms. My type of direct realism is content with the working out of indications, what I call a decipherment. There is a directed response and the use, in connection with it, of controlled sensory cues. Out of this combination arise *facts about*. Our common-sense world of behaving things emerges and, in our culture, scientific method adds to our information. In short, in my type of direct realism, there are knowable things but not, in the strict sense, *perceptible objects*. But even to put it this way is a little misleading. What I mean is that perceiving is not a grasping of transmitted qualities. The mechanism is more complex.

It is a little hard to know where to begin. Perhaps it is best to tackle Maritain and then, after that, to examine the Aristotelian outlook with which it is closely connected. We can thereupon bring out the change in Aristotelianism brought about by theistic creationalism. As I see it, the stress upon *esse*, the to-exist, as over against *ens*, or what is, makes its appearance at this point. I am a little curious as to whether this creative *esse* is regarded as manifesting itself in the perceptual experience. I think I have a strong sense of existence in my life and that this extends itself to my surroundings which impinge on me and which, quite obviously, have a career of their own. Certainly, we are led to make the distinction between imaginary dollars and real dollars. The touchstone is handling and use. This gives a world regarded as having causal efficacy and energy. It is in this context that perceiving operates. But let us turn to Maritain.

Maritain's first thesis, as presented in his book, *The Degrees of Knowledge*, turns on an appeal to immateriality. He holds that there is a rigorous correspondence between knowledge and immateriality. A being is knowledgeable in the measure of its immateriality. Why is this? Because to know is to *become* another thing than oneself.

I would query this dictum but it must be understood. Maritain holds that the knower, while seeking to keep its own nature intact, becomes the known itself and is identified with it. And this involves two kinds of existence. The knower is *in* the known in the form of an *esse intentionale*, intentional being. This kind of *esse* disengages the thing-object from its natural limits so that it comes to exist in the *soul* by another existence than its own. And the soul is, or becomes, the thing according to another existence than its own. What, then, is the means to this union of the knower and the known? It is the whole world of intrapsychic *forms* which, in the soul, are like the deputies of the object and which the Ancients called similitudes or species. Maritain suggests the term, presentative form, for these, but warns that the notion should be that of *making present* rather than presenting. This, I take it, goes with the idea of union.

It is to be noted that Maritain accounts for errors of sense in a causal way. The form, or sensible species, is perceived after it attains the sense, that is, after transmission through the internal, or the external, medium.

Let me now comment on this theory and its terms. It is through and through Aristotelian. Little is said of the nerves and their function. It is to be recalled that Aristotle did not know about the nerves and the brain as a system. Maritain thinks of forms as transmissible. They leave behind the passive and unknowable *hylé*. They can do this just because, in themselves, they are immaterial in the Aristotelian sense.

Leaving this point aside for the moment, it is clear that he must grapple with the difficulties of representative realism. His solution is in terms of the identity of what is *made present* and the form of the perceived object. It is in this way that the knower becomes one with the known. And this is why Maritain lays stress on immateriality and on the thesis that to know is to become another thing than oneself.

Here, of course, we have what De Santillana in his study of the origins of scientific thought speaks of as the tidiness of the Aristotelian corpus. But what has become of Aristotelian physics? I shall examine that question later.

I want next to consider other Roman Catholic thinkers. I shall take Coffey's work on *Epistemology*. It seems to me a scholarly product, well aware of controversies. He declares that scholastics have been divided between two views: perceptionism, which regards sense-perception as a process directly intuitive of external reality; and mediate, or representative, sense-perception which holds the external thing to be mirrored, or represented, in a mental datum from which, by a process analogous to inference, one would attain knowledge of the external reality.

It is interesting historically to note that Lenin's "reflection theory" is analogous to this second move. Of course, Lenin had the setting of modern physics in mind. But the problem is much the same. It may be recalled that I analyzed perceiving to bring in both directed reference to the object and the use of sensory material to be the point of departure for recognized facts about it. Cognitively, then, we are directly concerned with the object and use the "reflection."

I note that Coffey takes perceptionism to be the view generally held. The sensible species, or form, operated but it was not that which was perceived. As I see it, Maritain resorts to cognitional identity and intentional being.

Now I am one of those who wish to give honor where it is due. I agree with Gilson and Maritain that Cartesianism and modern philosophy turned away from sense-perception too abruptly. Or, at least, got puzzled. One reason for this was the rise of an intuitive kind of rationalism. The external world was, by definition, *res extensa*. Yet, as time went on, observation again began to be stressed. But technical philosophy moved toward positivism, phenomenalism and idealism. It has been hard to cut beneath this setting. And, of course, modern science had said good-bye to immaterial forms. At most, it had acknowledged arrangements and patterns. But this is a long story. And there was a resort to dualism in connection with the brain, which is only now being overcome. I shall try to bring all this to a head in my concluding remarks. I certainly cannot resort to immaterialism in the facile way Maritain does.

Maritain, in point of fact, impresses me as somewhat of a poet. He speaks of the *intuition* of Being. This is the act of existing, that victorious thrust by which the humblest thing triumphs over nothingness. It is this act which supplements *hylé* and immaterial forms to constitute an object. It is the Thomistic addition to Aristotelianism. Naturally, I have asked myself what I have in mind when I assert that there *is* a tree before me. It seems to me that I take my perceptual response to be directed at an object having a common status with my percipient self which involves my body. I can causally act upon it in various ways. Even at this level of common sense, I have the belief in an objective world made up of a vast variety of things. In perceiving, I select one of these and cognize it in terms of sensory indications. To which, of course, I may add far-reaching concepts, physical, chemical and botanical. In short, being, or existence, would be a *presupposition* tied in with reference and description. I know nothing in all this of a struggle against nothingness. That strikes me as mythical.

I am told that most neo-Thomists stress the judgment of existence with its tests rather than intuition. The question then is, What does this entail? So far as I can see, no more than the conclusion that a physical thing is out there to be handled causally and cognitionally. We are confronted with *ens*, with what is. But I grant you that both terms, the *what* and the *is* stand out. One way to put this is to point out that facts are facts about, that knowing presupposes something to know. Ontology cannot be reduced to epistemology.

But what is the nature of this world? As I see it, Maritain moves from essentialism and *hylé* to a creative *esse*, while I move from cognized facts *about* to theories of the categorial constitution of material things. I here take the path which modern science took. And this resulted from the inadequacy of qualitative Aristotelianism with its elements of hot and cold, moist and dry. In some measure, this shift is tied in with the theory of perceiving. Maritain, as we saw, held to a transmission of essences and thus to a cognitional identity of thought and object. I, on the other hand, think in terms of the referential use of controlled information. What stands out in science is the methodical search for additional information by means of measuring, weighing, clocking and so on; and the rise, in this context, of inertial facts, and combining proportions. The material thing now became the seat of constituents and new kinds of explanations. I cannot see the relevance to this sort of information of Maritain's cognitional identity of thought and object. It will, as we shall see, lead him to embrace a positivistic notion of the import of science. I, on the other hand, am a physical realist as regards atoms, electrons, photons, electro-magnetic fields. These become objects of enquiry. We gain facts about them. Yet to know about a thing is not to become it.

Creationalism and Gilson

I pass now briefly to creationalism and to the so-called proofs of a creator's existence. I turn here to Gilson.

He writes, "There is creation when there is absolute production of an act-of-being."* Thus, this conception, which we examined in Maritain, is foundational. Where there was *nothing* being appeared.

Now Gilson is quite right in pointing out that this notion of creation conflicts with the scientist's and secular philosopher's habits of thought. They stress movement and the conditions of movement, whereas the Thomist rests his case of what he calls the existential act. This is a built-in thesis which goes back to the question of what we have in mind when we affirm existence. So far as I can see, it is an affirmation of the justification of response and reference and connects their object with other objects in the world and with ourselves as both percipients and agents. In other words, it connects the object with the spatial-temporal-causal world in which we live and have our being. Reference is tied in with location in this world. It was this feature of perceiving which Hegel and the romantic idealists ignored in their stress on universals. So, I am, in a way, sympathetic with part of this Thomistic emphasis. But I cannot follow Maritain in his assertion of an intuition of existence. Yet one must be fair here and point to his qualification that existence is "affirmed and intentionally experienced by and in the mind. . . . And corresponds to the act of existing exercised by things."**

But there is a different context here. As an essentialist, that is, one who emphasizes transmitted forms as the *nature* of material things, Maritain would seem to need something additional. For me, knowledge-claims concern facts about the material thing of an informational sort. It is often of the nature of a reproduction of pattern, as when we run our hands over things or use our camera eyes. When we weigh things we get a relevant ratio. A realistic materialist thinks of the thing as out there in its complexity and wants to decipher it. He asks questions about it and gets indications. And so he builds up his thought of it. One must, I take it, follow the growth of the sciences to get the picture. Chemical formulae are good examples of the knowledge achieved. It is because Maritain identifies basic knowledge with cognitive identity that he so welcomes phenomenalism and positivism with their rejection of the realistic import of atoms, electrons, etc. The outcome for him is a return to "perceptible

---

*Gilson, *Christian Philosophy of Saint Thomas*, p. 121.
**Existence and the Existent*, p. 27.

things" as the external reality. But, of course, the positivist remains with sensory observations.

Nothingness and Creation

I cannot here give much space to the so-called proofs of a creator's existence. As I see it, these are tied in with scholastic terminology. God is a supreme essence united with existence. It is out of this Source that acts of creation flow bountifully and freely. But Thomism rejects the so-called ontological proof from the idea of God to his existence. Our human ideas as such never can attain this union of essence with existence. Hume and Kant developed this in pointing out that existence is not a predicate to be contained in an idea but something to be verified denotatively.

Aristotle's Unmoved Mover is transformed into a First Cause. The argument here assumes that motion in its causal nexus implies a beginning since an infinite series is unthinkable. Present-day mathematicians would deny this assumption. Physically it is held to-day that energy is intrinsic to the world. While many astronomers who speak of the big-bang cosmologically allow themselves to talk about creation, they do so carelessly from the semantic standpoint. All they seem to mean is an absolute beginning about whose antecedents they have no idea. I take it that the usual cosmological view now is that of a cycle of expansion and contraction analogous to that which Empedocles had in mind. Aristotle had an eternal cosmos with a teleological structure. Modern ideas are chiefly distinguished by their appeal to evidence.

The third proof puts stress upon necessity, not to be found in things which are generated and then decay. These latter things are contingent. But do they not have causes? There is much discussion these days about the status of necessity. Is it a purely logical idea of an analytic type? Or can it have a place in historical happenings? In any case, the Thomistic appeal is to something transcending history. But where is the empirical evidence for such transcendence?

I find the argument from perfection bound up with the argument from design. And it strikes me that the evolutionary approach has undermined both. One can account for adjustmental functioning by mutation and natural selection. Aristotle believed in a kind of dispersed purposiveness in nature. And the creationalistic approach would chime in with it. But proof has its own standards.

I conclude with many others, including Catholic thinkers, that the

Thomistic proofs do not hold. It would seem to follow that we must, like Margaret Fuller, accept the universe as both eternal and historical. Could it not have existed at all? That question has been raised. Theism, of course, starts with the aseity of God. I am inclined to hold that *nothingness* is not a primary, ontological category. We certainly work within what is.

In the next chapter, when we deal with existentialism, it will be human *Existenz* with which we shall chiefly be concerned, with authentic living and with death. In this context, nothingness will manifest itself dialectically.

It may be well to conclude this section with a contrast between panlogistic idealism, panpsychism, physical realism and Thomism. Hegel begins his logic with the dialectical movement from Being through Nothing to Becoming. These are categorial universals. The ingenuity is impressive. But Hegel has already rejected the particularity of perceiving. As we have noted in the previous chapter, panpsychism regards anything but experience as vacuous. F. H. Bradley expressed this to me as the impossibility of going beyond what appears. It is akin to Berkeley's move to the effect that to be is to be perceived. Now, in contrast, the physical realist takes perceiving to be at once denotative and cognitional. It affirms and cognizes in an elementary way. The objective unit is what is, the that-what of some writers. Now, so far as I can see, this unit can grow in comprehension with the increase of knowledge. There are categorial changes as energy, causality, and organization come to the front. There are factual insights as more detailed knowledge about is attained. All this, it seems to me, leads in the direction of evolutionary materialism, which signifies categorial and factual novelty. As has often been pointed out, both Aristotle and Saint Thomas accepted levels in nature but of a fixed sort because they did not accept temporal evolution.

What Is Existence?

But, to come back to existence, it would seem that the Thomist postulates an act-of-being intuited, or judged, pointing to creation. The physical realist, on the other hand, regards himself as immersed in existence as what is, as that-what. The denotative is filled out by cognitive claims. I suppose one divergence here is that I am not an essentialist with my what. One should recall Maritain's claim that in knowing one becomes the object. I do not think that is the case. Knowing is more of the nature of gaining facts about the full-blooded thing. And here, as I see it, science probes and asks questions about constituents and explanatory laws.

I am now going to discuss divergent trends in Greek philosophy and end up with an examination of the status of mind.

Philosophy began with the Ionians and their search for what things are made of, that is, with an attempt at physics, meteorology and cosmology. It was at once philosophy and science as against myth and tales. Cornford, an outstanding authority, speaks of Ionian materialism. This reached its climax in Democritean atomism, though both Epicurean and Stoic were, in their diverse ways, materialistic. I confess I was a little disappointed by Cornford's rather *ex cathedra* condemnation of materialism as unable to do justice to the spiritual. This was in his book, *Before and After Socrates*. An able historian is not always equally in touch with the movements of his day. But he should have remembered the Epicureans and the Stoics. Spiritual is a rather vague word associated with mind and values. Desire and the desirable are also involved. Socrates, I would say, moved too abruptly to the human level. And Plato reified Ideas and made them transcendent realities, all the more easily that he rejected the world of perception.

I want to do justice to the exploratory nature of Greek thought. If it began with materialism, it also investigated mathematics and the transcendent. But, alas! the culture weakened and lost its nerve. As we all know, modern science proceeded step by step from the inorganic world, in the large, to chemistry and thence to biology. The tie-in of science with technology assisted it. And it began with an accommodating dualism. Materialism never bulked large. And the only kind of materialism possible would be one which would do justice to mind and valuation. This I have called evolutionary materialism with a recognition of levels. If the Ancient World began with materialism, it may well be that the modern world will end with it. But it will be a sophisticated kind of materialism.

Tempted, though I am, to discuss Socrates and Plato, I must hurry on to Aristotle. I think it is true that Socrates gave a new direction to philosophy with his interest in morals and politics. But, unfortunately, he was too inclined to regard the older direction as useless. Plato developed a broad horizon and Aristotle continued it. What resulted was a kind of half-way house. It is usually called the qualitative view of the world. Aristotle turns back to perception much along the line that Saint Thomas and Maritain do. I have often asked myself just where and how they fell short of understanding the mechanism and reach of perceiving.

One reason, I take it, is their acceptance of forms as entities. Plato had made *forms* transcendent while Aristotle had made them constitutive of things. But are there such entities? If we think of perceiving as involving response-reference and the use of sensory information, it becomes a question of how we learn to think of things. Their behavior begins to stand out. They seem to be independent of ourselves and in a causal relation with one another. We can measure them and study their reactions. It was this line that Galileo took and so moved from *impetus*—a stage in medieval mechanics—to mass and inertia. It was not long before questions of constitution arose and modern chemistry was born. As a consequence of this development, we have the modern views of matter.

I recognize that the theory of the nature of perceiving lagged behind. We still have positivists and phenomenalists. But the point I want to make is that Aristotle moved from acceptance of forms to their transfer in perceiving. As Maritain puts it, to know is to become the object. I, on the other hand, regard perceiving as a kind of factual deciphering and as only the beginning of knowledge-about. Probing, experimentation, tested theory, all are needed. We thus get new facts about material things.

It is a matter of surprise that Aristotle was so dominated in his mechanics by such experiences as push and pull. Had he asked himself what would happen if friction were decreased, he might well have gotten the ideas of mass and momentum. We know that, in his astronomy, he was conservative and geocentric.

Plato had no concept of matter. He stressed the impermanent nature of particulars. I have always been astonished by Whitehead's estimation of him. But I have argued that Whitehead's theory of perception is not really realistic. As Solmsen points out in his book, *Aristotle's System of the Physical World*, "For Plato matter is and remains in the full sense of the word something unthinkable. . . . Plato's own approach remains 'metaphysical.'" That means, of course, here transcendental. That is why ontology is the preferable term.

Let us turn next to Aristotle's conception *hylé*. First of all, it is a principle of continuity in nature. Being does not arise out of non-being. Things, then, are combinations of two principles, the indeterminate substratum and the forms which alternate in relation to it. Matter is other than place and occupies it. Elements are constituted of this indeterminate matter and qualitative contraries. Earth is cold and dry; water, cold and moist, etc. One can understand alchemy arising, as it did in Alexandria under Aristotelian influence.

Qualities are perceived by sense after the manner of impressed shapes on wax. Aristotle had no notion of the function and mode of working of the nervous system. Here, again, he was strangely conservative. But we must do justice to Aristotle. He was the founder of logic and carried on investigations in biology and in politics. Though not an evolutionist, Aristotle recognized non-reductive levels in nature. There was a sort of chemistry in the inorganic world. Plants are living, while animals have also sense. Man is rational with a passive and an active reason. Aristotle seems to have been a Platonist for quite some time and a believer in the pre-existence of the soul. But he at last turned to an identification of the soul with the form of the body. This is a high-level affair. One might ask whether this could be translated in terms of a genetic code.

I have given little space to Aristotle's astronomy with its spheres and Prime Mover. In these days energy is thought of as intrinsic to the material world. It is a cosmos of galaxies.

There is much that is technically interesting in the Thomistic theory of thought. The stress seems to be upon an abstraction basis for universals. This is clearly connected with the idea of forms. But, if we give up such forms, the emphasis would shift to construction. An active mind thinks of possibilities and their implications and tries to relate them to observational tests. The notion of acceleration is a case in point. Newton's laws of motion follow the same pattern. Just as perceiving is active, so—but on a larger scale—is symbolic thinking. The correspondence theory of truth must recognize the rise of such constructive explorations. The world is as we responsibly think it. I look at the world around me and think of atoms, molecules, nucleic acids, hormones and enzymes and try to remember some of the steps taken in their formulation. And I suppose that it is because I think of perceiving as merely giving us indications and clues that I am as ready as I am to people the world with what are sometimes called "scientific objects." I have no doubt that I would think differently if, like Maritain, I regarded knowing as becoming the object. My critical realism is a physical realism of mass and energy, of atoms and of radiant pulsations. I now move back from these to observations relevant to them. The "perceptual world" has now become an appearing world which is yet not an illusion for it is a gateway to the material world within which it functions. But it functions in terms of the apparatus of sense-organs, sensations and referential thoughts which have been evolved within nature. It is no wonder that this collaboration of the internal and the external has puzzled man's mind. Which do we begin with, things or ideas? My form of direct realism is that we begin with both, for our ideas are taken as disclosing the external controls to which we are responding. Aristotle was not too far wrong in stressing touch, for touch leads to handling and taking hold of. The distance receptor gives us time to prepare our action. And our camera eyes also give us details about our world. Once set, science can add instruments of unbelievable delicacy. These give increased information.

But what shall we say of neo-Thomism? Surely, that it is a brave but mistaken effort. The motivations are evident. One wants God and immortality. We can all of us have admiration for Saint Thomas but he was, when all is said, a man of his time.

The modern world began, very naturally, with a dualistic outlook. There was matter and there was mind. And, to make matters worse, there was no clear theory of sense-perception. Ideas became terminal; and positivism, phenomenalism, idealism, Kantianism divided the allegiances of philosophers. Some, like Russell, even wanted to construct the world in a logical way out of sensations and sensibilia. The Thomists were convinced that all this was a mistake. But, in making perceiving objective in import, they resorted to a transfer of forms, or sensible species, and thus arrived at a cognitional identity of thought and thing. I, on the other hand, have explored another avenue, that of a production in the percipient of patterns and indications conveying information about their external controls. By the aid of these, the percipient is able to adjust himself to his surroundings and, cognitively, to arrive at facts about them. The processes involved in this kind of activity are complex and are only gradually being understood. But we can perceive without knowing these operations, just as we can digest without knowledge of digestive enzymes.

As I see it, the Thomistic-Aristotelian scheme is bound up with principles which science has bypassed. Our present idea of matter is quite different from *hylé*. Material things are thought of as massive and composed of constituents into which they can be broken down. Knowledge has been obtained of chemical bonds and patterns of organization. The various sciences move up and down the scale from the inorganic to the organic, experimenting, gathering evidence, theorizing. In all this, immaterial forms play no part. If then, perceiving can be given objective import without them, an essential bridge has been crossed. Here philosophy has a choice to make. I have urged a critical, physical realism to replace positivism, pragmatism and idealism. Thomism is a verbally tidy position but has difficulty in making any living connection with modern science.

I turn, in conclusion, to its doctrine of the soul. The soul is held to be a unitary, substantial form. It is immaterial and incorporeal and is the active form of the body. A man is the composite of soul and body. And here we come again to the assertion of the act-of-existing involved in what is, an act pointing beyond itself. The human soul has an act of existing which transcends the body.

A Sophisticated Kind of Materialism

Over against this construction, the evolutionary materialist accepts the emergence of life from the inorganic—a development still challenging investigation—and then the slow evolution of organisms with the hominids specializing in the role of the brain. Here the tradition of dualism is rejected and an identity, or double-knowledge, view proposed. As I see it, each of us is on the inside of his functioning brain aware of his feelings and sensations and using them in directed activities. The self arises as a center of coordination and control. Here we have a guided kind of causality. It is true that consciousness and awareness is not reached from outside, for external knowledge depends on the channels of sensory information about objects. But I can find no obstacle to such a unitary position. While the brain does not secrete thought, it is the organ in which awareness of signals, signs and symbols emerges. Here we have one of the greatest challenges to science. And it is a privilege of philosophy to help to clear the path of misunderstanding.

Maritain speaks of integral humanism and I of naturalistic humanism. But let it be humanism and a concern for human values. It is with interest that I note a biologist who is critical of the dominance of the physical sciences and their linkage with technology. In his book on *The Insects*, Url Lanham writes: "And above all, since man is part of the biological universe, there would be need for a nearly incomprehensible degree of humaneness in the face of the development of techniques that can change man himself." I felt this attitude in my friend, the great neurologist, C. Judson Herrick. Lanham appeals to Coleridge as the spokesman of the relation between man and nature.

"O happy living things! no tongue
Their beauty might declare:
A spring of love gush'd from my heart,
And I blessed them unaware."

Materialism has a bad name it has hardly deserved. This is a semantic question which requires investigation. I have concerned myself in this chapter chiefly with ontology and foundations. In the next I shall take up that odd movement called *existentialism* which wrestles with human *Existenz*. There will be need for clarification. Man has become self-conscious and now confronts the absurd, nihilism, the meaningless, and even the gulf of nothingness. Foundations may help.

10

THE HUMAN SITUATION
AND EXISTENTIALISM

Thus far, in this semi-autobiographical survey of recent philosophy, I have analyzed philosophical positions which were in vogue when I was inducted into the subject and movements in which I participated or with which I was confronted as alternatives. Hence the canvas has been broad. I have had to consider idealism, realism, pragmatism and positivism. To make my survey more complete, I have given serious attention to both dialectical materialism and neo-Thomism. But even this was not enough. One had to recognize currents of discussion such as those associated with the name of Wittgenstein with the ensuing stress on language.

When one thinks of all these movements and doctrines, one recognizes that it is difficult to keep one's balance and perspective. The task confronting a philosopher these days is not an easy one. But it may well be that one who has been immersed in philosophy for a long time and has worked out and defended a position has gained certain insights which are defensible. He has, of course, no right to be dogmatic. But I think he has almost a duty to explain his outlook and contrast it with others.

The reader is now aware that my thinking has led me to a form of realism which works in well with science. An ontology followed which stressed levels and novelty in nature. This gave an interesting framework within which to consider human living. Here values, the role of reasoning, and the question of the nature of human freedom came to the front. If the human mind evolved under the urgency of problem-solving, as some biologists and anthropologists hold, what was the import of this fact for the traditional claim to freedom? Very early in my thinking I had advanced the notion of levels of causality. It had not seemed to me reasonable to believe that one pattern of causality extended from the inorganic to the organic and thence to the activity of the mind-brain. At this stage there was, clearly, some consideration of consequences and weighing of alternatives. Thinking in terms of symbols, as an operation, could hardly be denied. How could such operations be assimilated into causality? There was much to think about. As a first step, I rejected predetermination. Decisions seemed to me to involve a certain openness. As we say, we have to make up our minds. At the moral level of conduct, this "making up one's mind" apparently involves the use of criteria and principles. It may very well be a rather tense affair. I became increasingly interested in ethics.

The Rise of Existentialism

Now it so happened that, between the wars and thereafter, there arose on the European continent a philosophical movement called existentialism. It had a lineage of its own. There was constant reference to Pascal, Kierkegaard, Nietzsche, even to Saint Augustine. One heard little of Locke, Hume, analysis, mathematical logic, empiricism, and not too much of recent epistemology. The movement seemed rather inbred. The terms one noted were rather different. Much was said of *Angst*, or dread, the absurd, the meaningless, death, nothingness, the subjective method, the authentic life, etc. There were atheistic existentialists and religious ones. It was, clearly, a kind of ferment of its own. One soon located Sartre in this ferment and then Heidegger, Jaspers, Marcel, Buber. Protestant religious existentialism was introduced in the United States largely by Paul Tillich. In England, one heard of Farmer and of Oman.

It became evident that this movement had to be reckoned with. Obviously, its domain differed from that of logical positivism and from the philosophy of science trends so dominant in the United States. I decided to look into it rather systematically. I would first try to understand it and then bring to bear upon it my own epistemology, ontology and theory of value.

There is a large literature on the subject; and I have read largely in the writings of the chief representatives. But this chapter must be looked upon chiefly as a critique; I hope a reasoned one. Because of the American situation I have devoted some time to the theses of Tillich. This comes more in the way of a conclusion. As I noted in connection with Maritain, I have long defended naturalistic humanism, writing one of the first systematic books on it in 1918, called *The Next Step in Religion*. It interested me that Father—now Bishop—Sheen commented on it in his doctoral thesis at Louvain. I may remark here incidentally that I have found Professor James Collins' book on *The Existentialists* illuminating, especially his treatment of Marcel on points conflicting somewhat with neo-Thomism.

The historical background of existentialism is furnished by Kierkegaard and Nietzsche. It got from these thinkers certain emphases such as the stress on the subjective approach and on negation from the former and on querying theism and conventional values from the latter. What they had in common was a turning away from the path of objective truth to the aphoristic and dramatic. Thus they reenforced one another, not in doctrine, but in attitude.

I was early introduced to Nietzsche. It was about 1903 when that occurred. And of course, extreme readings of his position on war and the will to power were common at the time of the First World War. In essentials, I took him to be a good European concerned with conventional trends and critical of them. He had recognized the Dionysiac in Greek life and became the prophet of something of the same for his times. He took a clue from Darwinism in his idea of the Superman. It is sometimes forgotten that his Superman must be hard on himself as well as on others. I did not take his biology too seriously and note that to-day biologists and anthropologists emphasize the role that group feeling played in the evolution of the hominids. Undoubtedly, the struggle for existence took too individualistic a form in the nineteenth century. I still read Nietzsche for his dramatic emphases which are challenging. "God is dead" signifies a loss of faith. It leaves a gap. Is there anything to take its place? I can understand why this poet-thinker appeals to the Germans. But did not Feuerbach and Marx raise similar questions earlier? As we shall see, existentialism represents a sort of third force in Europe. Even Sartre, though he flirts with communism, rejects materialism. I shall criticize Sartre's epistemology and ontology. He seems to me strongest in his psychology, especially in his qualification of Freud. The tradition of Cartesian rationalism makes itself felt here.

I turn now to Kierkegaard. There are two sides to Kierkegaard to consider, namely, his rejection of Hegel's panlogism and his dramatic version of Christian theology. It is sometimes forgotten that Feuerbach attacked the self-sufficiency of abstract thought at about the same time. In a measure, Schelling must also be counted here. When admirers of Kierkegaard emphasize an appeal to experience, they should not forget that British and American philosophy has long stressed the same appeal.

I find a certain resemblance between Kierkegaard and Tertullian. The latter advocated belief in Christian doctrine because it was, on its face, absurd. Kierkegaard turned inward and exalted the act of faith in a context of what William James later called the "will to believe." Christianity was replete with paradoxes. How could you pass from an historical Jesus to an eternal, or timeless, God? One must shut one's eyes and plunge into the abyss. One does this, surely, in fear and trembling. And Kierkegaard dramatizes the biblical stories of Abraham and Job. Some anthropologists suggest that the Abraham-Isaac tale reflects the passing of human sacrifice. If so, it is magnificently done within the framework of Jewish thought. But what does Kierkegaard make of it? A dramatic exposition of the paradox of faith. It is, for him, an instantiation of the soul's confrontation with the Absolute. It is thoroughly biblical and Protestant. I can imagine a gifted evangelist speaking in these terms. But it is clearly circular and assumes that faith will meet its object. On the whole, I prefer Pascal's wager or the Thomistic proofs.

But it was out of this subjectivistic, existential framework that the later philosophical movement derived many of its terms. There is metaphysical dread before death, confrontation with nothingness as an abyss. Out of this came a logic of negation analogous to the Hegelian, but couched in more concrete terms. To appreciate it, one had to live into it. I found it quite an effort. The atmosphere becomes one of awareness. I, myself, wanted to dig into the self but in an empirical way. I doubted that there were implications of the transcendental. I shall discuss this again in connection with Buber's "I and Thou." Is not the overarching Thou assumed?

Such are the antecedents. Let us move next to a study of outstanding representatives of what is generically called existentialism, though many reject the label. I begin with Sartre. I shall use my framework as a background to his theses. But, first of all, one must size up Husserl's outlook. Here was a continental thinker of first importance whose perspective was quite different from mine. He had, so far as I could make out, taken the path of presentational description and had not bothered himself too much about epistemology. He was, for instance, inclined to assume that Kant's distinction between phenomena and noumena, or things-in-themselves, was spurious. I, on the other hand, had attacked it by trying to show that perceiving was a referential affair engaged in using sensations as informational about external things. It was a kind of factual deciphering started biologically and lifted to a higher level by scientific method. In short, I held that the spuriousness of Kant's things-in-themselves came from his inability to see that his sense-manifold had cognitive relevance to external things. It was because of this that he constructed his phenomena and set them over against his unknowable things-in-themselves.

It is quite understandable, then, that Husserl, like Hegel before him, concentrated on conscious experience as ultimate. His first step was to follow Franz Brentano in stressing intentionality. Subjective processes are objectively intentional. What they intend are picked out, or selected. Here he sought to avoid *psychologism* because he was concerned with validity as in logic and mathematics. What is intended exists and so do its relations. Hence he distinguished between noetic acts and the noemata which they intend. His job, as a philosopher, was to concentrate on these noemata which he believed he could intuit in a somewhat Platonic fashion. To develop this method he adopted the scheme of bracketing. This was called technically an *epoche*.

By so doing, he argued that he could break with the natural tendency of presupposing the world and taking attitudes towards it. Thus he was left with painstakingly-made descriptions of what he could intuit. But this consisted of *ideas* tied in with noetic acts of a Transcendental Ego. In his last works he made explicit the implied idealism.

Husserl and Sartre

I can understand the effects of this teaching. If you have no way to break out into a cognitional realism and so undercut the Kantian constructive phenomenalism, it appears a logical path to take. As nearly as I can make out, Husserl was a clear and convinced thinker within his framework. And he had many able disciples. It was in this direction that Sartre moved in his year of study in Germany. I doubt that he had ever heard of American realism.

But Sartre did not like idealism and sought to dig a little deeper. He did this by making a distinction between the Reflective Level of Descartes and Husserl and what he called the Pre-reflective Level. In this fashion, Sartre produced a radicalization of phenomenology whose consequences we shall study. Keeping to intentionality as a basic feature of consciousness, he came up with two kinds of Being confronting one another which he called, respectively, Being-in-itself and Being-for-itself. These terms carry one back to Hegel's *An-sich* and *Für-sich*. It was this point that Iris Murdoch noted in her review of Sartre's major work, *Being and Nothingness*. In French, it is *Etre-en-soi* and *Etre-pour-soi*. These seem to be irreducible to one another.

Now Husserl's phenomenology may be called self-sufficient since it was merely descriptive of what is found. Sartre builds on this same priority in order to have his phenomenological ontology. Ontology just signifies a discourse about being; and being-in-itself is, for Sartre, just presented to consciousness, whose prime nature is awareness of it, that is, of something other than itself. Being is, accordingly, something presented.

It should be noted that ontology in this setting has a different texture than it has in neo-Thomism where it involves an act-of-existing pointing towards a Creator or in realistic materialism where it is something acknowledged both in knowing and doing and open to investigation. I shall later refer to Sartre's account of materialism as a kind of illusion. Here, of course, he runs counter to the Marxism which he sympathizes with in his social thought. It may be well to recall that, for me, the external world is disclosed and not presented. I cannot, therefore, accept Sartre's ontology. It seems to me nearer positivism or phenomenalism than realism. But it has an inertness which is rather astonishing and savors somewhat of Bergsonism. Certainly, it has nothing in common with modern science. But one must bear in mind here Sartre's dramatic desire for abrupt contrasts. His is a wholesale description of being-in-itself as inert plenitude alien to purpose and meaning. There is, supposedly, no evolutionary base for the emergence of these traits.

Sartre's Main Doctrine

Much has been made of Sartre's atheism which he seems to have inherited from Nietzsche. He paints the very idea of God as self-contradictory in terms of his ontology. It would involve a fusion of his two modes of being and is, therefore, impossible. The lineage of my own atheism with its emphasis on human values is, I believe, more in line with the development of secularism and naturalism. The burden of proof seems increasingly to be on supernaturalism. The traditional proofs for the existence of a God are hardly convincing, as even Marcel recognizes. As we shall see, Protestant defenders of the faith fall back on the claim that morality requires reference to a Transcendental Agency. In my own analysis of moral demands I can find no such ingredient. A sense of responsibility and of "oughtness," as I see it, grows out of group life but that does not mean that the group can dictate moral values. It is an affair of experience and of learning. But that is the case in politics, art and science also. In all this, humanism presents itself to me as an increasingly indicated perspective. But I am always ready to examine and weigh theistic arguments.

But I must hurry on. The other element of being for Sartre is the *pour-soi.* It is defined as a nothingness which negates. It is linked with, and yet differs fundamentally from, the inert *en-soi.* It is cognitional in an apprehensional sort of way. Let me point out again that I do not regard this as good epistemology. But it links up with, and continues, Husserl's presuppositions. Here we have the tradition of immanence set over against the only alternative of which the German philosophers could think, namely, the unknowable thing-in-itself. I repeat, perhaps *ad nauseam,* that it is possible to take the sense-manifold of Kant as informative about its controls and thus arrive at a realism in harmony with science. Cognizing would then be more than Sartre's awareness. I shall have to develop this theme in opposition to Jaspers' assumption that the subject-object relation is a limiting framework. I do not believe in any such *bounding relation* but in selective reference. I am led to refer to objects and to use evidence relevant to them. But this is to anticipate.

Sartre takes consciousness to be a kind of "hole in being" which thereby escapes causal determinism. It is gifted ontologically with an absolute freedom or spontaneity. This is his version of free-will. But it is, evidently, a non-moral affair and can support the will-to-power as readily as moral action. It is, then, needful to account for moral commitment and the authentic life. Sartre, accordingly, faces up to Dostoyevsky's challenge to the effect that if there be no God, then all things are permitted. Only one whose morality has been theocentric in an extreme way would think in such terms. The assumption is that human morality cannot justify itself. I think it can in terms of human well-being. But this must be worked out in terms of an integrative development of tested good reasons for this line of conduct and that.

It is at this point that one is confronted by the sharp contrast between essence and existence. I have never liked the term essence if it is taken to mean more than the cognizable *what* of things to be aimed at in terms of discoverable facts about them. That is, I am not an essentialist of the Aristotelian sort. Ontologically, I think more in terms of processes and dynamic organizations. I do not see how existence could precede such processes. I suppose what Sartre is protesting against is conventional fixity. But I had thought that moralists in general had emphasized responsible autonomy.

In this brief critique, I can only report that it strikes me that Sartre does not do justice to social psychology when he pictures individuals staring one another down. The stress should be on communication and discussion. But his account is dramatic; and he is a dramatist, as in *No Exit.*

I want now to sum up some points. For Sartre, things are profiles of appearances. Curiously enough, he here agrees with Ayer, the logical positivist. Both have in mind the Kantian thing-in-itself as the more than dubious alternative. But I have tried to show that sensory appearings are used to give facts about things. It is the thing that is known by means of its controlled appearings. This approach overcomes the unfortunate move of modern philosophy towards idealism and phenomenalism. It will be recalled that I praised neo-Thomism for its attack on the Cartesian move but argued that its appeal to a kind of literal transfer and identity would not do. We know more now—but not enough—about the mechanics of sense-perception and can argue that information about objects is achieved by a process of correspondent signals, cues and patterns which are taken up and used in behavior. Out of this matrix, locations and descriptions are gradually deciphered and verbalized. Testing is always going on. We move forward in our cognitive claims but can never achieve the kind of confrontation of which the naive realist dreams.

But to return to Sartre. He concludes that the idea of a material world as a totality is a construct and so rejects materialism. As a matter of fact, I think that his epistemology is quite inadequate and never reaches beyond appearances. The self is, for him, also a construct. And so he escapes from both materialism and idealism.

And yet, for all this criticism of his framework, one can have great admiration for his ingenuity and clarity. There is much in his work that has analogies with Bergson's vitalistic dualism. But it is more puckish in spirit. The times had also changed.

Marcel

I turn now briefly to Marcel. It is well known that he was first attracted to idealism and subsequently moved to what may be called a participative realism. I recall that Hocking expressed a certain sympathy with this emphasis on participation. I want to find out what it means. I shall, of course, use the method of contrast. It is interesting to note that Marcel moved away from idealism at about the same time the American realists did. But, as one would expect, he did so in a different atmosphere. He swung in the direction of intuition and sought to enlarge its scope. Now intuition is a rather treacherous term. I have myself always preferred an emphasis upon experience, upon something that could be analyzed. One can speak of the perceptual experience, for instance, but it is something that leads on to questions because it makes claims. One need not linger on Marcel's rejection of pure thought or on the identification of idea and being. That, we have seen earlier, is a very old story. Judging from Professor Collins' exposition, Marcel put to one side scientific realism on the ground that it is concerned with "essential objects or mental construct only remotely grounded in real things."* And this, in the days of the atom bomb, sounds pretentious. I remember talking to a logical positivist who shrugged his shoulders and asked me how I could get beyond sensations. Of course, I offered my analysis of perceiving, which refused to make sensations terminal. And we parted in good spirits. But I think we must keep this point in mind. It will be recalled that Maritain adopted much the same strategy with respect to the things scientists talk about, atoms, electrons, cosmic rays, etc. The epistemological dividing line is interesting. If we do not identify the things we perceive with transmitted qualities but regard sensations as preliminary appearings we can hope to supplement our knowledge by such operations as weighing, dividing, using retorts, etc. I find nothing disingenuous about these techniques and the information they further. But let us keep this point in mind if we are to participate in being.

Now I quite accept Marcel's criticism of Descartes. It would seem to be along the lines suggested by Hobbes. I walk, therefore, I am. C. S. Peirce had already questioned Descartes's rather artificial doubt. So I agree with Marcel that we must recognize the role of sensation in knowledge and the place of the body with regard to the self. I would quite acknowledge that we regard ourselves as coexisting with the things around us.

I am curious as to what he makes of this situation. When he rejects Cartesian dualism and asserts that whatever bears a relation to my body can be called an existent, I applaud. But then I am an evolutionary materialist. I am still looking for that which separates us.

Here it comes. We are told that God is being in an eminent sense. But how has he managed to bring God in? Existence is not a predicate, as both Hume and Kant saw. So far as I can see, the referential meaning grows up both in the context of our experiencing and in the denial of existential status to things merely thought of if they cannot meet tests, like Kant's imaginary dollars. In this setting I think I can understand the status of existence. But how, except by postulate, does Marcel jump from existence to God's being? Professor Collins seems to sense this difficulty. He brings in the scholastic notion of perfection and, I suppose, an appeal to the act-of-existing, a built-in path to God, as a creator. But the materialist

*Collins, *The Existentialists*, p. 124.

puts his feet down and accepts the universe and merely tries to understand it. This is an ontological affair. It involves knowledge about *what is*.

And so we come to Marcel's distinction between mystery and problems. The assumption seems to be that both science and philosophy have neglected the human situation. Now I am as opposed as anyone to a neglect of this sort and I had not supposed that it had occurred. And to the extent it had taken place it was a grievous fault. I can have sympathy with the criticism of impersonality and anonymity. But one must guard against a surreptitious smuggling in of mystery and transcendentalism. I have already criticized Jaspers' rather Kantian formulation of the subject-object framework. The evolutionary materialist is a realist and not a Kantian phenomenalist.

Just what, then, is this field of mystery which philosophy adds to science? It is called a metaproblematic approach to being. The argument seems to be of this sort. The sciences develop techniques for formulating and solving problems but, in so doing, miss the background of being. And, here again, the danger is that they concentrate on essences, which signifies, I take it, facts and theories about these facts. But the human situation involves something different, namely—evil, suffering and death. How can these features of human life be fitted into the scientific picture of the world? A mystery, Marcel holds, is a problem which is constantly encroaching upon its own data and thus going beyond the conditions of its own solution.

This is excellent rhetoric. But when I think about human problems I find myself engaged in an interplay of ethics, psychiatry, sociology and history. First of all, I must try to understand judgments of value for man is a valuing animal. Here I am concerned with standards of appraisal. These seem to involve both knowledge and feeling. I try to work out tests of what is satisfactory. I have found this domain very fascinating. One of the first to introduce me to it was a psychologically orientated sociologist, Professor Charles Horton Cooley. And I do think that progress has been made of late in this field. Man is here living and doing, thinking and feeling. This is a high level of existence which both Aristotle and the modern evolutionist recognize.

But what does Marcel do? He turns away from this approach and speaks of a new way in search of being. Being is somehow now seen as a participation in a creatively received gift of God. This, of course, is the transcendental motive. But how does he attempt to justify it? Much as Jaspers does by putting science within the boundaries of a supposed subject-object duality and setting up metaphysics as a discipline whose proper field is mystery.

And yet Marcel is cautious. He does not want to set up an unknowable. But he clings firmly to a metaphysics which concerns itself with the Divine Being and the human person as participative in being. It is clear that being has become a substantive term, reaching beyond the mere recognition of the status of existence. It is not clear to me how he makes this transition. He is somewhat skeptical of the Thomistic proofs and seems to turn to Saint Augustine, as we shall see that Paul Tillich does. To enter into oneself is to find the gift of being as it comes fresh from God's hands. This is assertive, or postulatory, and carries us back to his early turn from idealism to an intuitive kind of realism. He speaks in fact of *ontic intuition*.

From the technical point of view we have now covered the essentials of Marcel's program. As we should expect, he develops it bravely in such topics as "being and having" and "creative fidelity." In constrast, I can only put my own naturalistic outlook as having virtues of its own in its stress on human values and their achievement. Neither of us, I imagine, belittles the difficulties ahead for humanity. I turn next to Jaspers.

I was once asked by the President of the University of Chicago why it was so hard to get objective estimates of the standing of philosophers with a view to appointments. Those who read this book will, I imagine, have an inkling of the reasons.

There are fashions and alignments and these count very much. Also national traditions are operative. Germany is a case in point. It has a justified pride in its outstanding thinkers from Leibnitz through Kant to Hegel. Perhaps the isolation during and between the wars reenforced this bent. I refer to it because this bent comes out in Jaspers. We shall see that his outlook is built around that of Kant. And yet new motivations have entered in the persons of Kierkegaard and Nietzsche. It is in reacting to these motivations within the Kantian framework that he develops emphases which align him with existentialism.

Jaspers

Jaspers is a man of marked ability, erudite and a political liberal. It is well known that he opposed the Nazi movement.

I come now to my initial question. On what grounds am I critical of Jaspers' impressive, philosophical construction? To put it very briefly, it is because I am convinced that he did not weigh the naturalistic alternative carefully enough. In these days, naturalism goes with a stress on evolutionary novelty and, I would hold, with epistemological realism. Taken together, these give, I think, a simpler framework than Kantianism can offer. Much of my argument will be in the way of contrasts. I shall outline Jaspers' theses and then seek to show another framework. As I see it, his theses are imaginative but presuppose epistemological and ontological positions which are faulty.

The first point I want to make is epistemological. Following Kant, Jaspers sets up a subject-object structure. The principle here is that to know is to construct. Such construction is, of course, complex and involves an integration of sense-manifold, space and time forms, and after these come the categories. It is all a rather impersonal affair and holds for the thinking of all human beings. From this framework, it follows for Jaspers, as it did for Kant, that there is a strict correlation between knowledge and what is objective. That is, we know only our phenomenal constructs. These rest on a meeting of the sense-manifold and *a priori* frames. Hence *existence*, which lies beyond phenomena, cannot be reached and known. Kant had symbolized this postulated domain by such terms as noumena and things-in-themselves.

What Jaspers introduces at this point is the existential note to the effect that a person is aware of existing in his free activity and that this is the point of departure for an effort at transcendence. But this effort is balked, so far as cognition is concerned, since the human mind is shut into the subject-object structure. This acts as a kind of prison.

In place of Kierkegaard's leap of faith Jaspers now puts what he calls a ciphering procedure which is a sort of symbolizing which, however, always founders in face of its goal. It is just a fact that the noumenal world cannot be cognitionally attained. There is thus a yearning for transcendence at the same time that it is realized that it is beyond cognitional reach. It is this situation that haunts man and leads to adumbrations or ciphering. It is in this setting that Jaspers defines man as "the being who glimpses God." In a recent essay, entitled *What Is Man?** he goes on to assert that "only in this relation to Transcendence does man gain awareness of himself as a free being."

It should be pointed out that Jaspers, while a theist, is skeptical of revelation. To him, it would be an attack on man's freedom. He also rejects Christian doctrines as mythical and too easily leading to intolerance.

Let us now try to formulate the essentials of his outlook. The sciences

---

*_Universitas_, Vol. 8, 1965.

deal with phenomena which are cognitionally objective. But they do not reach existence itself. This is to be assigned to a noumenal reality to be called the Encompassing or, in German, the *Umgreifende*. This surrounds and plays into human situations but is transcendent to them. In the strict sense, existence, or being, as Santayana might say, is beckoned to but not intuited. The nearest to such awareness comes, I suppose, in what existentialists call *Angst* or metaphysical dread. But it is to be noted that Jaspers does not stress anxiety and even speaks of peace. "The immutability of God is a cipher of this peace."

The time has now come for rebuttal. The first point I would make is epistemological. I hold that we have knowledge about material things; and these are not phenomena. To know is not to construct but to achieve facts about. This operation begins with perceiving in which we referentially use the information about things conveyed in our sensations under the control of the things perceived. From this starting point, man builds up concepts of things and their relations in a controlled and tested way. This involves a process of learning. We do not have to appeal to innate forms but, at most, to abilities. Science adds methods of experimentation and interrogation. But I think it passes quite logically from molar things to their components. I cannot accept the view that so-called scientific objects are merely constructs. This stance was taken, it will be recalled, by Marcel and by Thomists in general.

The realism I uphold is this, a physical realism. How, then, do I think of what exists? Is it something which escapes cognition as Jaspers, with his Kantian background, holds? As I see it, existence is a term for *status*. When I ask the question, Do lions exist? or Are there lions? I am seeking to know whether there are living and perceptible things to which I can apply the concept lion. If so, lions have the status of existence. I recognize the importance of these little words, *am, be, exist*. They reflect a basic realism. They are ontological in import and connect up with perceiving and manipulation. Thence they spread out to apply to the components of things. If this foundation is denied, one founders and ciphers, as Jaspers does.

As a materialist, I am confronted with Thomist creationalism. In the next chapter I shall comment on Tillich's Augustinianism. As we all know, creationalism was a Hebrew and not a Greek idea. It belonged to the mythical and semi-magical outlook of tales rather than to the Ionian question of what things are made of. Dramatic, impressive tales, of course.

As I understand it, Thomism introduces a dichotomy of the metaphysical principles, essence and *hylé*, on the one side and existence, as a creative act of being, on the other. The materialist rejects both sides of this dichotomy. He, as it were, deflates them. Things and processes are factually knowable but this is a knowledge-about and not the grasping of an essence. Modern idealism made the mistake of trying to reduce *what is* to ideas. Its motivations were fairly clear, romantic desire and puzzlement. Thomism, on the other hand, approached from theistic beliefs to modify Aristotelianism. But I take it that Greek atomism had the sounder hunch, though largely speculative. Modern science has had to work *upwards* from the inorganic world while constantly modifying its principles. What I have tried to do is to furnish it with an epistemology or, at least, a direction for its epistemology. This is in terms of knowledge about, including a constant revision of categorial knowledge about space, time, causality, life, purpose. And I think that the master idea of evolution has been at work here. I do not think that Jaspers did justice to this, partly because he dismissed naturalism out of hand. One interesting feature of Aristotelianism is that it took levels in nature for granted but as something inherent in nature.

But let us leave epistemology and examine a sort of ontological question which scientific cosmology largely ignores but which has been thrown up by philosophy and theology as a sort of puzzlement. This can be called the question of *aseity*. Materialism locates aseity in matter and energy while theology locates it in God. The principle of conservation can, I take it, be correlated with that of aseity. Let us approach it from this angle. People sometimes ask the following question, Might the universe not have existed? If so, why did it come into existence? Obviously, the same question could be asked of theism. Why was there a God? The usual answer is that His essence involved existence. But it will be recalled that I was skeptical of the validity of this notion of essence. The materialist does not consider that it is a metaphysical principle.

In these days, one turns to what is called the logic of language which, of course, is the logic of concepts. One asks what the question means. It is hardly a factual question. If one decides that it is meaningless to say that the universe exists by a sort of logical necessity, it follows that, logically speaking, it might not have existed. They are the two sides of one coin. It seems best, then, to consider the universe as an existential fact. It clearly is and seems to conserve itself. Is there, then, any good reason to assume that it had a beginning? That would be to suppose that it was either created or came out of nothing. The first horn of this dilemma would seem to beg the question and the second seems to be meaningless. Hence the conclusion that the universe is eternal, that is, always was. That is the meaning, as I see it, of aseity.

To come back to Sartre, I was surprised by what he seems to read into the contingency, that is, the undeducibility of the world. It seems to imply for him irrationality and meaninglessness, on a cosmic scale. But undeducibility and irrationality are not identical. Here I see a divergence of background between our empirical traditions and those of the continent. There can, clearly, be order in the inorganic world. As for purpose, that is an ability which has slowly emerged in the biological realm. This view undercuts much of Sartre's rhetoric. Matter, as conceived to-day, is also not an inert plenitude. That seems to go with his inspectional type of realism, his consciousness of. It all strikes me as a *tour-de-force*. But this does not mean that I do not take seriously questions of philosophical anthropology. Man was nature's most remarkable experiment. What will he do with himself? Make living pleasanter by the integration of loving kindness and intelligence? Or will it be drift? Or will it be self-annihilation? I do not think it is predetermined. In social affairs I find that I largely applaud Sartre, just as I am impressed by Camus.

Heidegger

I come, finally, in studying this cluster of labelled existentialists to Heidegger, a rather enigmatic thinker. I understand that he regards himself as primarily an ontologist. Like Jaspers, he wrestles with Kant but also interrogates early Greek thought for verbal cues. It appears that he resorts to his own versions of etymology to wring secrets from words. I, myself, see him immersed in a framework and traditions quite different from my own. I have read some painstaking expositions which, at least, cast light on his endeavors. I judge that Heidegger departed from Kierkegaard, Kant and Husserl. He seems to have departed from Husserl's bracketing to throw man into the world.

The first stage of his thought involves a concern with the world of practical life. Here he sounds rather pragmatic as, I understand, Dewey recognized. There is also this stress on projects and the future in Sartre. I, of course, have nothing against it.

Taken thus, the world into which man is thrown is a world of things at hand. It is by their very nature that they can be made into tools and put to use. But reflection brings a break and one passes to a kind of speculative distancing, to what Heidegger calls, in German, *Vorhandenheit*.

It is from this outlook, he argues, that Greek and Western thinking in general has taken its departure. Out of it has come stress on substance, independence and impersonal repetition. It is, I take it, fundamentally descriptive. Now it is Heidegger's aim to come back to what he regards as the more primary outlook which centers in man. Here, if anywhere, one can get a new look at Being. And so we find the stress on care, on time as a projective activity and on death as a disclosure of Nothingness. Negation comes to the front, not as merely logical, but as a *Nicht*-ing, a destroying. Out of this approach arises a new understanding of Being, as something turbulent and not merely repetitive. One is, I suppose, more on the inside of Being.

In this way, ontology gets a new foundation. It is qualitatively deepened. In the very texture of his life man becomes aware of Being. And, at this point, there is the note of vertical transcendence which might point to theism, though Heidegger, unlike Jaspers, is reluctant to press it. This awareness of Being should bring with it a demand for authenticity in life. Sartre made somewhat the same move in trying to authenticate moral engagement. The note of moral valuation enters. The average human life is a *falling away* from Being to the things around him. Heidegger's vocabulary is vivid and colloquial. Being is hidden. Being seems to function as a substitute for the God of a theocentric ethics.

Now I, as a naturalist, would lay more stress on the emergence of self-consciousness in the context of group-life, drives, and value appraisals. I would be quite willing to call this an emergent level of existence, with features of its own. I would hardly personify something called Being.

Technically, what is interesting in Heidegger is a turning away from traditional approaches to a search for something more of the nature of an intuition. One is reminded of Marcel's ontic intuition. One is not surprised, then, when Heidegger turns away from the correspondence theory of truth to what he calls an *unveiling*. It is this shift, I suppose that leads Heidegger to explore language and poetry for hints. He also turns to early Greek philosophy for indications of this unveiling. One finds references to Goethe, Hölderlin, and Rilke with this in mind. Thus in his *Satz vom Grund*, he quotes these lines from Goethe.

"Doch Forschung strebt und ringt, ermüdend nie,
Nach dem Gesetz, dem Grund; Warum und Wie."

It is the old search of speculative philosophy for a path to a transcendent Source of Being. And it has its own vocabulary. The stress is on intuition. One can see the continued influence of Kierkegaard in this search for unveiling.

And yet, as I reread Heidegger's *Introduction to Metaphysics*, I find that I can see an analogy with my own physical realism. To me, knowing can be regarded as a disclosure, a factual unconcealment. I take the term, true, to stand for an endorsement of a knowledge-claim. But I stress more the mechanism of human knowing. I, also, am an ontologist, a realist. *What is* includes both being and becoming and, at the human level, appearing and thinking. But, for me, existence signifies the assignment of a status and a recognition of what is. And I feel less, perhaps, than Heidegger the contrast between being and nothing. It is within the immanence of the material world with all its variety and richness that the sciences are working.

It is fairly clear, then, that Heidegger is trying to work beyond Kant while Jaspers retains his boundaries.

And this concludes my analysis of continental existentialism. One can understand the emotional reaction of the logical positivists. But it would have been better if they had not sought to brush aside points in epistemology and ontology with such disdain. And I am still curious as to why all these movements saw no appeal in materialism. In this, I fear, they were socially conventional.

What, then, is the human situation? I think we are becoming increasingly aware of its uniqueness and its precariousness. As I see it, man's life is not predetermined but is more of the nature of a continuing exploration. There is the element of freedom, which goes back to his problem-solving equipment. But it is a freedom which always works within a context of personal and social history. Absolute spontaneity of the Sartrean sort would be a disaster. But the hope is that wisdom with its mixture of restraint and intelligent appraisal will increase to qualify habit and impulse. In asking about man, in a somewhat melodramatic fashion, existentialism made a contribution. In the next chapter, I shall examine some theological reverberations. In these days of linguistic consciousness they are taking rather startling semantic forms. There is, sometimes, an almost Elizabethan richness in vocabulary. John Donne might feel at home.

11

RELIGIOUS EXISTENTIALISM, SECULARISM AND HUMANISM

Since this book is semi-autobiographical, I shall begin this chapter with some quotations from my first book on religion, *The Next Step in Religion*, which introduced humanism in a systematic way to the English-speaking world. This was before John Dewey, Sir Julian Huxley and others became spokesmen for a similar outlook. I followed it by a later book, called *Religion Coming of Age*. Both of these books have long been out of print but they had some effect in helping to initiate the humanist movement. And it led me to compose the *Humanist Manifesto*, as sponsored by a group of humanists and signed by many distinguished men. So it would seem that I have some historical standing in the field of religion as well as in epistemology and ontology.

The Next Step in Religion

Glancing over the books on religion, I find that I was more rhetorical than I would be now. I was, obviously, under more tension. I quote: "But, having explored the universe by telescope and microscope, and having thus come to some understanding of his world, man must return again to his own pressing problems and possibilities, to his need to interpret his own good, to his desire to further and maintain those interests and activities in which he finds self-expression. His own life, as a realm of affection and action, must rightly be for him the significant center of the universe. These urgencies, interests, possibilities, satisfactions, loyalties are inalienably human and valid. He can no more ignore them than he can his hunger for food and his thirst for water. Nothing can rob him of the values which he has created, nor can any one take from him the burden of courageous endeavor. He is the master of his own destiny and the prompter in his own drama. In his tenser moments, the physical spaces around his planet will but contain: "the endless, silly merriment of stars.""

"As religion learns to relinquish theology and accept the modern view of the world, the spirituality it has fostered will mate with reason. Reason by itself is not enough; feeling by itself is not enough."*

And so I go on to a question of semantics about the status of such terms as religion, theology and philosophy. Such status will, of course, be settled only by the drift of social thought. I find that Americans like now to speak of *their* philosophy, that is, of their outlook in business, politics, what will you. Religion is still regarded as something inherited. They are Protestant, Roman Catholic or Jewish. Here a feeble dialogue is, at most, beginning. It is not good form to press issues.

But, if I am not mistaken, philosophy is becoming more outspoken and radical. I wrote some fifty years ago of religion learning "to relinquish theology." Such a phrase is two-directional. It hints at a changing religion as well as the relinquishment of theology. In between, as more or less symbolic, can arise the question of a new theology. Or the expression, Philosophical Theology, can be adopted as by Anthony Flew and Alastair MacIntyre.** Here even the question of whether the existence of God can be disproved is raised. And, even as I write, an American book comes to hand querying the existence of God.*** And, astonishing enough, the Nietzschean question, Is God dead? is debated in campus and seminary. It is clearly a new day. More is on the cards than a disavowal of the biblical and Medieval three-story universe.

Under these circumstances, I thought it well to examine the basic alternatives which are manifesting themselves. On the one hand, I shall take Paul Tillich as an outstanding exponent of an identification of Being-Itself with God. Here we get down to ontological fundamentals. And man, we are told, is a metaphysical animal. And, in a way, I think the reflective man may well be so, that is, concerned with foundations on which to build. And here I take the evolutionary perspective with its stress on locality and novelty. Tillich speaks alternately of Abyss and of Transcendence. I, of this earth, this might-be *demi-paradise,* were man not his worst enemy. And, as a realistic materialist, as one who stresses levels in nature, I stand out against what I consider bad traditions in philosophy; also against the denigration of those interwoven realities, matter and energy, which come to flower on the surface of this planet. As I understand it, molecular chemistry is giving a hand to biology and physiological behaviorism, in its turn to psychology.

---

*Sellars, *The Next Step in Religion,* 1918, Macmillan, p. 218.

**New Essays in Philosophical Theology,* Macmillan.

***Matson, *The Existence of God,* Cornell.

Fortunately, I have been able to prepare the way in preceding chapters. Thus, I have spoken out against Cartesian dualism and against the odd kind of subjectivism which ensued in British empiricism. I have tried to show the objective import of perceiving and its mechanics. Upon this objective import of human knowing man, I have sought to show, grafted his appraisals and norms in which his feelings are brought to bear upon his projects. The ground is thus laid for a humanistic approach to ethics which avoids both supernatural commands and arbitrary relativism. This is in line with the "good reasons" outlook which is beginning to dominate ethical theory. "Ought" is a socially evolved category which, as Konrad Lorenz has shown in his recent remarkable book on *Human Aggression*, has its analogues in *animal ritual*.

T₁illich and Whitehead

In connection with Tillich, I shall make some comments on White-head's reformed subjectivism. I met Whitehead first when I was in London in 1922 to give a lecture before the Aristotelian Society on my double-knowledge approach to the mind-body issue, a form of the identity theory. In this chapter I oppose Whitehead's panpsychistic *process* analysis to my own "causal process," emergence outlook. Here I stress integrative causality with novelty as against Whitehead's Principle of Concrescence. The idea of causal process is an older idea than White-head's and I protest the arrogance of Whiteheadians in designating theirs as the sole process theory. But that is the way "winds of doctrine" go. I, at the same time, protest against the caricature of the category of substantiality common to Russell and Whitehead. Organization and dispositional properties must be recognized. There need be nothing static about dynamic equilibrium in chemistry or physics. And factual knowledge-about does not, in my epistemology, imply properties stuck on like cloves into an unknowable substratum. What we know is the composition and modes of behaving of denotable things.

So much in the way of anticipation. I want to be, in the confrontations before us, as determinate as possible. But before I take up Tillich and Whitehead, I wish to say a few words on the topics of secularism, scientism and humanism. It is on the interplay of these attitudes in human society that the future of mankind will depend.

Secularism, I take it, expresses a concentration on human affairs of a this-worldly type. It connects up with interest in the economic sides of life along with literature, politics and science. It is usually regarded as involving a turning away from the religious perspective and its motivations. Its rise in the modern world is usually associated with the Renaissance and with the eighteenth-century Enlightenment, though its massive and impersonal development has gone with industrialization and large-scale means of communication.

Scientism usually appeared as a term of mild reproach against tendencies of being dominated by the scientific outlook and its procedures and methods. These tendencies are regarded as inimical to the religious outlook, its traditions and perspective. Often the stress is laid on the inorganic sciences with remembrance of the so-called warfare between science and religion. Anthropology and psychology are, however, now coming to the front.

There are both positive definitions of humanism and dissuasive ones. The dissuasive ones ordinarily take the form of protest against the reduction of Christianity to "mere humanism." A true humanism, it is said, is an integral one. As I see it, the core of humanism is an emphasis on human activities and values and a rational concern for their clarification and extension.

Humanism, so taken, has tended to be an ingredient qualifying both secularism and scientism and calling attention to the need for broad horizons and the human touch. I take it that it has in this much in common with the traditions of philosophy. Both aim at viewing the whole scene comprehensively, while regarding nothing human as alien. The standing of humanism has varied but I shall try, in this chapter, to show that developments point in its direction.

It is not the strategy of a professional philosopher to avoid problems but, rather, to face them. And it is for this reason that I shall give so much space to Paul Tillich and religious existentialism. And it is, likewise, for this reason that I make my comments on Whitehead and his followers. I am persuaded that the time is at hand when the nature and mechanism of human knowing, as a well-prepared achievement, are at last being deciphered. And man is being seen in his ontological, epistemological and axiological context. That is, as a Being, a knower, and an appraiser. I early began such a synthesis and realized that it would involve the explicit restatement of materialism in emergent and evolutionary terms. It is understandable that philosophers have largely shied away from this task. It involved a breakthrough in epistemology for which they were not prepared, a grappling with the locus and status of mind, an appreciation of the objective import of valuation and its linguistic differences from descriptive knowledge. All this was no easy matter. Yet it had to be done, somehow together. I think that both Dewey and Russell made efforts in this direction but not incisively enough. I have in mind Lange also and how, finally, he held back and retired to the Kantian compromise. Huxley took the path of Hume in his discussions with Tyndall; and we owe to him that weasel word, agnosticism. But I think the time has come for basic confrontations and decisions. Man is a child of nature.

What Is Man?

But what is man? Not, as the existentialists are fond of saying, a mere thing. Let us run over some definitions advanced. A tool-making and using animal, now full of gadgetry. A social animal. A language-employing animal. A rational animal. An historical animal. A metaphysical animal. He is all of these and, thereby, unique for this earth at least. But, just as there are *dissuasive* definitions of humanism so there are dissuasive definitions of animal. Man, it is said, is not a mere animal. But he is the paragon of animal life except that he has learned to be a killer at long distances in an institutionalized way. He is an intra-species killer, as hardly any other animal is. His morality has not caught up with his abilities. But I must leave this topic to my planned book on political and social philosophy called *Social Patterns and Horizons*, which I plan as a sequel.

It is time that I plunged into religious existentialism and White-headism as positions I want to confront. To them and to their allied "Encounter" strategies I want to oppose my reformed, or new, material-ism and humanism. It should at least be stimulating.

I have already made my objections to philosophical existentialism clear. It was not that it stressed the human condition but that it added so little to the technical equipment of philosophy and did not "engage" with science in a comprehensive debate. It had about it the touch of the parochial, of the culturally isolated. It seemed to ignore the logical, linguistic and epistemological explorations of British and American philosophy. Its chief novelty seemed to be its emphasis on *Angst* and metaphysical dread. I did not object to its contrast between being and *nothingness* for the logical contingency of the world had to be understood. But I could not see that Kierkegaard had faced up to the alternative we are pondering in our day, namely, naturalism, in his dramatic leap of faith. To turn to him would be like turning to Emerson's Transcendentalism, which no one thinks of doing. This raises the question of perspective. For instance,

I ask myself just why did Sartre turn to German philosophy for his foundations. Was it because he got a chance to study in Berlin? Or was it because British and American philosophy did not seem to him to have the proper dramatic touch? Well, it is my belief that grappling in earnest with materialism as an ontology can supply that. I tried to show that he brushed off materialism too jauntily. And it should be evident that I hold that British and American philosophy did not dig deeply enough. Logical positivism is already *passé* and I would not bet on a long life for "ordinary language." These are "winds of doctrine." When, then, I speak approvingly of British and American philosophy I have a longer tradition in mind. It is this that I have tried to bring to the front in prior chapters. Just because Marxism is materialistic in outlook is no good reason why we should ignore materialism. It had its intriguing queries all along the line. If analytic philosophy has sharpened philosophy's tools, this is a good area in which to use them.

Perspective

What I am going to aim at in this chapter is perspective. Consequently, a brief review may be in order. It is my intention to pass from it to a consideration of overtly religious forms of existentialism and to confront these with the naturalistic humanism which I, myself, regard as the preferable alternative.

I began with a consideration of Sartre's foundations and principles. I concluded that neither his epistemology nor his ontology was well founded. I studied perceptual claims rather than his "consciousness" with its postulated awareness of being-in-itself. And I argued that even elementary cognitive judgments rested on a biological foundation of sensory equipment and behavioral use of sensory information. In so using sensations we gain factual knowledge about the objects around us. Knowledge is, accordingly, a mediated achievement, arrived at step by step. It has had a long, evolutionary preparation.

Sartre, on the other hand, based his outlook on a modification of Husserl's phenomenology, an attempt to dig deeper within it to avoid its stress on the self. But I think that he still gives what he calls consciousness a rather magical ability to inspect something other than itself. I, on the other hand, regard awareness as a resultant of an interplay in which sensations are used as cues to referential response. It is as though we looked through the visual field at the object. It is as though we inspected it. As I see it, it is in this fashion that we develop the notion of *consciousness of*. What we really gain are informationally transmitted facts about objects, quite an achievement.

All this is important. Because Sartre builds so much on the status of spontaneity he has taken consciousness to be a sort of hole in causal being. I take freedom to connect up with abilities of problem-solving, involving my own view of consciousness as resting on the informational use of sensations and images and the development of symbol-thinking. I would stress here agential causality rather than predetermined actions.

All in all, then, I find Sartre stimulating rather than foundational. Turning to Marcel, my complaint was that he moved too quickly from the human situation, dominated by the human body and the sense of existing or living. That is, he adopted a metaphysical extension of being of the Thomistic sort as over against what I would call a naturalistic recognition of existence as status assignable to the causal, spatial and temporal realm of which we humans are a part. To say that what we describe exists is to give it a referent in this realm and thus existential status. I cannot, myself, find any indication of a special act-of-being and assume that it reflects the idea of creating out of nothingness, that is, adding to essences. The burden of proof seems to me to rest on theism and creationalism. I just accept the brute fact that there are things, that is, describable actualities.

I was rather puzzled by Marcel's mysteries. I can understand problems but they seem to me to point to factual comprehension and then to adjustment. Just what is this participation in being which Marcel sets up? I could not but feel that a remnant of idealistic epistemology operated in it, as Hocking supposed. Of course, we engage ourselves with other beings and even communicate with some, even with cats and dogs; but is this literal participation?

There is a good deal of literary philosophy in Marcel and that has both its good and its bad sides.

Turning now to the German existentialists, I find a more marked appeal to Kierkegaard and Nietzsche. But there is a divergence between Jaspers and Heidegger. Jaspers stays more within the Kantian framework while Heidegger seeks to escape from it by concentration on ontology. We saw that Jaspers stresses the desirability of transcending the Kantian subject-object frame. He postulates boundary conditions which, while not permeable by cognition, invites to ciphers and symbols. I, on the other hand, reject the Kantian construction and hold that it is the external world, itself, that we perceive and decipher by means of the use of sensuous indications. This approach undercuts Jaspers' effort at a semi-thwarted transcendence of the subject-object frame. I have the impression that German thinkers have not explored the idea of evolutionary levels and the rise therein of awareness, knowing and appraisal. Cultural isolation, undoubtedly, had much to do with this neglect.

Turning to Heidegger, I have the impression that he seeks to press through to an ontology in a less wavering way than does Jaspers. So far, so good. He turns back to Greek origins and to poetry for his inspiration. He takes truth to be an unveiling of reality and is thus rather Platonic in his perspective. Being is contrasted with nothingness, on the one hand, and with becoming, appearing, and thinking, on the other. Sheer linguistic intuition is demanded. I recognize his intensity. And yet here, too, as in the case of Jaspers, I note the Kantian subject-object frame. It is within this that his verbalized intuition works. It strikes me that this perspective limits his endeavor. That is, he is trying to press through an artificial barrier, almost by will power and verbal ingenuity. I suggest, again, that a more empirical and realistic approach might have freed him from these shackles. Man is not so much "thrown into the world"—his contingency—but born into it with an inherited genepool. Perceiving is an activity which has slowly emerged from humble beginnings. Out of this come factual claims and references and, at long last, scientific method. I would confront, more than Heidegger does, the mind-body equation and the emergence of novelty in nature. A new kind of materialism might then become a living option to replace the reductive type of the past. I would welcome a man of Heidegger's ability to such an exploration and it would represent a breaking down of cultural blockages. I cannot help thinking that such a development might well stimulate American thinkers who, so often, look abroad in a mood of discipleship. It would lead to a vital interplay of minds. For I am one of those who have the belief that American thinkers have not been idle.

To conclude this summary, I would say that an emphasis on human *Existenz* was desirable but that it was given a background of "fear and trembling" which was dated. Undoubtedly, the great wars had something to do with this stress on "metaphysical dread." And it may well be that it aided the revival of ontology as against the smugness of logical positivism. A certain wonderment about existence, a standing back and looking at nature and life, should be encouraged. It might even take the interrogative form of the question, Why is there anything and not merely "nothingness"? But such an interrogation should not be allowed to get out of hand but be encouraged to lead to disciplined thought. It has its semantics and its logic. Popular thought has been taught to take the road of theism and creationalism. But there is an alternative which should also be explored, that of the acceptance of nature. A debate between these two stands should be interesting. It is for this reason that I am now going to examine religious existentialism and confront it with naturalistic humanism. The whole spectrum of philosophy will be involved from ontology to theory of knowledge and to recent theories of the nature and status of values. I am going to put particular stress on the role and status of values for there has been too much obscurantism here. I, myself, hold that there are good and relevant reasons to *justify* moral and other appraisals and that the old contrast between relativity and absoluteness is outmoded. Essentially, absoluteness signified something of the nature of commands, theocentric, or traditional, while relativity indicated contextual qualifications of such demands and the setting up of new norms. As I see it, the requirement of justification shifts to an emphasis upon experience and reflection. Working rules are judged in terms of consequences for human well-being. Morals turns out to be an affair of intelligent appraisal with its own language. In this context, Hume's contrast between *is* and *ought* has its explanation.

Tillich Again

I am going to examine in considerable detail Paul Tillich's philosophy and theology. Barth and Brunner did not pretend to be philosophers but devoted themselves to the Christian message, or *Kerygma*. Revelation was just a fact to the man of faith. The Reverend "Billy" Graham belongs, of course, to this tradition. If I am right in my analysis, such evangelism belongs to an historical stage which is being outgrown. That will, naturally, take time, especially when the powers that be favor it. But I anticipate that, when history is rewritten, wars and persecutions will be seen in a better perspective. I am told that the "angry young men" of the present generation do not think highly of the wisdom of their parents. Since I always disagreed with these parents, I sympathize with them. But human affairs are always a tangle.

There is one feature of Tillich's philosophy and theology to which I want to direct attention. It is the identification of God with Being-Itself. Seeing the increasingly recognized weakness of the Thomistic proofs of God's existence, that was good strategy. But what if Being-Itself turned out to be matter and energy and that it was from this that life and intelligence emerged? We shall keep this alternative before us. I think the Ionians were nearer right in asking what things are made of than the Jews in postulating a Creator. But what a dramatic setting the Jews achieved with covenant, punishment, and mercy from on high? It was mythopoeic construction of the highest order. But where was the testing? We are now reminded of Buber's "I—Thou" encounter. It is a gambit which will be replayed many times. What I shall be concerned to show is that there is an alternative which should be taken seriously and explored. Man must learn to stand on his own feet, know himself for what he is and his world for what it is.

But let us come back to Tillich. He was entirely Germanic in his training. He was at once a philosopher of the Kantian, Husserl, existentialist perspective and a Christian theologian, taking pride in working on the boundaries between the two disciplines. While teaching at Marburg, he came in contact with Heidegger. He speaks also of Bergson, Schelling and Böhme. So far as I can make out from some autobiographical remarks of his, his epistemological training was of the neo-Kantian variety. Kantianism is opposed to a direct, physical realism such as I worked out in connection with an analysis of perceiving. One gets *into* a cognitive framework instead, that of a subject in relation to an object. But it seems clear to me that we make things objects and gain facts about them. This is the line of breakthrough from Cartesian dualism and phenomenalism. But it forces one to take materialistic naturalism seriously.

Now, in scanning Tillich's statements, I have found no awareness of *this sort of approach*. It was rather distinctively American and went with the growing interaction of philosophy and science taking place here. Even the Viennese logical positivists seem to have had no consciousness of this kind of epistemological development for they made sensations terminal. And I have argued that Russell's type of empiricism had much the same, traditional framework. Since I am going to move from my kind of direct realism to emergent materialism and naturalistic humanism, this different foundation should be noted. We have pointed out the Kantian framework in Jaspers and Heidegger. Let me here call attention to a statement by Tillich in his reply to his critics, a statement very definite in import. It is on page 334 of the book, *The Theology of Paul Tillich*. There he asserts, "The unsymbolic statement which implies the necessity of religious symbolism is that God is being itself, and *as such beyond the subject-object structure of everything that is.*"

Here we find, in a nutshell, the foundation of his ontology and of his apparently daring assertions that God does not exist. That is, that He is beyond existence. He is the Abyss, the Ground. It is for this reason, among others, that he rejects the Thomistic proofs for the existence of God. God is not a being among other beings. To set up anything and give it divine status is idolatry. As we well know, Niebuhr and others have used this schema very effectively in their political and social rhetoric. God should not thus be mocked.

But, from the side of philosophy, there remains the question, What is the basis of this ontology? How does Tillich get to Being-Itself, to this Ground, or Abyss, to which all symbols are tied? Well, as nearly as I can make out, he moves to it along Platonic and Augustinian lines. A modern realist is immediately suspicious for he remembers how Plato dealt with sense-perception in the *Theaetetus*. Perceptions are affairs of flux and the impermanent. They are more non-being than being. To get knowledge one must turn to intellectual apprehension of constants, such as forms. Mathematics is a better starting-point than perception.

It will be recalled that Aristotle sought to get back to perception and away from Plato's supersensible realm of Ideas. But he still had enough of Platonism to postulate immaterial forms as transmitted to the percipient. But we need not go into our criticism of neo-Thomism and its *sensible species*, so ably presented by Maritain. It is more relevant to consider the Augustinian view of knowing. It is interesting to remember that Protestant thought turned away from Aristotle and scholasticism to Plato and Saint Augustine. I think that Professor Randall is right in treating Tillich as belonging to the Augustinian tradition as enlarged by German idealism. Certainly, Tillich paid little attention to Locke and empirical developments. He was a liberal, however, and valued modern science and art highly.

What I am concerned with then is perspective and emphases. As a theologian he was existentially concerned with God as Being-Itself and with what he accepted as the Kerygma, or message, contained in the bible. He differed from Brunner and Barth, who did not dabble in philosophy but were expositors of what, by an act of faith, they regarded as God's Word.

As I see it, then, Tillich began with a theistic ontology in an Augustinian way and fitted his epistemology to it. Kantian epistemology was to be subordinated to it as relevant to existing things. What is primary, then, for a knowledge terminating in basic ontology is a kind of participation in true being, a participation which unites love and cognition. But this kind of cognition seems to work largely in terms of symbols elicited from encounters. This gives what Tillich called a "belief-ful or self-transcending realism." It is existentialist in that it is tied in with what he called ultimate concern. In its orientation, it is a theocentric religion of the Hebraic-Christian type. Now humanism is often called anthropocentric, though it does not neglect the scientific view of the world and locates man's place in it as indicated by the best knowledge obtained. I do not think that anthropocentric means selfish but what the existentialists of the philosophical line would call a recognition of the human situation. Maritain seeks to unite the two orientations in what he calls integral humanism. As we have noted, Tillich identifies being with God. His outlook is theocentric. God is the Totally Other, the Unconditioned. And yet his message tells us that he accepts us and becomes a *Thou* to our *I*. Faith must give us the courage to be.

I do not belittle the dramatic intensity of the outlook which has back of it Jewish priestly and prophetic thought and the brooding reflections of Christian saints and theologians. To me, however, it is a mythopoeic creation, a projection of thoughts and feeling in pietistic or in logically systematic form. And, as I shall indicate later, I have great admiration for many of its dialectically patterned constructions. But I want now to contrast the two paths which seem to me open, the naturalistic one and the theistic. Justice must be done to both. It is, after that, a question of personal decision.

The two philosophical entrances are epistemology and ontology; and I want to study both. I shall examine, first, Tillich and add, for good measure, some remarks on the Whitehead-Hartshorne panpsychistic, process perspective. After that, I shall present the kind of emergent naturalism which seems to me to go with my view of the rise and development of our knowledge of the world. It will be recalled that Tillich seems not to have explored the possibilities of the Lockean gambit. I, on the other hand, sought to press beyond it to a direct, critical realism.

The matrix of Tillich's philosophy, if I judge correctly, is a fusion of Kantianism, Platonism and German idealism with undertones of Husserlian phenomenology. This is a heady mixture, especially when it is suffused with theological motivations. Through it shines a very honest and enlightened personality. But is it valid?

Let us now see to what it leads. Back of phenomenological analysis of essences or structure is to be found a kind of awareness of reality as a whole. Human experience contains encounters which indicate this confrontation with Being-Itself. This is the sense of the Unconditioned, which is analogous to Jaspers' transcending *Ungreifende* and clearly has a similar existentialistic provenance. Tillich admits the need of a kind of epistemological "justification by faith." Let us bear in mind the point that Being-Itself, which is thus affirmed, is to blossom into a God beyond the God of Thomistic proofs. This is because it is that which underlies existing things. It is the Ground, the Abyss. It is both transcendent and an underpinning. Böhmean mysticism fuses here with Platonic transcendence to produce something analogous to Anselm's ontological argument. As is well known, there were anticipations of this in Hegelian idealism and in Hocking's version of it in America.

I think that I must permit myself to set in contrast the much more matter-of-fact confrontation with material things which I have emphasized in perceiving, handling and behavior. Even Marcel started here though he soon extrapolated to Thomistic Being. I must confess that I am very skeptical of Tillich's by-passing the world around us, which we deal with in everyday life and which science is investigating so meticulously, to try to peer into something called Being-Itself. I cannot help feeling that Plato and Kant gave bad leads here which Tillich is following. I antedated logical positivism, which seemed to me epistemologically naive, in favor of a direct, physical realism. I have only noted one reference to materialism in his *Reply* and that is on page 333. And that merely points to the fact that the materialist must have his theory of the rise of thought in man, something I grappled with in *Critical Realism* (1916) and in later writings.

What, then, I am calling attention to is that Tillich makes his precarious leap of faith to Being-Itself in the setting of philosophical traditions very much alive in the Germany of his time but being challenged in the United States of my era. It is in this way an importation of the post-war period of what is usually called neo-orthodoxy. I met this "wave of the future," somewhat to my surprise, as modernism was making its transition to humanism. I taught a course in the *Philosophy of Religion* at the University and had to keep familiar with religious currents. I must confess that I was rather astonished by Barth, Brunner and Niebuhr. I tried to size them up as between liberalism and biblical fundamentalism. I shall later say something about them. None of them pretended to be philosophers and Barth had some derogatory remarks to make on philosophy of religion. But Tillich, as we have noted, worked on the boundary line between theology and philosophy. What I am trying to bring out is the divergence between his approach to philosophy and my own. And I think it would hold in some measure for the pragmatists, though, as I have tried to show, I was not satisfied with Dewey's use of the word, *experience,* and what seemed to me a shying away from epistemology. I said that I would give some attention to the Whitehead-Hartshorne "reformed subjectivism" approach, which, of course, is frankly adverse to my form of emergent materialism. I think that man emerges and must learn to stand on his own feet—not always an easy thing to do, especially when he gets too much technical power. I have always thought of Whitehead as a sort of magnificent "last hope" of idealism.

But to return to Tillich. I take his Being-Itself as an echo of Kant's noumenal world beyond phenomenal existence. It is much the sort of thing one has in Jaspers and Heidegger. It comes to a reification of what I have called the *status of existence* apart from existing things. And then he begins to inflate it in terms of what he calls the "depth of reason" and an ontological reason which grasps and shapes reality to attain an approach to an objective Logos, all of which savors of romantic idealism. I would have some hope in his technical reason but that it is too merely instrumental and is of the same vintage as Heidegger's first stage of practical dealing with objects before he is shaken by "metaphysical dread" into his effort at intensive intuition. I would, myself, distinguish the practical and the theoretical in a less ecstatic manner and would have the theoretical play back into the practical. Dewey sought to do this but he was, I think, handicapped by a kind of experientialist foreshortening. He was too afraid of what he called "mirroring" an external world. I have argued that things supply information about themselves—something science makes the effort to increase—and that human cognition is a kind of aided deciphering.

As I see it, Tillich turns his back on this kind of orientation with its stress on evidence and proceeds to inflate—I know no better word—a supposed supersensible world of Being-Itself which, as I said, must be regarded as a reification of the status of existence cut off from existing things. As we should expect, this device has its antecedents in both Plato and Kant, though formulated differently. I am convinced that it is a temptation which philosophy must live down. I have always had a respect for Aristotle's effort to do so. And I think that Thomism was a gesture in that direction but burdened too much as yet with the demands of Christian supernaturalism. That I can understand; I have a well developed historical sense. But I suspect that Saint Thomas, or his intellectual peer, if living to-day, would have a different perspective. I cannot quite raise Maritain to this level, even though I respect him highly.

Significance and Fact

A few words now, in conclusion, about Tillich's rationalization of revelation and his Christology. As I understand it, he holds that "ecstatic reason"—more or less a term for the emotional leap of faith—takes "sign events" as indications of significance bearing on God's plan and purpose. This is linked with man's "ultimate concern." I take it that Tillich avoids physical miracles in the fundamentalist sense and its view of the supernatural. His emphasis is on God's working in history, much as Niebuhr's is. I, myself, find it hard to see how this belief can be tested in the multiform currents of history. I would stress detailed knowledge of events and circumstances and such light as cultural anthropology, economics and sociology would add. I could say much on this topic for I have been a teacher of political and social philosophy but this is not the place. I may say that Niebuhr has, for polemic purposes, exaggerated the naiveté of liberalism. Professors Lovejoy and Frankel have made some good points in rebuttal. I have listened to recent "dialogues" of the fashionable sort but they always struck me as rather low level. I sometimes fear that American culture tends in these matters to be of a second-class type. Foreigners always remark on the inhibition of discussion in American society. I am sure that Tillich would not have favored such inhibitions. My regret is that his own teaching was so much of a *red herring*, at once intriguing and bewildering. It burst in from outside and was, I hold, already anachronistic. I should myself like to see Americans wrestle with Marxism in a less scared way and Marxism, itself, confront liberal, realistic thought.

Tillich's affirmation of the revelation of "the new Being in Jesus as the Christ" is, of course, theological. I am here only as an historian and have followed the results of scholarship with great interest. It is generally acknowledged how little we know of the origins of Christianity. The "form" technique stresses the attachment of Christian literature to the churches. But the inception of these is lost as yet. It may well be that the Essene communities are the key. The Dead Sea scrolls will probably have much to tell us of divergence from Jewish orthodoxy in the silent centuries. But it cannot be doubted that Christianity was formulated in an age of intense mythopoeic activity. Its setting is not that of science but that of astrology and gnosticism.

One final remark. I sense in existentialism a tendency to put assigned significance above historical fact. Even Bultmann and Niebuhr flirt with this propensity. I do not think it has reached the stage of "two truths" but may well encourage an almost unconscious duplicity. I have asked questions. Unfortunately, Tillich is no longer here to give the theological answers. I turn, accordingly, to Hartshorne. I was impressed by the high level of his conceptual dialectic.

The first point I would make with Whiteheadians is a questioning of the assumption that theirs is the only philosophy of process, and that their panpsychistic version can be set over against a kind of static substantialism as *the* alternative.

Now, as a realistic materialist of the emergentist variety I had always stressed causal processes, much as science does, but with more emphasis, perhaps, on what I called integrative causality with the emergence of novelty. I distinguished between transeunt causality, immanent causality, and that variety of immanent causality which I called integrative. Here I emphasized organization.

As I saw it, organization was not static but dynamic, an affair of functioning patterning. There were dispositions, modes of acting under certain circumstances. History had its relevance as in synthetic and in analytic chemistry and in the development of organisms. Since I was not a Lockean, I had not gone down the arid pathway of treating substance as *something I know not what.* I held that, as in science, I had tested knowledge about objects, their composition and powers.

It is important to keep in mind this kind of materialist ontology since Russell had attacked it because he could not fit it into his Humean kind of empiricism. The point is that he had made sensations the primary termini of his knowing and of his logic, whereas I regarded sensations as *sources of information* about the objects we looked at, handled and measured. Here, I suppose, my outlook would fit more into what these days would be called the "ordinary language" approach but it would have an epistemology to back it.

To make a long story as short as possible, Whitehead sought to find a path *beneath* positivism in a reformed subjectivism. His ingenuity, as we should expect, is extraordinary. Though he begins with sensa, he puts them in a semi-Leibnitzian context. He now stresses *occasions* and teaches that each occasion originates by including in itself a transcendent universe of other sensa, given objective immortality, and such other factors as can be intuited as operating, factors he calls "eternal objects." From this base he moves upward to a kind of Platonic theism with stress on process and participation.

In many ways, Whitehead is a Berkeleian. Things are as they seem. I, on the other hand, regard sensations as signals of use in giving facts about their external controls. I move in the direction of an objective realism, while Whitehead used all his ingenuity in transforming subjectivism into a closely knit integration of monads with the supreme monad, God, at the top. It is a panpsychism, yes, but a hierarchical one. Every principle he employs has its role. But it should be noted that he refuses to regard sensations as originating in the brain and having a function in its economy, that is, as events. Instead, they are given a status in quite another setting. They are factors in concrescent occasions which constitute the very stuff and composition of reality.

What motivations lie back of this striking construction? Many. A dislike of superficial positivism, on the one hand, and of traditional, reductive materialism, on the other. Like F. H. Bradley, he did not see how we could get beyond appearances to realism. A world of atoms and electrons seemed to him *vacuous* without the warm reality of sensations and feelings. He could not make his home in the entities science sets up. And there was a strong religious predisposition as well into which I need not go.

My own perspective starts from biology and anthropology. I have moved from man's warm participation in his organism to the larger world that science has disclosed. Of that we have only descriptive knowledge-about. And that I think is, itself, a great achievement. But I was intrigued by the question of the status and role of awareness and consciousness and mental abilities and their functional location in connection with the brain of man. Here I early moved to a form of the identity theory which I called the double-knowledge approach. I decided that we participate in cerebral activity and that its outcome was not predetermined As I saw it, this was the highest type of causal process. Only of late has science been grappling with it; and it promises to give it headaches enough. As Konrad Lorenz, the great Austrian ethologist points out, the nervous system has an autonomy of its own.

Hartshorne and Whitehead

But I must come to Hartshorne's theism. As I indicated, it has a Whiteheadian base and is no stronger than its foundations. Being-Itself is, for Hartshorne, Process-Itself. But, just as Being-Itself is not ordinary being—as it is for the materialist—so Process-Itself is not ordinary process. It is this assertion of transcendence in both which I find unjustified, for I am an immanentist. For both Hartshorne and Whitehead, God, the *Principle* of Concretion, that is, of the selection of compossibles for actual occasions, is not the world but the *valuation of the world*. This means that Hartshorne is a *panentheist*, making the world internal to God. This establishes his form of transcendence.

I find many of Hartshorne's categorial remarks acute. For instance, the status of the past. He holds the past not to be inactual, save for our knowledge. But I hold that, *as an event*, it has ceased to be, though that event may well have left determinate patterns behind it, as in tape-recorders or D.N.A. My colleague, De Witt Parker, wanted to survive in the memory of his Omega System, akin to Whitehead's Consequent Nature of God.

When all is said, contrasts stand out as basic. Any adequate material-ism needs a better epistemology than academic philosophy has deigned to give it. This I have tried to supply in my form of critical realism. And there must go with that epistemology a clarification of ontology. More justice must, of course, be done to time and causal process. Much the same holds for the idea of substantiality, which must take into account, in its conceptualizing, such items as photons and mesons, elements cooked up in the stars, chemical compounds, living organisms, etc. The idea of qualities stuck into a substratum is, surely, outmoded but should be repeated as a target to shoot at. I am a causal-process thinker but reject emphatically the essentially Berkeleian-Leibnitzian framework within which White-head and Hartshorne work.

A few words, in conclusion, on the cultural reorientations indicated by terms like secularism, scientism and humanism. It is fairly easy to state what they connote. It is generally granted that their foundations are this-worldly. And I have supported them in that I have argued against a transcendent other-world.

It would, I think, be granted by all that a laissez-faire secularism has its dangers. There is needed a concern for human values. That is, there must be guidance as to goals. This means that secularism must pass to a more self-conscious, constructive level. I cannot, myself, help feeling that the churches have as much impeded as furthered this development by their traditionalism and other-worldly orientation. Very often, they have supported conservative tendencies and institutions because of their insti-tutional alliances. And I would add that they have not, on the whole, encouraged vigorous and uninhibited thinking. But I am not a fanatic in these matters. Much, I think, will depend on the scope of education. Questioning and problem-solving must be encouraged. And I doubt the validity of appeals to mysteries and to an over-arching *Mysterium*

Tremendum. Yet I have a feeling for curiosity and wonderment. This universe in which we find ourselves is terrific in complexity and range. I have watched the growth of physics with excitement and my fascination with new developments in biology and psychology has not been less. And, all the time, I have tried to reconstruct philosophy to adjust it to this orientation. If thus grounded, it may with new vigor take up old responsibilities and seek to see life clearly and as a whole. I certainly hope so.

Like secularism, scientism is often defined in dissuasive terms. The burden of these varies from fear of its naturalistic import to criticism of overspecialization and to neglect of concern for misplaced applications, as in the case of the atomic bomb. But there is a lively debate going on, on these points, among scientists themselves. A social consciousness is manifesting itself. I read this literature with interest. My old friend C. Judson Herrick was one of the first to make me aware of this debate. No, I do not think that scientism is a great danger. There is much that is self-correcting about it.

And, finally, a few words on naturalistic humanism. Humanism is an attractive term. It symbolizes a concern for the human scene. I would emphasize a well-tempered perspective. I have not found in myself any Nietzschean, or Sartrean, tendency to want to become God. That goes, as the French would say, *sans dire.* Nor do I exalt man in any romantic fashion. I wonder at him as a product of biological and cultural evolution but recognize that, as one biologist put it, he has a precarious life. Both Greeks and Hebrews recognized this fact. That, at least, they had in common. It did not take Niebuhr to teach me that there was wickedness as well as goodness abroad. I saw, however, no need to embellish this with the myth of original sin. Sufficient to an era are the myths of that era. I cannot help feeling that crisis theology is subsiding, as it is recognized that it was more emotional than constructive.

I have become so familiar with the humanist outlook through the years that I have come to identify it with perspective and emphases. It is, essentially, a redirection of thought to the human scene, a frank acceptance of the human situation. And I believe it does this with courage and not with "metaphysical dread." When I read and think about Kierkegaard, I do not regard him as a model. I am, in point of fact, rather sorry for him. But I respect him, admire him, while thinking his approach is dated.

One could say that humanism stands for the thesis that what men have called the spiritual is not alien to his condition but is something of the nature of projection, aspiration and even of dreaming which, though good on the whole, needs repeated revision and, if I may say so, tidying up. The word seems to me on a boundary line ambivalent in its attachments.

Trends and Depth Psychology

In conclusion, I want to make some comments on trends. Here I shall limit myself to religious and philosophical ones. In a more inclusive text, I would speak not only of crisis theology but of crisis politics. Power seems on the loose.

Quite naturally, I am skeptical of the ability of "depth theology" and "encounter theology" to meet the situation arising from cultural development. This is very broadly based.

These new theologies are, I gather, supposed to aid an imperilled rational tradition. They have an homology with Kierkegaard's subjective method. Now it is my belief that the subjective should, so far as possible, be correlated with the objective, as the best behaviorism is now trying to do.

Depth is, of course, a metaphor. Let us take depth psychology as an illustration. Intellectualism in psychology had too much neglected instinct, feeling, the subconscious, motivations, genesis in favor of sensations, images and associations. Depth psychology united with psychiatry in prying out genetic factors and odd devices such as rationalization. This is a work of supplementation and was all to the good. It did not seek to escape from biological contexts.

But depth theology and *encounter* claims seem to me to belong to a different gambit, that of mysticism. The idea is that one can dig down to God and the supernatural. Feeling is, as in mysticism, supposed to have epistemological disclosures. The dyad, "I and Thou," come into play.

Now, of course, I take feeling very seriously in the economy of living things. It is indicative for reaction. But I would stress its role in adjustment and appraisal rather than in cognition. The "heart" has such "indicative" reasons. Description is not enough for action. One has to note impact and bearing.

Mysticism is a complex topic which has been much discussed. It must be studied historically and culturally. Orthodoxy has often been rather arid, as has been shown in Islam, Eastern Jewry, and in pietism. But mysticism must also be studied psychologically and epistemologically. Here *processes* and *claims* are involved. I note that critics of Encounter have stressed the difficulty of verification. Brought up among psychologists, I would also note studies of the "sense of presence." A child develops expectations with regard to its mother and tends to see her at any signal. We have something analogous in dreams and their apparent objectivity. It is not a matter of sensation and images alone but of an attempt at perceiving. The pattern is that I dream of my dead wife and seek to talk with her. But objective verification cannot be secured for these cerebral efforts. We have efforts rather than controlled cognitions. Now these motivations can be enforced by religious traditions' techniques, such as fasting. But I take this to be a blind alley.

What I offer in naturalistic humanism is an outlook which works within the world, stressing exploration and creative mastery. What I would emphasize is what is traditionally called wisdom. I would speak of a stress on the quality of life and of new levels. I would here follow the lead of the Greeks at their best. I would think of self-knowledge, fellowship, moderation and creativity. Of course, I would emphasize cultural developments in science, art and technology but yet not break with older insights. The Jewish traditions stress will, love and revelation.

Now I just don't believe that traditional religion and theology symbolize the right direction to take. I quite acknowledge that Judaism, Buddhism, Christianity had their virtues, just as group fellowship has its bonds of affection. But the frameworks were misleading and somewhat primitive. There tended to be *dogmas* of a carefully cultivated and indoctrinated type. Some of these linked up with superstitions. And idealism and conservatism are often oddly combined.

I judge that ecumenical efforts will increase as dogmatism declines in this changing cultural atmosphere. I have been unable to take the dialogues I have read very seriously in any other context. They do not concern foundations and are not very incisive. I expect shifts will come with the years, as secularism, scientism and humanism have their cultural effects. Man's status will be better understood.

One last word about the situation in philosophy. As I have shown, I have moved within American philosophy some sixty years, not without being aware of developments in other lands. I think there has been a fair increase in technical competence. But often epistemology and ontology were too much ignored. Take linguistic analysis and logical positivism as examples. From the beginning I sought a breakthrough beyond dualism and subjectivism. The reader must judge my leads.

I shall now pass to a study of value appreciation. It has its own categories, like good, bad and ought. These can, I believe, be given a naturalistic status. I stress *role* in the human economy.

12

IN WHAT SENSE DO VALUE
JUDGMENTS AND MORAL JUDGMENTS
HAVE OBJECTIVE IMPORT?

I am concerned here to do some tidying up in my general outlook. As I see it, it is not so much a matter of "second thoughts"—to use Ewing's expression—as of more adequate thinking within a *framework* more or less implied by science and modern culture. I take this to be realistic and naturalistic. But that is only a beginning.

On the side of theory of knowing, it was necessary to reanalyze perceiving to bring out its two main ingredients, namely, external reference and the use of information fed into the organism by the senses. I connected reference with responsive activity and thought of this as guided and informed by the senses. Here I spoke of a from-and-to circuit. As I saw it, this was the foundation of the natural realism which finds expression in conduct and speech. I see a tree over there and walk towards it. I distinguish such natural realism from naive realism which is a naive form of epistemology which thinks of perceiving as a sort of direct *intuition* of the object. In contrast, critical realism is an attempt to explore what is involved in natural realism. I ended up with the view that we decipher the external thing to which we are responding through, and by means of, the information fed into us by the same object. There is a good deal of selective and exploratory activity here. Recent psychology speaks of the discernment of sensory patterns and the growth of concepts. Children have much to learn before they perceive objects in a stable way.

I take perceiving to consist of deciphering referential claims which are constantly being tested. From this base, we work out our cognitive claims about things, relating and describing them. It is a remarkable achievement, if you will, but well founded. *It is in the recognition of what is involved that critical realism exceeds natural realism.* Modern philosophy got off to a bad start because it did not understand the causal circuit in perceiving and made sensations terminal.

---

*This was first published in *Philosophy and Phenomenological Research*, 28, 1967, pp. 1–16, and is reprinted by kind permission of the editor.

I am accustomed to say that critical realism moves between presentation-alism and representationalism in that it is referentially direct and yet recognizes the informative role of sensations.

So much for epistemology and its framework. I want now to pass to a consideration of two other, human activities essential to human living, namely, valuing and normative morality. Neither, it seems to me, has been adequately understood. I shall begin by making a few relevant statements which I shall later explain and apply.

The first is to the effect that the great task of the present is to fit *moral philosophy* into *natural philosophy* and show that it is a culmination of the latter. I take it that the theory of evolution, as it is being developed today, along with clearer notions of valuation and moral judgment, is making this possible. I adopted this perspective quite early in my career in terms of emergence and levels of causality. I stressed organization and integrative causality. But I could not foresee recent developments in the bio-chemistry of genes. Here one speaks of codes, pattern replication and interplay. But I am even more interested in discoveries about the working of the nervous system. Man's "big brain" must be taken into account in natural philosophy. Language, communication and culture would seem to rest on its capacities.

But philosophy cannot do the work of science. Its job is to set its own house in order. Yet it must keep its eye on science.

Accordingly, I turn to the handling of values and morality in modern philosophy. And I shall begin with a few theses of my own.

The first is about value judgments. My idea is that these are culminations of a way of thinking about referents of all sorts, such as projects, states of affairs, things, the self, other selves, institutions, etc. It is a way of thinking essential to the human economy and feeds into choices and decisions. While it interplays with cognition, it is not reducible to it.

As I see it, this way of thinking is concerned with the *role* of the referent in the human economy. That is, how it connects up with desires, plans, needs, etc. The dominant concern is with the *bearing* of the object valued upon these dynamic interests of self or group. I speak of the value assigned to the object or objective. I take this not to be an *attribute*, natural or non-natural, but an appraisal of the role of this factor in this setting. This involves a way of thinking with its own categories and terminology. As I see it, it is objective after its kind. This sort of thinking takes into account whatever it regards as relevant. But, while purely cognitional thinking concentrates on facts and descriptions founded on sensory data, this is engaged in the task of estimating, or sizing up, the *role* of the object in the human economy. It is led to note how the object bears on, and affects, the interests at stake. It is thus reflexive and relational but focuses on the object to appraise it. That is why the value-assignment has objective import. And yet, because it is not cognitional, it is not descriptive. One can see now why I think that British intuitionism had a bad lead. So far as I can make out, G. E. Moore felt that the intuition of the "good" was the sole means to escape subjectivism of the form, "I, personally, like that," or the statistical summary, "Most like that." By means of this objective intuition of "good" he believed he had found anchorage away from both subjectivism and naturalism. Naturalism was defined—a little uncertainly—as the substitution of a descriptive property, such as complexity in evolution, for this simple, indefinable property which he thought he had found. This was his so-called "naturalistic fallacy." Though not technically a fallacy, it presented people with a bad choice which has still continued to intimidate thinkers. Being a thorough philosopher in his own framework, he added his question technique: You call pleasure, or something else, good, but is it really good?

It goes without saying that I looked upon the expression, naturalistic fallacy, as badly chosen. It would have been better if he had spoken of a descriptive fallacy. Naturalism had already been preempted by philosophy as a position in opposition to supernaturalism. And naturalism was wide-spread in the United States, as in evolutionary naturalism. It seemed to me clear that man had the capacity to value objects as well as to describe them. In the preceding paragraphs I have argued that a very important way of human thinking is to note the role an object plays in relation to desires and needs and to appraise it accordingly. Such appraisal sizes up the valuational status of the object but does not involve an intuition of a non-natural property.

It is just an historical fact that most American thinkers of my generation, Perry, Pratt, Rogers, Dewey and myself, for example, were unable to intuit Moore's quality, and they raised the old questions about self-evidence and what to do when opinions varied. But the path largely taken in the United States was that of axiology, dealing with the nature and status of values. Great Britain did not seem to take to this effort kindly. Ethics had historical primacy and Moore had set a pattern. I shall say something about axiology later and show where I differed from R. B. Perry. My stress was upon a way of thinking and upon value judgments and the sort of claims they make. But, at present, I want to run over British moves. I can do this in a very summary fashion since they have been examined so thoroughly.

The next move, primarily in ethics, was made at Oxford by Prichard and Ross. Both were intuitionists but stressed the right and duty as the key terms. Within the moral point of view they made some good points. Ross held that the rightness of moral rules was intuited. This was an intrinsic feature of them. Some of his critics suggested that he moralized too much as an English gentleman and did not appreciate fully the work done in the history of morals and in cultural anthropology. Another point sometimes made was that he was dominated in his epistemology by the traditions of classical rationalism and by older views of mathematics, now displaced by postulational methods. Soon the full impact of logical positivism would challenge his outlook. But, then, I was persuaded that logical positivism had oversimplified matters, as I shall point out.

Let me take up for a moment Ross's criticism of Perry's axiology. It is to the effect that "when we call something good we are thinking of it as possessing a certain attribute" and not of having an interest in it. Now, while I think Perry was right in stressing interest, I do not think that he did justice to the way of thinking involved in valuation. As I see it, we focus on the object and appraise its role in a context of the *interplay* of interest and object. The aim is not primarily cognition, though facts are recognized so far as they are relevant to appraisal. But, in this type of thinking, we are concerned with the way in which the object bears on our interests. It is not a purely cognitional affair; and we must expect a different category than description and attribute. To say, with Perry, that a value is any object of any interest should be merely the beginning. My own feeling is that the new realism stressed a kind of presentational confrontation—here interest and object—and did not do justice to the complexities of thinking, whether cognitional or valuational. On the other hand, Ross's demand for an intuitable attribute is equally mistaken. To estimate the role an object plays in the human economy is an objective endeavor in its own fashion. I would, myself, speak of a justifiable value-assignment. There is often a great delicacy in working it out. And it shifts with circumstances, as does living itself. I have great respect for norms and standards and the mode of their establishment. But my respect is accompanied with inquiry.

I am now ready to deal with the linguistics of valuation and moral judgment. Here I embark on what is called these days metaethics, that is, a clarification of the words and concepts used. Important as words are, one must have concepts and theories to go with them or else they become opaque. As I see it, words are tied in with thoughts. Even perceptual claims rest on sensations, functioning as disclosures or appearings, and the concepts that have been worked out in exploratory activities. Let me begin with cognition. Here we have the key words, true and false. There is quite a range of uses of these words. They vary from equivalence to "That's so" to recognition of what is involved in a knowledge claim. As an epistemologist, the first move seems to me an *endorsement* of the knowledge claim. In effect, it is to say that the proposition endorsed is a correct description of the state of affairs denoted. It states the facts about what is the case. But, for the epistemologist, there follows the second move. How is this knowledge achieved? What does it involve? I would put my own position this way. It is a form of the correspondence theory. Beginning with perceiving, the object feeds information about itself to the percipient and this is constantly being renewed and supplemented. Concepts *about* the object are developed and the logical need for the avoidance of contradiction is realized. Science just continues this procedure with new techniques and instruments. But the upshot for the critical realist is neither presentationalism or representationalism but direct *knowledge-about* based on information fed into the knower. It is, of course, a complicated achievement but it gives us a picture of the world which enlarges and deepens, has application, and is coherent. Pragmatism and coherence-idealism strike me as weak in their epistemology.

Now I want to show these two moves from endorsement to explanation in both valuation and moral judgment. But, first, a few words about the nature and function of morality.

I think it is generally agreed by the historians of morality and by cultural anthropologists that moral rules arose out of the need to help people to live together. This is the stage of customary morality and we need not idealize it. There was no innate wisdom and groups varied in their emphases. But there was a kind of working consensus. As society became more complex, old rules were modified and new ones developed. But I need not go into all this, since it is so well known.

I take it, then, that morality is prescriptive, directional, and concerned with living together. By its very status and function it is public and an affair of convictions. Hume was quite right in emphasizing its distinctive language.

The first move here is to recognize that "right" is a term of endorsement, much as "true" is. One says that's the way to do it. These are the rules to keep. Moral education enters here, as does tradition. Aristotle saw this clearly.

But the next move is the question, Why? What is the ground or reason? Reflection cannot avoid this move.

Now I think that intuition is not the answer. I agree with Professor Frankena that it has been undercut by psychology and by postulationism in mathematics. What, then, is its strength? It is a simple explanation of the fact of endorsement; and it has appeal until a more adequate explanation is worked out. It has, for example, a defense of objectivity. Rightness is an intrinsic claim made by rules. Another strength it has is the weakness of supposed alternatives. Paulsen points out that Kant's rigorism was, in part, a reply to a sentimental degeneration of ethical theory in the Germany of his time. The virtues were spoken of as pleasant and charming. For Kant this was a prostitution. And so he worked out his categorical imperative. The "Practical Reason" was given a job it could not accomplish, that is, to disregard the consequences of actions. As I see it, it is the very nature of morality to have these in mind. But in what terms shall we consider them? Here we come up against non-moral values. And it is to these that I return. One last remark is, however, in order. It is to the effect that deontology reflects linguistically the first move, the emphasis on rightness as an endorsement of *prima facie* duties. This operates constantly along with some awareness of the consequences point of view.

I turn now to the semantics of "good." The Oxford Dictionary emphasized the meaning, commendation, along with some recognition of an *implication* of the existence in a high, or at least satisfactory, degree of characteristic qualities which are either *admirable in themselves* (what does this mean?) or useful for some purpose.

This is a complex. I grant that commendation, a feeling of approval, a pro-attitude is one element in it. But I take it that there is the second element of a judgmental kind concerning the object or state of affairs. This concerns the role of the object as it connects up with needs and desires. To use C. D. Broad's expression, it is good-making. But, unfortunately, Broad had Moore's idea of good in mind. As I see it, good here stands for a favorable appraisal of the way the object connects up with needs and desires of self or group. It is not a descriptive term but it is meaningful in a referential way. And it supports the attitude. When we are doubtful in detail, we make what are called *evaluations*. Thus we hear of job evaluations, institutional evaluations, etc. All this is conceptual as well as verbal. It means that cognizing alone is insufficient for human living. We must learn to discover how events, objects, plans, patterns of human living fit into our lives.

To sum up this semantics angle: I have argued that the first definitional move is often that of affirming claims without reasons being explicitly given. That knowledge-claim is to be endorsed, the other rejected. And afterwards may come ground and explanation. Historically, this has been in terms of correspondence, coherence and pragmatic working. I have argued for a correspondence but in terms of an epistemology which recognizes that objects feed in information about themselves which is used referentially. This is the second definitional move and is debatable.

Turning to morality, I suggested that much the same development occurs. "Right" and "wrong" are contrast terms which function in the vocabulary of morality as terms of endorsement and rejection respectively. They are indices of the code. But here, again, moral thought has asked the question of ground or reason. And so we make the second definitional move and may get puzzled. Conscience and intuition are linked candidates. And then come the varieties of "consequences" moves. F. C. Sharp made a life-study of usages and reactions. For him, the first definitional move was to say that right *means* that the refusal so to act would be blameworthy. The second definitional move was to seek the ground of this in consequences. But here he was more of a hedonist than I. I think of pleasures and pains as guides and indicators for activities rather than primary objectives. But, of course, there are complications here. Ethical hedonism is, certainly, nearer the goal than psychological hedonism. It stresses satisfactions and dissatisfactions as guiding criteria rather than ends. But we come back to the nature of value judgments. And here I return to the notion of role and interplay. As I understand it, ends, or objectives, stand out and these are estimated in complex ways, taking account of other ends, drives and feelings. It is a kind of balancing affair which issues in choices of goals. And there is always what we call to-day feedback. I certainly have no objection to pleasures but would, on the whole, take them in their function as indicators. As I understand it, cortex and thalamus play supplementary roles. I shall argue that this interplay rises to consciousness in a compresent awareness of *cues* which can be verbalized in deliberation. I shall say more about this in my consideration of the mind-body problem, which is today largely the mind-brain problem. The kind of causality that goes on in the brain is, as I see it, mental in type. It involves analyzing, summarizing, communication, the use of cues, the establishment of dispositional sets, patterns and methods of operation. In all this there is functional action-as-a-whole. It is, of course, an astonishing organ. But my point is that the self and its activities arise within it as centers of control and direction. *I am not an epiphenomenalist but a participationist.* It seems to me clear that perceiving, itself, involves a from-and-to circuit in which sensory cues stand out as signals guiding response. The very causality of signals must be explored. And this schematism is open at both ends, inviting both increased information and selective response. It was upon such a pattern that the brain-mind was built.

But I must return to British ethics. It had, for the time being, culminated in such intuitions as the good and the right. And it held to the kind of objectivity these seemed to imply. Now I have been arguing for external reference and informational input in cognition. But in valuation, as I see it, our concern is with the *bearing* of all sorts of referents—objectives, plans, possibilities, ways of living—upon our needs and desires. Here, also, our outlook is objective enough. As Heidegger would say, these things are *zuhanden.* Our outlook is likely to be that of what I called natural realism, built on perceiving. But we are concerned with the role and import of these things for our lives. This is an objective quest in which the objective interplays with the subjective to work out justifiable appraisals. The context is simply more reflexive and relational. *In this setting, objectivity takes a new shading.* It is a doing justice to what is involved. Moral objectivity, for instance, consists in setting aside private involvements and stressing reciprocity and long-run consequences. But it would seem that British intuitionists *cognitionalized* all this and believed in a sort of Platonic apprehension.

And then came the challenge of logical positivism. To my way of thinking it was mistaken in many of its theses. I was, as has been noted, a physical realist with much concern for science. In fact, I was an emergent, or evolutionary, materialist. This rather impatient crusade was not only phenomenalistic but had little use for epistemology. Carnap held, in fact, the stalemate theory that idealism and realism were locked in a futile dispute. As a realist with what I regarded as a breakthrough in the analysis of perceiving, I could, naturally, not accept such an approach. But I did admire the new logic. I could understand his impatience with German speculative philosophy and with existentialism. But the range of his acquaintance with American realism was, clearly, limited. He is, however, a fair-minded and a persistent thinker.

First, there was the dispute about the verificational theory of meaning. This, I take it, has subsided with the development of semantics and its separation from the question of the nature and meaning of truth.

As a matter of fact, Carnap moved from position to position under the pressure of criticism and his own realization of inadequacies.

Let us now turn to Ayer, a very clear expositor. I remember that he gave a lecture at the University of Michigan on alternative positions in his early days. It was clear that he had never heard of critical realism. I had, of course, become used to this sort of thing but it has led me to stress the need of cross-fertilization in philosophy.*

Now it is with the challenge to British intuitional ethics by logical positivism that I am here concerned. It was an expression of *scientism* at a stage which did not take into account the development of psychology and the social sciences. Now it so happened that I had been brought up on the psychological form of sociology pioneered by Charles Horton Cooley. In fitting the *human conditions* into natural philosophy I had always had biology, psychology and the social sciences in mind. The other day I leafed over a book on the new science of *personology*. It aimed at putting behaviorism, psychiatry and introspectionism together, much as I would. But, back to logical positivism, its thesis was to the effect that only scientific sentences and logic statements were meaningful. It followed that moral statements must be regarded as commands (Carnap) or the evincing of feelings (Ayer). This did not mean that normative ethics was not important but that it was a non-scientific activity. The challenge to theology along the same lines intrigued me since I had published a book on humanism in religion in 1916, called *The Next Step in Religion* (Macmillan). My argument was that naturalism had the preference over supernaturalism if it could be worked out to do justice to the human situation. As a philosopher, I had never liked Huxley's coinage, agosticism. Tyndall seemed to me a more forthright soul who had to take Huxley's ribbing. The chemistry of giant molecules was in the future. And I may say the need for new views of causality, such as those involved in feedbacks and patterned systems. As I see it, much of the difficulty about the mind-brain problem rests in bad epistemology and refusal to recognize *that new types of causality* operate in the brain which is an organ of communication and control.

It was in 1926 that I began to investigate valuing as a way of thinking different from cognizing but a way of thinking which has its own categories. A good deal of knowledge is involved but the emphasis is on the *interplay* of the objective and the subjective or, as we might put it, recognition of the bearing, or connection, of objects on desires, plans, etc. It is within such a context of interplay that appraisals are made. As I have

---

*See an article of mine called "Existentialism, Realistic Empiricism, and Materialism" in *Philosophy and Phenomenological Research*, March 1965. I might also mention my study of British Theories of Sense-Perception in *Methodos*, 1962.

argued, they are objective in import but not cognitively descriptive.

One can see, then that, while I agreed with the positivists in rejecting intuition and the *truth* of moral judgments, I thought their approach quite inadequate. Man had the job, like other animals but in a higher degree, of sizing up the bearing of objects on his life and prospects. And as pragmatists and existentialists say in common, he is full of projects and lives in the future.

I hope the reader will excuse another reminiscence of an old man. It so happened that Ewing was teaching at the University of Michigan summer school in 1926. I asked him to read my chapter on valuation and moral judgment in my book *The Principles and Problems of Philosophy*, which was then in galley. He was rather horrified, I think, by my thesis that moral judgments are not true or false but justifiable. I have read his books carefully and with the respect due to careful exposition and find his shift to reasonable from fitting and to the "good reasons" analysis is in my direction. He, however, still emphasizes the naturalistic fallacy which, for me, would just be a confusion between descriptive cognition and valuation. As I pointed out, what Moore had in mind was the difference between fact and his alternative, the intuition of the quality good. One reason why I did not like the adjective, naturalistic, so used, was that I wanted to put the operation of valuing *within nature*. I shall say something about that when I come to the topic of fitting moral philosophy into natural philosophy, which seems to me rather a culmination. As a philosopher by profession I have taken rather a pride in naturalizing perceiving and studying the higher ranges of cognition as cultural developments. This is an extension of what biologists are coming to call *anagenesis* (another term for emergence).

While recognizing the stature of Ayer and Carnap and their motivations, I shall now concentrate on Stevenson. There seems to be some ambiguity here which I want to chase down, the more so that he has an excellent feeling for words. I shall argue that attitudes are functions of knowledge and valuation, even though they are affectively *pro* and *con*. And both of these activities seem to me to have a logical texture. That is, we can give reasons for both our cognitional claims and for our appraisals. The latter were traditionally brought under the heading, the Practical Reason. I would call attention to Hobhouse's book, *Rational Good*, which, I think, was too neglected. Philosophy seems sometimes to have only the thin edge of bursts of local contemporaneity. To me, it should be a dialogue in depth. And it would stress deep-seated problems which, in this age, have a cultural background with science playing a major role. Stevenson presents two models. The first is, "This is wrong" means "I disapprove of this; do so as well." Now I cannot accept this model for it combines a factual assertion of personal attitude, with no attempt at justification, with a supplementary command. The second model focuses on the descriptive element within ethical terms and supplements it with an emotive meaning. "This is good" is said to have the meaning of "This has qualities or relations X, Y, Z—and good has as well a laudatory, emotive meaning which permits it to express the speaker's approval, and tends to evoke the approval of the hearer." Here, again, I think that Stevenson's analysis falls short because it does not recognize that moral valuations are objective in import and involve the appraisal of the qualities and relations, X, Y, Z, in their bearing on moral demands and convictions. Surely, the moral point of view must be taken into account. And, as we have noted, this outlook is connected with the very function of morality, namely, to direct and control conduct in the public interest. At a reflective level, there may well be revision and greater awareness of the consequences of behavior. But the setting remains. What may well happen is the search for justification of the moral judgment which brings together facts and their valuation. This, I hold, is a way of thinking with its own concepts and categories. As I see it, logical positivism rightly rejected intuitionism but was so dominated by the traditions of cognition that it was unable to do justice to what takes place in moral valuation. There is no need to reduce the *ought* to the *is*. What should be done is to bring out the role of duty and oughtness in moral thought. And these terms must have critieria for their application.

In what sense is morality and its categories "in nature"? Just to the extent that man and his endeavors are in nature. As I see it, morality and its categories are developments connected with the complexities of human living. Just as cognizing and its achievements are developments whose mode of operation we are learning to understand in an *anagenetic* way, so the supplementation of prudential valuing by moral valuation and its categories stands out as a cultural growth within nature, as enlarged by man's uniqueness.

Stevenson in his able book, *Ethics and Language*, stresses a division into beliefs and attitudes while admitting that changes in belief may lead to changes in attitude. But the term, attitude, is rather treacherous. It seems to have offered itself to Richards, Barnes and Stevenson as something supplementary to the factual. But, as I see it, *pro* and *con* attitudes emerge from evaluations resting on the interplay of feeling and recognition of the linkage of objects with persons and groups and the way one feels as a result. In this area we establish norms and rules which seem to us to satisfy this interplay. And, of course, language has worked with this kind of thinking. We speak of projects, objectives and standards. I suggest, then, that Stevenson did not sufficiently link up the dynamic and emotive with judgment. That is, he did not explore the valuing activity. In reading Baier's book, *The Moral Point of View*, I had the feeling that, in criticizing Stevenson, he overstressed epistemology with its concern for knowledge and the true and false as over against axiology and its stress on justifiable appraisals. These are non-descriptive, yet may conflict. It is along these lines that I would work out my own metaethics. There seem to have been anticipations of this approach in both Hume and Mill.

In final comment, may I remark that the very simplicity of logical positivism in its epistemology, that is, its phenomenalistic reduction of perceiving to sense-contents may well have encouraged a similar simplicity in the treatment of values as the *evincing* of feeling and attitude.

With Toulmin's stress on *good reasons* for moral judgment and Hare's careful study of moral language, a pathway between intuitionism and emotivism was being opened up. Now I find myself very much in agreement with Toulmin's emphases. He seems, however, to have reached them by way of Wittgenstein's later freeing of language from restraints put on it by intuitionists and emotivists. I, on the other hand, belonged to a different tradition, that of realism and axiological theory. Like most American thinkers, I had rejected intuitionism. Hence my job was to understand what was involved in valuation and in the framework of morality with its demands or prescriptions.

Taking Toulmin, Urmson and Hare together, I find a recognition of the practical reason and of the interplay of criteria and attitude in evaluation. This emphasis is also taken up by Nowell-Smith. All of this seems to me in the right direction. When Hare defends Moore's criticism of naturalism, he has in mind the difference between factual description and valuation. But, surely, both of these activities are natural though diverse. It still seems to me better to emphasize the human context and to recognize that the aim of knowing is different from that of valuing. These are two types of thinking and each has its logical peculiarities. Valuing concerns itself with a wide range of objectives and relates them to situations and needs. Morality comes in in a supervisory way to judge objectives in their bearing on welfare as envisaged in an accepted way of life.

I conclude that the *reductionism* of logical positivism forced metaethics to the forefront. It is interesting to see how British thought reacted. It gave up intuitionism and took the path of a careful study of valuational and moral language. But, as I have indicated, American axiology had taken much the same path with more stress on concepts than on words. This was a difference in technique. I have considerable sympathy with the definist efforts of Perry, Sharp and Parker. Only I would make the value judgment more explicit. While Perry defines "good" to mean "being an object of favorable interest," I would define it as "a value term expressing commendation on the basis of recognized criteria bearing on the role of the object in the human economy." Perry seems to me to limit himself to a precondition and does not go on to the kind of thinking which ensues. As for his definition of "right," I would make a similar amendment. The first definitional move is to bring out the point of moral endorsement. The second, to stress the ground, or justification, namely, that it tends to bring about happiness or welfare. Perry stresses this second, teleological approach. It seems to me that both definitional moves are necessary to do justice to what I would call the two poles, subjective and objective, in morality. And I would again call attention to a similar dichotomy in the definition of truth. Here the first move is an acceptance, or endorsement, of a knowledge-claim. The second concerns the ground, namely, that the knowledge-claim rests on informationally mediated correspondence.

My amendment of Sharp would be on much the same lines. Where he defines "good" as "desired upon reflection," I would add "and considered desirable."

It may be recalled that Dewey with his stress on scientific method found "desirable" a hard word to deal with. I would argue that value thinking is a native feature of man's adjustment to his environment. It concerns the connection of things with his life. It was only because science began with astronomy and physics that it was led to envisage a world without 1 The existentialists begin at the other end with man thrown-into-the-world and the human condition. These are the extremes. The new naturalism seeks to do justice to man in the world.

I want now, in conclusion, to take up briefly the questions I flushed out, here and there, in my argument. I shall begin with questions about the human economy and lead on to what I called the fitting in of moral philosophy onto natural philosophy but which is, in effect, a comprehending of man in nature. Here the uniqueness of man must be recognized, as a knower, a valuer and an agent. But, surely, that does not make the rest of nature absurd. Merely, we must not have false expectations. I, for one, can get quite enthralled in following the patterns of activity discovered by scientists.

The best procedure might well be to start with animal life and then consider the complications introduced by man's biological and cultural evolution. This would, at least, give perspective. One could note the interplay of the cortex with the sensory areas, on the one hand, and with the thalamus and hypothalamus, on the other. As I see it, there are broad patterns of functional integration. There are centers which interplay. Pleasure and pain centers act as indicators to modify responses. It is almost as we would deductively expect. An animal must combine cues of information with signals as to how it is affected. It is out of this interplay that awareness and what we call consciousness emerges. There is a compresence which rests on this interplay. It involves a kind of causality hinted at by feedback and interaction. Here we have arrived at selective action as a whole, unified response. It will be recalled that I favored what I called a participative view of the mind-brain economy. Here we have a level of causality featured by the role of cues and indicators. It is a kind of communicative causality. Learning, dispositions, the summarizing role of symbols were added to this communicative type of causality. And this made possible new techniques and methods. Here cultural evolution played its part in *anagenesis*. As I see it, a level of causality arose which required criteria for its guidance. When we make mistakes we try to correct them. Man is a self-correcting and learning organism. I argued in this fashion against the unidirectional notion of causality then held. I take it that the chemistry of giant molecules and developments in computer technique and in the electrical study of the working of the brain have been modifying our notion of causality.

As against epiphenomenalism, I argue for our participation in brain-mind activities. Here meet two kinds of knowledge, knowledge resting on external perceiving and knowledge based on careful introspection. These two kinds of knowledge should supplement one another. Hence I speak of a double-knowledge approach to the brain-mind. A good epistemology feeds into this outlook. So taken, I can find no need for a conflict between behaviorism and introspectionism. The flaw in traditional introspective psychology was that it had no clear theory of perceiving and doing. Behaviorism came in as a protest. It was often rather crude.

Let us now look at the *self* from this context. As I see it, the self arises in connection with the need for direction and control. It has deep roots in the basic functions of inhibition and enforcement. And it grows with the role of criteria and purposiveness. It is referentially symbolized by the pronoun *I*, which gains in meaning by social contrast. But this meaning is embedded in the recognition of the function of control and direction. It gradually rises in man to self-consciousness, which is not a discovery of some peculiar sensory factor *a la Hume*, but a recognition of learned controls resting on judgment and valuation. It goes with adopted plans and purposes and outlook. Social psychology has done much towards our understanding of its genesis. It certainly is in accord with my participative view. This level could not have developed without language, though I think I note an early stage in the higher animals, in a dog, for instance. But I cannot go into that here. Suffice it to say that domestic animals, like the pig in Polynesia, may reflect, in some slight measure, human attitudes. I conclude that the self stands as the center of developed control and outlook. It is in this fashion that the brain furthers the human economy. A little care in language can avoid dilemmas.

I want now to comment on hedonism. While pleasure and pain function as indicators, they may become goals, as in the pleasure-seeking man. Recent experiments in stimulating centers in the thalamus show how a function can be disturbed. But I have argued that pleasure and pain normally play the role of signals or indicators of the satisfactory, or unsatisfactory, working out of projects. I take it, then, that Bishop Butler and William James were correct in their rejection of psychological hedonism. Needs, drives, desires, purposes are the dynamic setting within which feeling operates. And I have argued that value judgments involve an interplay of feeling and recognition of the bearing of an objective upon the self or the group. Criteria and feeling are thus interwoven.

The strength of hedonism has rested on the weakness of mere tradition, on the one hand, and intuitionism, on the other. In the search for justification of behavior, the reflective individualist falls back on his feelings. These are considered *intrinsic values, terminal ends*. As I see it, however, the moral economy concerns itself with conduct having social consequences. How are these valued? Surely, in a kind of summarizing way through observation of the reactions of those affected, deepened by sympathy and well-wishing. Communication plays a role here. But I very much doubt that the hedonistic calculus throws light on people's reactions. Attitudes seem to me to express a summarizing response *pro* or *con*. And I have argued that these rest on value judgments having objective import. Language has many forms to express these. I may say I am not happy about the effects of that line of conduct. Or, simply, I do not like it for the following reason.

The weakness in hedonism, accordingly, seems to me to be that it isolates feeling from its context and makes it the sole end, whereas its normal function is to operate as an indicator in the interplay involved in valuation. By such isolation, it tends to favor self-love and selfishness and to move away from the function of morality. Needless to say, I welcome happiness as a condition of life. The pursuit of it requires moral rules and awareness of the consequences of actions for others.

In this connection, one might well criticize Hume's famous thesis that the reason is the slave of the passions, that is, that it has only to do with means. But, surely, we deliberate about ends and look at them in terms of value judgments. As I see it, the flaw in traditional empiricism is that it made sensations and feelings terminal rather than as informational and indicational. By making them terminal, it disregarded their function. And this outlook made it difficult to escape from a kind of solipsism or self-centeredness. This alignment appears in both Mill and Russell, who, however, struggled against it. Kant had earlier swung back to a Reason able to spin out rules from the logical principle of avoiding self-contradiction. It is more than doubtful that he escaped the importance of consequences. I would, myself, stress the practical reason as tied in with a kind of thinking ranging from prudential concern with means and ends to social, moral thinking concerned with living together in a satisfying way. In this context, justifiable demands are formulated as "oughts." I can see nothing non-natural about this development. I grant that it is not purely cognitional and descriptive. But it is natural as a development of what is involved in living. Man is an *agent* and not a mere thing. On this point, the existentialists are right but more in a forensic way than in terms of systematic thought. But I have taken this point up elsewhere.

In fitting moral philosophy into natural philosophy, it is well to take one's departure from biology, psychology and the social sciences. There is, as yet, somewhat of a divide between philosophy and even these sciences closer to man. It is my belief that a well-thought-out naturalistic epistemology which explained man's natural realism and lifted it to a critical realism in harmony with scientific method might well serve as a conciliating step. After all, science presupposes man's cognitive capacity. And no one science has undertaken to explain it. If philosophy in touch with science can do so, this should aid. And, I take it, much the same holds for man's valuations, non-moral and moral. The "ought" has bothered the social scientists. In attacking the transcendent and, with it, absolute standards, they have fallen back on what they call "relativism." But, surely, what is needed is an emphasis on justifiable and relevant standards in a forward-moving culture. The horizon should be as broad as that of cultural anthropology. No provincialism should be accepted, but there should be open-mindedness about ways of living. As I see it, the job here is that of working out criteria for goals. And I would stress what I call interplay. At the human level, science cannot expect to find fixity. It has the task of supporting any promising approach. Not absolutism or an opposed relativity but relevancy and adequacy should be looked for. The emphasis should be upon tentative goals and their criteria. No one who has worked in social philosophy, as I have done, can escape the sense of exploratory openness. It is an affair of experimental growth, much of which is a fumbling. It is not a question of being *wertfrei* but of being value-conscious in the right way. And, philosophy at its best can, surely, help. It can work away at perspective, criteria and goals. And I suspect it might help to bridge the gap between science and the humanities, so much spoken of to-day.

* * * * *

So runs my tale, a tale of many ways of going wrong, along with an accumulation of subtle analyses and techniques. It is this mixture which is often so exasperating.

My own thesis is fairly simple. It is to explore the stages in the emergence of human cognizing. I begin with animal perceiving and note the role and function of sense-organs and sensations in the guidance of the animal. Perceiving is here a response activity of objective import. And sensations play a role within it. They are not subjectively terminal but have a function to perform. As I see it, what I call natural realism is but a continuation of this kind of operation. In it, cognizing has developed. Words and concepts have been contextually added. The informational role of sensations is being stressed. They mediate what are called looks, glimpses, appearings. Out of this setting emerges empirical knowledge-claims. That thing I am perceiving is round and hard. Here I achieve external reference founded on directive response and the informative role of sensations. This is, basically, all there is to transcendence.

But, alas, modern empiricism divorced itself from this natural setting and made sensations subjective and terminal. Critical realism is a return to it to develop what it implies.

Because they had ignored this setting in which sensations guide and inform perceiving, men like Dewey and Blanshard thought I was misled when I put sensations in the brain. But where else could they be to play this guiding and informing function? And perceiving must be linked with directed response including the indicative role of feeling.

What, then, does human cognizing turn out to be? It is of the nature of a well-founded claim to arrive at mediated facts about objects. Common sense busies itself at this job and science develops techniques to carry it further. It is in terms of these stages that human cognizing has emerged. And it is a remarkable achievement. I think that science should be interested in it.

This is *my* story of American realism. Much can be added. Our enlightened men of good-will must pool their moral resources in an ecumenical mood to work towards a solution. Nature has gone as far as it can. Man must now take over in a responsible way.

INDEX